Inside Math
Books 5–8: Rational Numbers

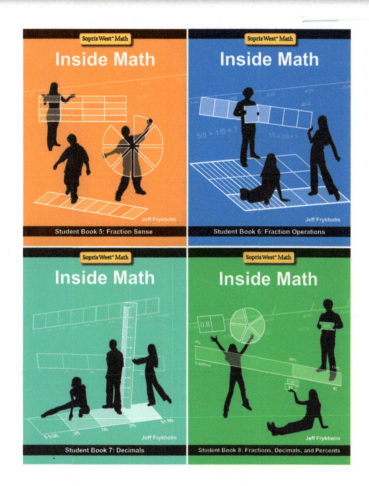

Teacher Edition

Jeff Frykholm, Ph.D.

BOSTON, MA | LONGMONT, CO

Copyright 2009 by Sopris West® Educational Services

All rights reserved.

3 4 5 6 7   FRD   10 11 12 13 14

ISBN 13: 978-1-60218-790-0
ISBN 10: 1-60218-790-8
167759/2-10

No portion of this work may be reproduced or transmitted in any form or by any means, electronic or mechanical, including photocopying or recording, or by any information storage and retrieval system, without the express written permission of the publisher.

Printed in the United States of America
Published and Distributed by

Cambium
LEARNING®
Sopris West®

4093 Specialty Place   Longmont, Colorado 80504
(303) 651-2829   www.sopriswest.com

With grateful thanks to my parents,
for a lifetime of support and encouragement.

J.F.

ACKNOWLEDGMENTS

I am greatly indebted to the many talented people who helped move *Inside Math* from a rough idea to an innovative resource for teachers and students.

It was important to me to develop this textbook series based in part on the expertise and knowledge of practicing teachers. Over the course of nearly four years of development, more than 30 teachers participated in the project, and the books are certainly stronger by virtue of the feedback they gave me from the initial planning stages through the end of the pilot testing. To mention several individuals in particular, Craig Schneider provided invaluable assistance in reviewing and enhancing earlier drafts of the manuscript and engaged the tedious work of providing the answer key for the entire manuscript. Pilot teacher Schuyler VanZante worked with the team to enhance access for ELL students. Pilot teachers Jennifer Whitten and Julie Soja illuminated our thinking about how beginning teachers engage these sorts of innovative methods and materials. As *Inside Math* neared completion, pilot teachers Paige Larson and Michael Mattassa collaborated with the development team to enrich and refine the content and to examine implementation issues. They improved the program immeasurably. Their enthusiasm in sharing these models with their students provided the necessary momentum for all of us as we turned the final corner toward production. Mary Pittman, Director of Mathematics for Boulder Valley School District in Colorado, provided vital support for this novel approach to mathematics education by sponsoring the pilot implementation.

The editorial, design and production staff included Jane Brunton, Sherry Hern, Judy Pleau, Geoff Horsfall, Jeff Dieffenbach and Holly Bell. Steve Mitchell, the publisher of *Inside Math*, encouraged and supported our team throughout the project.

As project director, Jack Beers was indispensable. This program would not have been completed without his leadership, vision, insights, and steady hand. Jack made key improvements to the instructional design, helped to underscore important mathematical ideas in the manuscript, and kept the project on course through its final phase. Finally, Christine Willis, as sponsoring director, is the reason this program exists at all. She believed in my first ideas for this textbook series, and her enthusiasm, encouragement, and persistence in the very beginning led to the signing of the project. Chris carefully shepherded the manuscript through its early stages, directed the pilot study and envisioned the *Inside Math* multimedia professional development component of the project. Without both Jack and Chris, this program would never have experienced any wind in the sails, and to both of them, I am both indebted and truly grateful.

J.F.

ABOUT THE AUTHOR

Dr. Jeff Frykholm is an Associate Professor in the School of Education at the University of Colorado at Boulder. A former high school mathematics teacher, Frykholm has spent the last 15 years of his career teaching and researching issues pertinent to the teaching and learning of mathematics. He is widely published in academic journals and recently authored an award-winning integrated mathematics and science curriculum. He was a member of the writing team for the NCTM Navigations series, and continues to be active in promoting mathematics education reform at all levels. Frykholm is recognized nationally and internationally as a top-tier scholar and teacher/educator, recently receiving the highly prestigious National Academy of Education/Spencer Foundation Fellowship, and a Fulbright Fellowship to teach and research in Santiago, Chile, in 2006.

CONTENTS

Book 5: Fraction Sense

Book Five Overview: Fraction Sense 2
Professional Background...4
Section A: Developing Fraction Sense 8
Section B: Fraction Circles 25
Section C: Fraction Strips...34
Section D: Fraction Sense Applications...47
End-of-Book Assessment 61

Book 6: Fraction Operations

Book Six Overview: Fraction Operations..68
Professional Background...71
Section A: Informal Addition and Subtraction of Fractions 76
Section B: Adding and Subtracting Fractions Using Common Denominators.......92
Section C: Multiplying Fractions Informally 104
Section D: Multiplying Fractions in Context 114
Section E: The Fraction Multiplication Algorithm 119
Section F: Dividing Fractions 128
End-of-Book Assessment 141

Book 7: Decimals

Book Seven Overview: Decimals 154
Professional Background...157
Section A: Introduction to Decimals...161
Section B: Formalizing Decimals and Beginning Operations 171
Section C: Measuring With Metrics 182
End-of-Book Assessment 193

Book 8: Fractions, Decimals, Percents

Book Eight Overview: Fractions, Decimals, Percents 200
Professional Background...203
Section A: What Is a Percent?...206
Section B: Ratio Tables and Percents 213
Section C: Number Bars and Percents..229
Section D: Tipping 252
End-of-Book Assessment 262

Corrections to Student Books

Inside Math supports the development of key mathematical concepts through the use of a handful of visual models. Correct models and accurate mathematics are necessary to guide students to an understanding of the mathematical procedures.

In some instances, the mathematics or the models are inaccurate as presented in the first printing of the Student Books. Those inaccuracies that would mislead students and teachers have been corrected in this second printing. The corrected pages appear in the Teacher Edition; student versions of these pages are available for download at www.sopriswest.com/insidemath.

The changes encompass the following pages:

- Student Book 1: Pages 13, 16, and 18
- Student Book 3: Page 17
- Student Book 4: Pages 15 and 30
- Student Book 5: Pages 15 and 22
- Student Book 6: Pages 1, 4, and 21
- Student Book 7: Page 11
- Student Book 8: Page 9

Corrections that affect only the answers in the Teacher Edition are included in this printing.

Book 5:
Fraction Sense

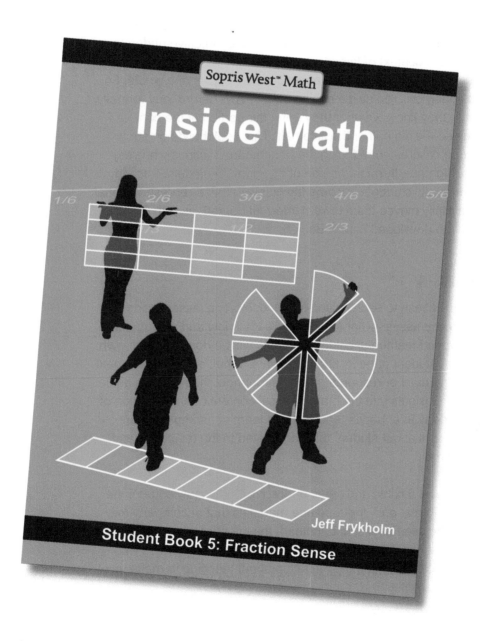

Book Five Overview: Fraction Sense

Introduction

This book is the fifth in a series of eight that are geared toward helping middle-grade learners acquire both facility with, and understanding of, the basic mathematical procedures and concepts that lay the groundwork for more advanced mathematical study. In particular, this series cultivates understanding of a number of mathematical tools that students learn to use with facility in various mathematical and real-world contexts.

Book Focus

This book engages students in situations that help them develop an informal, intuitive understanding of fractions. Students will explore their intuitive understanding of fractions through the context of fair shares. Research has indicated that even young children have an intuitive sense about fractional parts of a whole. For example, watch two young children split a cookie in half. Well before they formally learn that 1/2 + 1/2 = 1, they know whether they got a fair portion of the cookie, or whether they received the big half or the little half. This book builds on such native intuition of young children, introducing the benchmark fractions—halves, thirds, fourths, sixths, eighths—through the use of two primary models: fraction circles and fraction strips. As students become familiar with these representational models, this book gradually moves them toward informal operations with fractions. Formal operations will be developed fully in Book 6.

How to Use this Book

There are two primary sections to each lesson in this book. The lesson starts with a discussion that helps you assess what students already know and a suggestion for how to model the type of mathematical thinking they will be doing on their own. A reduced version of the student page includes answers. What follows on the next page is an accompanying teacher resource guide. Throughout the resource guide, you will be provided with insights into the mathematical content of each section of the book, pedagogical ideas to enhance teaching and learning, samples of anticipated student work, insights about student thinking related to the topics at hand, and ideas about assessment.

This program is meant to be flexible and relies on the craft and knowledge of the teachers who will use it. To that end, the resource materials that accompany this text are not intended to be used as a script. Instead, the intent of this program is that teachers will apply their knowledge of students, their own experiences with some of these mathematical tools, and their intuition about teaching to make this program as effective as possible.

Models of Implementation

This program has been designed to be as flexible as possible. While this series of books may be used as the primary curriculum for the classroom, it was not designed as the full curriculum for any given grade level. Rather, it was crafted to support teachers as they help students understand the number operations and concepts that precede more advanced work in algebra. Teachers may choose to use this program as a guide for whole-class explorations or as the text for smaller, pull-out groups of students. In either case, it is important to note that the program is designed on the principle that students learn mathematics in large measure through interactions with each other.

Throughout this series, you will find numerous questions that ask students to explain their thinking. These occasions should not be taken lightly. It is in the sharing and comparing of solution strategies that students begin to build a firm foundation of understanding. The social dynamic of learning mathematics is important to recognize. Participation in mathematical discourse may be the most powerful impetus for learning mathematics available to young learners, and you will want to take advantage of every opportunity to encourage students to talk about their mathematical thinking and processes. Given a commitment to this principle, this program is likely to be most successful when students are progressing through the problems with their peers.

Assessment

At the conclusion of each section, you will find several problems that may be used for formative assessments. These problems review the key concepts discussed in the section. At the end of the book you will find additional assessment problems that cover the content of the entire book. These problems may be used as a cumulative assessment of student understanding of the key concepts in the book. The teachers' guide contains insights as to how the assessment problems might best be used and what they are intended to measure.

Assessment rubrics and scoring guides for every assessment may be found in *Assessment Teacher Edition*. Detailed instructions regarding assessment in general, and the use of the program rubrics in particular, are included in the introduction of *Assessment Teacher Edition*.

Professional Background

Perhaps the greatest mathematical challenge students face in the elementary grades is the understanding of fractions. It is not surprising that many middle school students also have difficulty with conceptual understanding of and computational facility with fractions. National and international test results have consistently confirmed that U.S. students have a weak understanding of fraction concepts; make limited connections among fractions, decimals, and percents; and generally struggle with fraction computation.

Some mathematics educators have suggested that the root of the problems young learners have with fractions lies in the fact that students are too often rushed to learn the algorithms and procedures for fraction operations. Without a firm understanding of the nature of fractions, or of the conceptual models that make fractions transparent, students easily become confused by a host of rules: When adding, find a common denominator and add the top, keep the bottom; when multiplying, multiply the top and multiply the bottom; when dividing, flip the second fraction and then multiply. What is it about the nature of fractions that supports these mathematical maneuvers? Without proper understanding of fractions, it is no wonder that by middle school many learners have given up on understanding fractions, relegating them to the magic of mathematics that will always be beyond them.

The next two books of this series deal with the topic of fractions. In this book, a solid foundation of the nature of fractions will be established in order to prepare students to use the various strategies for combining and operating on fractions in the next book.

The Big Ideas

There are several key ideas on which this book is based. These ideas form the basis for students to develop a richer understanding of fractions—what they are, what they mean, and how they are connected to other math constructs—that many students never develop.

Big Idea #1: Defining Fractions Fractional parts might be thought of as equal-sized portions—*fair shares*—of a whole, a unit, or a collection of objects. In what is often a troubling idea for students to grasp, the unit or collection of objects is counted as one and is often represented on a number line as the distance from zero to one.

Big Idea #2: Parts of a Whole Fractional parts have names that tell how many parts of that specific size make up the whole. We might think of fourths or thirds. There are 4 fourths that make up one whole. Also, 3 thirds, 2 halves, and 6 sixths each make up one whole. This book will emphasize the benchmark fractions of halves, thirds, fourths, sixths, and eighths. In what may be counterintuitive to students, the more fractional parts used to make a whole, the smaller the size of the fractional part. For example, although the number eight is greater than the number three, eighths are significantly smaller than thirds. Imagine cutting a whole pizza into three pieces or eight pieces. Clearly, the thirds are much larger than the eighths.

Big Idea #3: Numerators and Denominators A fraction has a structure that many students do not ever fully comprehend. The denominator may be thought of as the number of equal-sized parts into which the whole has been divided. In the fraction 3/4, the denominator 4 indicates that the whole has been divided into 4 equal parts. So, the denominator is a divisor—it divides the whole into a certain number of equal parts. In so doing, the denominator names the fraction—halves, fourths, thirds, and so on. The numerator of a fraction is a counter. It indicates the number of fractional parts (the size of which are determined by the denominator) that are presently under consideration.

Big Idea #4: Equivalence Equivalent fractions may be thought of as two or more different expressions of the same part. Equivalent fractions describe the same part by using different-sized fractional parts. For example, imagine two pizzas of the same size. The first is divided in half. The second is divided into four equal parts. One half of the first pizza is equivalent in size to 2/4 of the second pizza. We have cut the same amount of pizza into a different number of slices, and so two different fractions may be used to describe the same amount of pizza.

Big Idea #5: Relative Size The size of a fraction depends on the size of the whole. For example, imagine asking a friend, "You could have 3/4 of the money in one of my pockets or 1/4 of the money in my other pocket. Which pocket do you choose?" The answer to that question becomes nothing more than a guess, because, for example, 1/4 of $100 is clearly more than 3/4 of $4.

Teaching Ideas

Consistent with the intent of this text series, students' sense of fractions is most likely to be enriched through contextually based problems that gradually lead them from the informal to the formal. This book begins with several contexts that allow students to reason intuitively about fractions. The contexts are specifically designed to motivate them to use concrete models that can be helpful in both understanding and operating with fractions.

The book begins with the idea of a fair share. Students are asked how to fairly divide different groupings of candy bars among friends. When given bars to model these contexts, students quickly determine various ways to accomplish the task. In the case of three candy bars shared equally among four friends, students are likely to choose one of the following strategies:

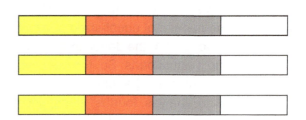

Strategy One: Divide the first two bars in half and the last bar into four equal parts. Everyone gets one half and one fourth, or 3/4 of a candy bar.

Strategy Two: Divide each candy bar into four equal parts. Each friend then gets 3 pieces, each 1/4 of the bar, or 3/4 of a candy bar.

It is important to recognize that students may intuitively be introduced to fraction equivalence through the use of pictures. In this case, they may see that 1/2 is the same amount as two parts that are 1/4 of a bar when they are trying to determine how much of a candy bar each person gets.

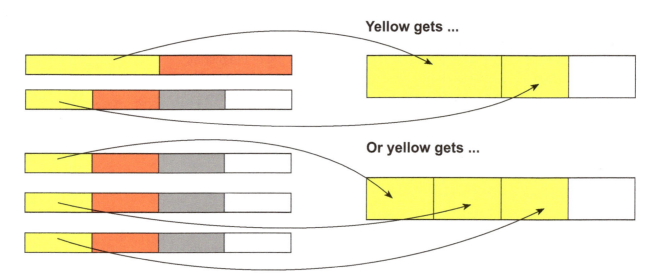

Please note how the problem's structure lends itself to a fraction-strip model. In subsequent pages this model is increasingly formalized through other contexts such as sharing plots of land or folding pieces of paper into equal-sized portions.

A second fraction model, developed after the fraction strips, is the fraction circle. Many students are familiar with pizza or pies as contexts for illustrating fractions. Indeed, the fraction circle is a helpful tool for many students, especially those who may not have fully understood fraction strips. In this series of problems, children are asked to cover the whole, and, in so doing, discover that there are many ways to divide a circle into equal parts. We might divide it in half, resulting in two equal halves. We also might divide the pizza in half, and then divide one of the halves into thirds, which are sixths of the entire circle. In this case, students can see that 1/2 + 1/6 + 1/6 + 1/6 will cover the entire circle. So, prior to introducing formal algorithms for addition and subtraction of fractions, students experience many informal contexts in which they are recognizing families of fractions (halves, fourths, and eighths; or sixths and thirds, and so on) as well as combinations of fractions across families that can combine to cover the whole (or add to one).

In the third section of the book, fraction strips and fraction circles are used to compare fractions and express equivalent fractions. Once again, students are asked to use the models, now formally, to find combinations of fractions that are equal to one. Earlier, students were allowed to play with the fraction circle parts to come up with combinations that could cover a circle. Now students are asked to use the models and to make the transition from the models to symbolic representations of fractions in the common form of, for example, 1/3.

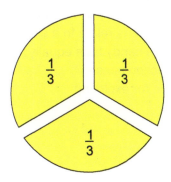

The final section of the book provides students with numerous examples to solve problems through contexts that require understanding of fractions and their use. It is interesting to note in these problems just how often the students are implicitly adding, subtracting, and even multiplying fractions without any formal algorithms to do so. These problems become the basis for the next book, in which the procedures for operating with fractions will be explained with conceptual models, practiced, and used both efficiently and with understanding.

As teachers, we must resist the temptation to rush students to using fraction algorithms. Each of the problems in this book can be solved by using the rather simple, but powerful, fraction models (strips and circles) developed in the book. If students are comfortable with these models, they will be much more likely to excel with the fraction operations. The moral of the fraction story should sound familiar. If we can take our time in the development phase of these concepts, we will reap the rewards rather quickly as students apply their understanding to procedures and algorithms with confidence.

Section A: Developing Fraction Sense

SECTION A PLANNER

THE MATHEMATICS CONTENT AND GOALS

GOALS
Students will:
- Explore the notion of fair shares as they build on their intuitive and informal fraction sense.
- Explore the benchmark fractions (halves, thirds, fourths, sixths, eighths).
- Represent their thinking about fractions with visual representations.
- Locate fractions on a number line.

> **LANGUAGE DEVELOPMENT**
> **Mathematical language in this section includes:**
> *Fraction:* A number used to name a part of a group or a whole. The number below the bar is the *denominator* and the number above the bar is the *numerator*.
> *Fractional Part:* Fractional parts might be thought of as equal-sized portions—fair shares—of a whole, a unit, or a collection of objects.
> *Numerator:* The numerator of a fraction is a counter. It indicates the number of fractional parts (the size of which are determined by the denominator) that are presently under consideration.
> *Denominator:* The denominator may be thought of as the number of equal-sized parts into which the whole has been divided.
> *Fair Share:* A fair share might be thought of synonymously with fractional part—equal sized portions of the whole.

PACING
The projected pacing for this section is 2–3 class periods (based on a 45-minute period).

PROBLEM SETS: OVERVIEW

Set 1 (pp. 1–4; problems 1–13)
Students begin this problem set by thinking about different ways to share candy bars among friends. Students intuitions about a fair way to share the candy bars are used to develop understanding about what fractions are and how fractional parts relate to a whole. Various methods for dividing the candy bars equally help students develop their fraction sense and begin to set the foundation for exploring fractional equivalence.

CONCEPT DEVELOPMENT (Pages 1–4)

INTRODUCE THE CONCEPT

ASSESS STUDENTS' PRIOR KNOWLEDGE
Students' understanding of what constitutes a fair share can motivate them to understand fractions.

Ask:
Suppose you and a friend found $4 in coins and bills on the street. What would be a fair way to share the money? What if you were with two other friends? Would there be a way to share the money so that each person got the same amount?

Listen for:
Students may ask which coins and bills were found. As you discuss this problem with them, elicit that they could change any coins and bills they found into equivalent amounts, such as 10 pennies for 1 dime.

- Two people would get $2 each.
- It is impossible for three people to share $4 and get the same amount. There would be 1 cent left over.

MODEL MATHEMATICAL THINKING
Model the thinking for another example by asking, *What would be a fair way for five friends to share $4 in coins and bills? How could they be sure that each friend gets a fair share?*

Talk Through the Thinking:
In the problem about you and a friend finding $4, you saw that it could be shared equally—the friends split the money so that each one gets $2. One way to share the $4 among five friends might be to start by changing all the money into pennies and making five equal groups of pennies. That would take a lot of time. Another way might be to share the money a little bit at a time until it is all gone. First, I could give 25¢ to each person. If I did this, it would mean I had given out $1.25. I could do it again, this time giving 50¢ to each person. That is another $2.50, for a total of $3.75 given out so far. That leaves 25¢ to be shared among five people.

Ask:
Could I give another 25¢ to each friend? Why not? What could I do next?

Listen for:
- You could not give another 25¢ to each friend because that would amount to $1.25, and you only have 25¢ left.
- You could change the 25¢ into all pennies and then count out the pennies, one by one. You could also change the 25¢ into 5 nickels, and then give each friend 1 nickel.

LAUNCH THE PROBLEM SOLVING

Have students work individually to solve the problems on page 1. As they work, you may want to circulate and monitor their recorded answers. When students finish each problem, have them compare and discuss their answers with a partner. Then have each pair share their answers in a class discussion of the problem. Refer to the **Teacher Notes: Student Page 1** for more specific ideas about the problems on this page.

As students work and report their conclusions, focus on these issues:

Encourage Language Development – As students work through the page, look for opportunities to encourage their use of vocabulary related to fraction sense, such as the naming of the fractional parts: halves, thirds, and fourths.

Facilitate Students' Thinking – Encourage students' use of intuitive and informal strategies as they divide the candy bars into equal parts.

Allow Waiting Time – As students struggle to explain their thinking, be sure to allow them at least 20 seconds to organize their thoughts (this may feel like a long time).

Student Page 1: Problems and Potential Answers

Section A: Developing Fraction Sense — Set 1

Who Gets the Most?
Students are trying to share candy bars equally. Use the models below to show how much of the candy each student gets.

Group 1: Stan, Tim, and Cody have 2 candy bars to share.

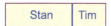   

Group 2: Ellen, Mark, Scott, and Sheri have 2 candy bars to share.

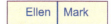   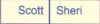

Group 3: Bob and Mary have 3 candy bars to share.

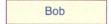

Group 4: Susan, Brian, Dan, and Jonathon have 3 candy bars to share.

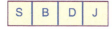   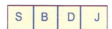   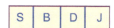

1. In which group does each student get the most candy? __Group 3__ How do you know?
   Group 3 because each student gets $1\frac{1}{2}$ bars.

2. In which group does each student get the least candy __Group 2__? How do you know?
   Group 2 because each student gets only a half of a bar.

Book 5: *Fraction Sense*

TEACHER NOTES: STUDENT PAGE 1

The context of fair sharing used to introduce this book is extremely important. Even very young children know when something has been divided evenly. You might ask your students with younger siblings to do a fun research assignment. Have them get a cookie, candy bar, or some other food item that is desirable to a younger child. Have them divide the item into two unequal pieces, and then ask the younger sibling to choose which piece he or she wants. Almost all young children (ages 3–5 or so) will recognize the difference in relative size of the pieces and choose the larger piece. The notion of a fair share is deeply ingrained at an early age. This book, and these first problems in particular, attempts to take advantage of this kind of informal and intuitive understanding of fractional parts of a whole.

Problems 1 and 2: *Teaching Strategy:* As students answer these problems, discuss the different ways of partitioning the candy bars. Take several minutes to allow students to share their thinking and strategies in response to each of the questions. *Watch for:* Students who are not using benchmark fractions in their responses. Rather, they may say things such as, "Well, for group 3, there are more candy bars than people. So, each person gets at least one whole candy bar."

CONTINUE THE PROBLEM SOLVING

Have students work individually to solve the problems on page 2. As they work, you may want to circulate and monitor their recorded answers. When students finish each problem, have them compare and discuss their answers with a partner. Then have each pair share their answers in a class discussion of the problem. Refer to the **Teacher Notes: Student Page 2** for more specific ideas about the problems on this page.

As students work and report their conclusions, focus on these issues:

Validate Representations – When several students use different drawings to partition the candy bars, have them compare drawings and discuss whether all are correct.

Validate Alternate Strategies – Different students may use different strategies to decide how to share the candy bars. Be sure to have them share their strategies with their classmates. Have the class discuss whether a chosen strategy is valid for the particular problem.

Allow Waiting Time – Because students may use several representations and strategies, it is especially important to allow them ample time to organize their thoughts before explaining their thinking.

Student Page 2: Problems and Potential Answers

Section A: Developing Fraction Sense Set 1

3. Stan, Tim, and Cody share 2 candy bars equally. How much of the candy does Tim get? _____
   Explain your reasoning, or show the amount Tim gets on the models below.
   $\frac{2}{3}$ of 1 bar, or $\frac{1}{3}$ of each of the 2 bars

4. Ellen, Mark, Scott, and Sheri share 2 candy bars equally. How much of the candy does Ellen get?
   _____ Explain your reasoning, or show the amount Ellen gets on the models below.
   $\frac{1}{2}$ of 1 bar, or $\frac{1}{4}$ of each of the 2 bars

5. Bob and Mary share 3 candy bars equally. How much of the candy does Mary get? _____
   Explain your reasoning, or show the amount Mary gets on the models below.
   $1\frac{1}{2}$ candy bars, or $\frac{1}{2}$ of each of the 3 bars

6. Susan, Brian, Dan, and Jonathon share 3 candy bars equally. How much of the candy does Dan get? _____ Explain your reasoning, or show the amount Dan gets on the models below. $\frac{3}{4}$ of a candy bar, or $\frac{1}{2}$ of each of the 3 bars

   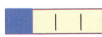 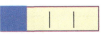

TEACHER NOTES: STUDENT PAGE 2

Problems 3–6: The most important idea in these problems is that there is usually more than one way to divide the candy bars into equal portions. Each illustrated answer simply shows one way to do the problem. There are others ways that students should recognize. For example, in order to share 2 candy bars equally among 3 people, two common strategies are likely to emerge:

Strategy #1: Divide each candy bar into 3 equal parts.

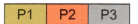 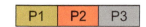

In this solution, P1 receives 1/3 of the first candy bar and 1/3 of the second candy bar. So do P2 and P3. So, each person receives 2/3 of a candy bar.

Strategy #2: Split each candy bar in half; then divide the remaining portion into thirds.

In contrast to the first strategy, in which each person gets the same part of each candy bar, a second popular method that you might look for in students' work involves a different kind of thinking. Using this strategy, a larger part, 1/2, of each candy bar is first given to each person.

Next, the leftover portion of the candy bar is divided into thirds, with each third distributed to each of the three individuals.

Each person then receives the following parts:

Teaching Strategy: If possible, students should discuss and compare these two strategies. *Watch for:* Students should recognize that with both strategies, the total amounts of candy each person receives are the same. *Watch for:* Some students may begin to assign labels to the fractional parts and operations, for example, 1/2 + 1/6. This observation will be pursued in subsequent sections of this book and in Book 6. *Teaching Strategy:* Take advantage of this opportunity to foreshadow future work with fraction labels if it arises in your classroom.

Problem 4 and Problem 6: The strategy that students use for separating the bar into fourths will tell you what the students are learning about the relationship of halves to fourths. *Watch for:* Some students will separate the candy bar into halves, then subdivide each of the halves into two equal parts to get fourths. This takes advantage of the fact that it is easier to separate a region in half than into thirds, fourths, or any other number of equal pieces. *Teaching Strategy:* Have students explain to the class why they chose to create fourths in this way. Have students suggest other fractions that could be created using the same strategy.

CONTINUE THE PROBLEM SOLVING

Have students work individually to solve the problems on page 3. As they work, you may want to circulate and monitor their recorded answers. When students finish each problem, have them compare and discuss their answers with a partner. Then have each pair share their answers in a class discussion of the problem. Refer to the **Teacher Notes: Student Page 3** for more specific ideas about the problems on this page.

As students work and report their conclusions, focus on these issues:

Validate Representations – When several students partition the candy bars in different ways, have them compare and discuss their representations to determine whether all are correct.

Look for Misconceptions – Some students may not understand that, depending on the size of the whole, the same fraction can refer to a different amount or quantity. If students draw candy bars that are different sizes for problem 1, it would be a good opportunity to discuss whether the method of sharing by giving each person a whole candy bar would be fair — it would not because the 3 thirds in each candy bar would be different amounts.

Facilitate Students' Thinking – Some students may need to be reminded that the denominator of a fraction (the number below the fraction bar) names the total number of equal parts of the whole and that the numerator (the number above the fraction bar) names the number of equal parts that are being considered.

Validate Representations – There is more than one way to show the partitioning in problem 7. Have students discuss and compare their diagrams to determine whether all represent a solution to the problem.

Explaining Thinking – Students are encouraged on these problems to explain their thinking. Take time to discuss and model the various strategies one might follow to solve the problems, being particularly attentive to the ways students describe their thought processes and strategies.

Student Page 3: Problems and Potential Answers

Section A: Developing Fraction Sense Set 1

7. Three friends share 4 candy bars. Draw a diagram to show how much of the candy bars each friend gets.

8. Divide the model of the candy bar into 6 equal parts.

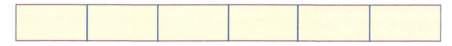

If you get two parts, what fraction of the bar do you get? $\frac{2}{6}$ or $\frac{1}{3}$

9. Four friends share one candy bar equally. The piece below is the size of one of the pieces of the candy bar. Draw the whole candy bar.

10. Show how the bars below can be divided into the given number of equal parts. **Label** each fractional part of the bar.

2 parts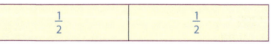

4 parts

8 parts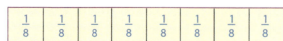

TEACHER NOTES: STUDENT PAGE 3

The problems on this page introduce formal notation for fractions. This is a good opportunity to help students understand how fractional parts are written and what they mean. Even those students who have worked with fractions before may not recall that the number below the fraction bar (the denominator) indicates how many equal parts there are in the whole. The number above the fraction bar (the numerator) indicates how many of these equal parts we are interested in. It is worth the time to model several examples, being clear to connect the visual and symbolic representations. For example:

Three of the equal parts are shaded. So the numerator is 3.

$$\frac{3}{4}$$

The bar is divided into 4 equal parts. So the denominator is 4.

Problem 7: Strategies and representations may vary. *Watch for:* Students should use either of the two methods discussed in the **Teacher Notes: Student Page 2**.

Problem 8: *Watch for:* Check to make sure students are partitioning the bar into equal parts. *Teaching Strategy:* This problem offers a good opportunity for a class discussion of the symbolic representation of fractions. The denominator, 6, indicates how many equal parts; the numerator, 2, indicates how many parts are shaded. *Watch for:* The method that students use to create sixths will tell you how much students are internalizing about the relationships between fractions. If students first draw halves and then separate each half into thirds, this shows an advanced understanding. Similarly, they may create thirds first and then halve each of the 3 thirds. *Teaching Strategy:* Have students explain their thinking to the class and discuss the possible advantages of the strategy they used.

Problem 9: *Watch for:* This problem will indicate whether students understand that the parts of a fraction indicated by the denominator need to be of identical size. Scan your students' drawings. Look for parts of the candy bar that are not fair shares. Also look for students who create fourths by doubling both the length and the width of the shape they started with. These students are taking advantage of the ease of doubling a figure.

Problem 10: *Watch for:* Students who see the relationship between halves, fourths, and eighths will build eighths by first separating into halves, then subdividing into fourths and then eighths.

On the Lookout for Misconceptions

One of the ideas students have difficulty with is that a **fraction** may actually refer to a different quantity or amount depending on the **whole** that is being divided. For example, 1/2 of one dollar is a very different amount of money than 1/2 of 10 dollars. Although the fractional representation 1/2 is the same, the amount it represents varies as the whole varies.

As an example, a child might be asked whether he or she would rather have 3/4 of one pile of coins or 1/4 of another pile of coins. You might try this experiment in class to illustrate the point. Depending on what coins are in the pile, e.g., quarters vs. pennies, the value of 1/4 of one pile of coins may be much greater than the value of 1/2 of the other. This idea illustrates why context is so vitally important when introducing fractions to young students. Particularly early on, be sure to anchor your use of fractions in meaningful contexts to prevent the proliferation of such misconceptions.

Fraction Sense Teacher Edition

CONTINUE THE PROBLEM SOLVING

Have students work individually to solve the problems on page 4. As they work, you may want to circulate and monitor their recorded answers. When students finish each problem, have them compare and discuss their answers with a partner. Then have each pair share their answers in a class discussion of the problem. Refer to the **Teacher Notes: Student Page 4** for more specific ideas about the problems on this page.

As students work and report their conclusions, focus on these issues:

Look for Misconceptions – Fractions name equal parts. As students work on problems 11 and 12, check to be sure that they are partitioning the bars into the correct number of equal parts. See the Teacher Notes below for more information. **Facilitate Students' Thinking –** You may need to remind students of the meanings of the numerator and denominator of a fraction. You might suggest that they ask themselves how many equal parts in all and then write that number as the denominator, writing the number of shaded parts as the numerator.

Allow Waiting Time – When students struggle to explain their thinking, be sure to allow ample time for them to organize their thoughts.

TEACHER NOTES: STUDENT PAGE 4

Problems 11–13: These problems provide students with further practice in naming and identifying fractions. Emphasize the meanings of the denominator (number of equal parts) and the numerator (number of parts we are interested in).

Problem 11: Students should use the relationship between thirds, sixths, and twelfths to help them partition the figures.

Watch for: Students should realize that the easiest way to draw sixths is to draw thirds and separate each third in half. Similarly, they can build twelfths by separating the sixths in half.

Teaching Strategy: Have students explain how they know that this strategy will create the correct fractional parts. Then extend the discussion by having students think about a way to create tenths (by combining partitioning in fifths and partitioning in halves).

Problem 12: Students can shade any of the sectors. For example, in part a, students may shade the second half instead of the first half.

> ### On the Lookout for Misconceptions
>
> Students may have an understanding that for 1/3 of a whole, the whole can be sectioned into 3 parts, as in problem 11. But it is important for them to know that the three parts must be of equal size in order for one of the parts to represent 1/3 of the whole.
>
> When students are breaking and shading the bars into the appropriate numbers of parts, make sure they understand that the size of the parts are equal. This may not be apparent in the students' drawings. It's important to discuss this idea of equal size with students as discussion will either reveal a misconception about fractional parts or reveal their difficulty with fine motor skills.

Student Page 4: Problems and Potential Answers

Section A: Developing Fraction Sense — Set 1

11. Show how the bars below can be divided into the given number of equal parts. **Label** each fractional part of the bar.

Example: 2 parts

3 parts

6 parts

12 parts

12. Shade the given fraction on each bar below.

a) $\frac{1}{2}$    d) $\frac{2}{4}$

b) $\frac{1}{3}$    e) $\frac{1}{4}$

c) $\frac{3}{6}$    f) $\frac{2}{3}$

13. What fraction of each bar is shaded?

a) $\frac{3}{4}$ 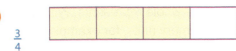   d) $\frac{1}{2}$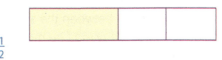

b) $\frac{2}{3}$ e) $\frac{4}{8}$

c) $\frac{1}{4}$ 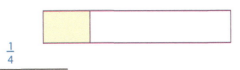   f) $\frac{6}{8}$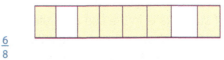

4 Book 5: *Fraction Sense*

SECTION A ASSESSMENT (PAGES 5–6)

LAUNCH THE ASSESSMENT

Have students turn to the Section A assessment on page 5. An additional copy is found on page 78 of the Assessment Book. Have students work individually to solve the problems and write their explanations. As they work, circulate to be sure students understand what they need to do for each problem and that they are completing each part of the problem. For example, for problem 1 students need to analyze the models to determine whether they both show the same fractions. Then they need to explain their reasoning. You may find it helpful to read through the directions for all the problems before students begin, discussing the types of responses they will need to make for each problem.

Encourage students to use whatever space they need to explain their thinking. If the space on the page is inadequate—it probably will be for some of their explanations—they should use an additional sheet of paper or the back of the page. Refer to the **Teacher Notes: Assessment Problems for Section A, Student Page 5**, for more specific ideas about the problems on this page.

Evaluate Student Responses

Use the assessment rubric on page 77 of the Assessment Book (pictured on page 24 of the Teacher Edition) to evaluate student responses. The Assessment Book has some general suggestions for using the rubric that you may find helpful.

TEACHER NOTES: ASSESSMENT PROBLEMS FOR SECTION A, STUDENT PAGE 5

Problem 1: This problem provides a context that makes explicit the two partitioning strategies presented in Set 1. *Teaching Strategy:* Use this context to motivate students to see and understand the connection between the strategies and to decide which strategy may be most useful, depending on the context of the problem. Be particularly attentive to the explanations students give to support their conclusions.

Problems 2–3: Perhaps the most common application of fractions on a number line in the daily life of students is in the use of a ruler. Whether measuring inches or measuring miles, number lines are powerful models for expressing distance or length. *Teaching Strategy:* Take advantage of these two problems to help students connect the bars they divided in previous problems to the number line that has already been partitioned. To help avoid misconceptions, review the notion that any fraction has meaning only when one knows what the whole represents. With a tape measure in customary units, for example, the whole being referenced by any fraction is 1 inch. As an extension activity, you may wish to have students measure objects with both metric and customary rulers. Doing so will illustrate in a meaningful way that 1/2 centimeter is a very different length than 1/2 inch.

Student Page 5: Problems and Potential Answers

Section A: Problems for Assessment

1. Four neighbors are trying to divide three plots of land at the community garden equally. Two strategies are shown below. One of the neighbors wonders whether both strategies are fair ways to divide the garden plots. Do both strategies result in the same answer? Explain your reasoning using words or pictures.
   Yes, each family is getting an equal share of the land. Explanations may vary.

Strategy #1

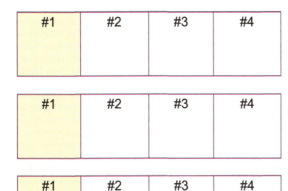

Strategy #2

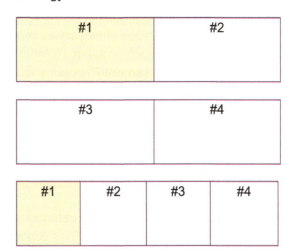

2. Graph each fraction on the number line below.

   a) $\frac{1}{2}$ b) $\frac{1}{3}$ c) $\frac{2}{4}$ d) $\frac{1}{6}$ e) $\frac{2}{3}$ f) $\frac{3}{4}$

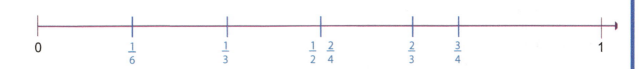

3. Start at 0. Use sixths above the line and thirds below the line to extend the number line to 2.

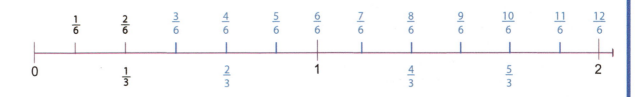

Book 5: *Fraction Sense* 5

CONTINUE THE ASSESSMENT

Have students turn to the Section A assessment on page 6. An additional copy is found on page 79 of the Assessment Book. Have students work individually to solve the problems and write their explanations. As they work, circulate to be sure students understand what they need to do for each problem and that they are completing each part of the problem. For example, for problems 4a, c, and d students need to name each fraction in two ways. You may find it helpful to read through the directions for all the problems before students begin, discussing the types of responses they will need to make for each problem. Refer to the **Teacher Notes: Assessment Problems for Section A, Student Page 6**, for more specific ideas about the problems on this page.

Evaluate Student Responses

Use the assessment rubric on page 77 of the Assessment Book (pictured on page 24 of the Teacher Edition) to evaluate student responses. The Assessment Book has some general suggestions for using the rubric that you may find helpful.

TEACHER NOTES: ASSESSMENT PROBLEMS FOR SECTION A, STUDENT PAGE 6

Problem 4: This problem explicitly introduces the concept of equivalent fractions. This concept is extremely important, yet is intuitively obvious to most students if presented in meaningful contexts. *Teaching Strategy:* Be sure to return to the definition of a fraction as students think about how to name a fractional part in different ways. Using the standard graham cracker as a model, for example (4 equal rectangles comprise the whole cracker), it is relatively easy to illustrate that breaking the cracker in half and distributing one piece to two people is a fair share. Next, show that dividing the cracker into its 4 equal rectangles and then giving 2 rectangles to each person results in another fair share.

Comparing the amounts (1/2 of the whole vs. 2/4 of the whole) reveals that they are equal quantities. So, 1/2 and 2/4 of the same whole is the same amount of cracker. Other visual and conceptual models may be equally effective. Be sure to take the time to provide physical demonstrations of equivalent fractions to emphasize that a fraction is simply a convention we use to identify what part of any one thing we have when compared to the whole.

Some of the fractions have obvious equivalents. The equivalents of others, such as 3/8, are not so obvious. For the interested and advanced students in the class, challenge them to find a way to represent such fractions by renaming them as equivalent fractions. This activity will require them to consider ways to break the units into smaller parts. In the case of eighths, sixteenths is the most obvious option.

Student Page 6: Problems and Potential Answers

Section A: Problems for Assessment

4. What fraction of each model is shaded? Use more than one fraction to identify the shaded part when you can.

a) 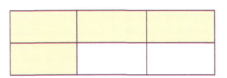 $\frac{4}{6}$, $\frac{2}{3}$

b) 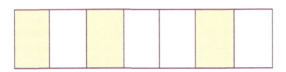 $\frac{3}{8}$

c) 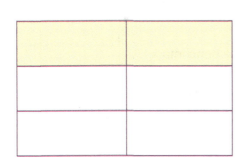 $\frac{2}{6}$, $\frac{1}{3}$

d)  $\frac{3}{6}$, $\frac{1}{2}$

e) 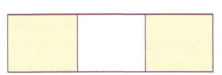 $\frac{2}{3}$

f) 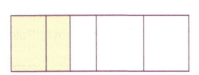 $\frac{3}{8}$

6   Book 5: *Fraction Sense*

Fraction Sense *Teacher Edition*   23

SCORING GUIDE BOOK 5: FRACTION SENSE

Section A Assessment
For Use With: Student Book Pages 5–6

PROBLEM DESCRIPTION	SCORING: WHAT TO LOOK FOR	SCORE AND COMMENTS
Problem 1 Two sets of fraction strips, with three strips in each set. Add the fractional amounts from each set of fraction strips, and compare to each other. Real-world context. Level 2: Tool use Level 3: Connection and Application Level 4: Synthesis and Evaluation	Do students: • Understand visual representation of fractional pieces? • Use informal strategies to add fractional pieces? • Compare fractions to determine which is greater? • Appropriately articulate strategies they use?	 Points: _____ of 4
Problem 2a–f Locate fractions on a number line. Level 1: Comprehension and Knowledge	Do students: • Understand the relative size and position of various benchmark fractions? • Appropriately place benchmark fractions on a number line? • Use common denominator families (1/3 and 1/6) to place fractions?	 Points: _____ of 6
Problem 3 Extend a number line using thirds and sixths. Level 1: Comprehension and Knowledge Level 2: Tool use	Do students: • Appropriately extend the number line? • Recognize equivalent fractions (e.g., 1/3 = 2/6)?	 Points: _____ of 3
Problem 4a–f Name fractions based on a visual representation. Level 4: Synthesis and Evaluation	Do students: • Recognize fractional quantities? • Understand visual representations of fractions? • Recognize equivalent fractions (more than one way to name a fraction)?	(problem a) Points: ___ of 2 (problem b) Points: ___ of 2 (problem c) Points: ___ of 2 (problem d) Points: ___ of 2 (problem e) Points: ___ of 2 (problem f) Points: ___ of 2

TOTAL POINTS: _____ OF 25

Section B: Fraction Circles

SECTION B PLANNER

THE MATHEMATICS CONTENT AND GOALS

GOALS
Students will:
- Be introduced to fraction circles as a model for illustrating fractional parts.
- Use fractional parts of the fraction circles to make a whole, thereby informally exploring addition of fractions.
- Use fraction circles to find equivalent fractions.
- Use fraction circles to compare fractions.

LANGUAGE DEVELOPMENT
Mathematical language in this section includes:

Greater/more: In the context of comparing fractional parts in this unit, greater or more refers to a comparison among fractional parts, selecting the largest fraction while assuming the unit whole is the same for each fraction compared.

Least/less: In the context of comparing fractional parts in this unit, least or less refers to a comparison among fractional parts, selecting the smallest fraction while assuming the unit whole is the same for each fraction being compared.

Part: Fractional parts might be thought of as equal-sized portions—fair shares—of a whole, a unit, or a collection of objects.

Whole: The entire unit being evaluated.

Fraction Circle: A fraction model/manipulative in which the unit circle is divided into triangular wedges that indicate various fractional amounts.

Fraction Strip: A fraction model/manipulative in which a rectangle representing the unit whole is divided into rectangular sections that indicate various fractional amounts.

PACING
The projected pacing for this section is 1–2 class periods (based on a 45-minute period).

PROBLEM SETS: OVERVIEW

Set 1 (pp. 7–8; problems 1–9) &
Set 2 (pp. 9–10; problems 1–12)

The problems in this section are designed to introduce students to fraction circles as physical representations of fractions. Fraction circles are tools that help students visualize and conceptualize fractional parts, compare fractions, find equivalent fractions, and begin to explore operations with fractions. Such uses of fraction circles are explored in this section of the book.

Fraction Sense Teacher Edition 25

CONCEPT DEVELOPMENT (PAGES 7–10)

INTRODUCE THE CONCEPT

ASSESS STUDENTS' PRIOR KNOWLEDGE
Draw these shapes on the board:

Ask:
Into how many equal parts is the rectangle divided? What fraction does each equal part represent? How can you draw lines on the circle to show the same number of equal parts? (For the last question, you may wish to have a volunteer demonstrate rather than describe the action to take.)

Listen for:
- The rectangle is divided into 4 equal parts.
- Each equal part represents 1/4.
- You can draw one line through the center of the circle. Then draw another line through the center that is perpendicular to the first line.

MODEL MATHEMATICAL THINKING
Draw a circle on the board. Draw lines to divide it into eighths. Shade 6/8 of the circle. Then ask, *Suppose this circle were a pizza and the shaded parts represent the slices eaten by some friends. How could we tell what part of the whole pizza was eaten?*

Talk Through the Thinking:
First, let's find the number of slices the pizza was cut into. I see 8 slices. I also see that all the slices are exactly the same size. So, each slice represents 1/8 of the pizza. Now, let's count the number of shaded parts, the number of slices that were eaten. There are 6 shaded parts. So if there were 8 slices in all and 6 of the slices were eaten, this means that 6/8 of the whole pizza was eaten.

Ask:
Is there another fraction you could use to tell what part of the pizza was eaten? If so, what is that fraction?

Listen for:
- Yes, there is another fraction. The fraction is 3/4.

LAUNCH THE PROBLEM SOLVING

Have students work individually to solve the problems on page 7. As they work, you may want to circulate and monitor their recorded answers. When students finish each problem, have them compare and discuss their answers with a partner. Then have each pair share their answers in a class discussion of the problem. Refer to the **Teacher Notes: Student Page 7** for more specific ideas about the problems on this page.

As students work and report their conclusions, focus on these issues:

Help Make Connections – You may need to remind students that, just as when we divided candy bars into fair shares, fractions name equal parts.

Encourage Language Development – Encourage students to use correct terminology when talking about fractional parts of a circle.

Validate Representations – Students may wish to make their own drawings. Encourage them to do so. There is value in allowing students to struggle a little bit with these concepts, because it helps them to develop visual clues and strategies, an important part of fraction sense.

Allow Waiting Time – When students struggle to explain their thinking, be sure to allow them ample time to organize their thoughts.

TEACHER NOTES: STUDENT PAGE 7

Although fraction circles are different visual models from the candy bar models used previously, they are used in much the same way. Take advantage of students' intuitive understandings of candy bar models and help students transfer the concepts to fraction circles.

Problems 1–8: These problems introduce students to the fraction circle model, at first in the form of a circle graph. *Watch for:* Many students will recognize the basis of the questions being asked and concepts probed on this page from earlier explorations with candy bar models. *Teaching Strategy:* Be sure to help students transfer conceptual understanding across models. Pause at problems 6–8 in particular to make sure students see how benchmark fractions such as halves and fourths are related.

Student Page 7: Problems and Potential Answers

Section B: Fraction Circles — Set 1

Fraction circles are used to illustrate fractional parts of a whole. You could use one type of fraction circle, called a circle graph, to show how students typically spend their days.

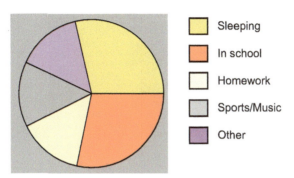

In this example, it looks as if students spend about $\frac{1}{3}$ of their day in school. (How many hours per day would that be?) It also looks as if students spend about $\frac{1}{4}$ of their day participating in either sports or music, or other activities. Let's explore how fraction circles can help you understand fractions better.

Here are some common fractional parts, which are shaded in purple:

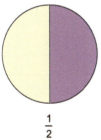 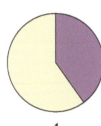  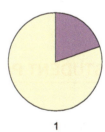 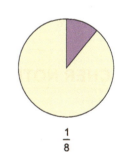

$\frac{1}{2}$ — One Half $\frac{1}{3}$ — One Third $\frac{1}{4}$ — One Fourth $\frac{1}{6}$ — One Sixth $\frac{1}{8}$ — One Eighth

1. How many halves are needed to make one whole? __2__
2. How many thirds are needed to make one whole? __3__
3. How many fourths are needed to make one whole? __4__
4. How many sixths are needed to make one whole? __6__
5. How many eighths are needed to make one whole? __8__
6. How many fourths are needed to make **one half**? __2__
7. How many sixths are needed to make **one third**? __2__
8. How many eighths are needed to make **one fourth**? __2__

Book 5: *Fraction Sense*   7

CONTINUE THE PROBLEM SOLVING

Have students work individually to solve the problems on page 8. These problems should be pretty straightforward. As they work, you may want to circulate and monitor their recorded answers and watch how they count the sections. **Refer to the Teacher Notes: Student Page 8** for more specific ideas about the problems on this page.

As students work and report their conclusions, focus on these issues:

Allow Processing Time – Be sure to allow students enough time to label their models and to explore their fraction circles.

Help Make Connections – The easiest fraction to recognize in the circular model is any fraction that represents 1/2, 1/4, or 1/8. This is because it is easy to see when a circle has been halved or quartered but harder to see other fractions. Ask students if they could cover half of the fraction circle and still figure out the fractional value of each sector. Have students explain which fractions they could identify this way and how they know.

TEACHER NOTES: STUDENT PAGE 8

It is extremely important for students to be able to physically manipulate these fraction models. While fraction circles can be purchased from any number of educational suppliers, you can also use thick card stock to print templates of them for later use by students. In any event, it is important that they have these models readily available throughout this book and the next book, which will focus on operations with fractions.

Student Page 8: Problems and Potential Answers

Section B: Fraction Circles — Set 1

Making Fraction Circles

9. Label each part of each fraction circle. The first fraction circle, the halves, has been done for you. When you finish, your teacher will give you similar fraction circles that you should label. Then carefully cut along the lines to make your own fraction circles.

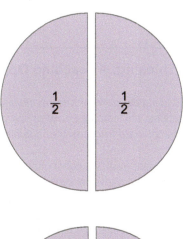
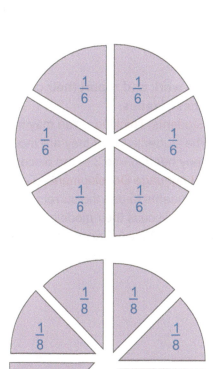
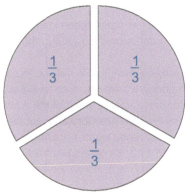
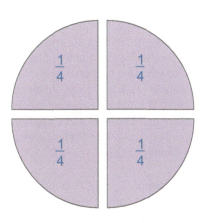
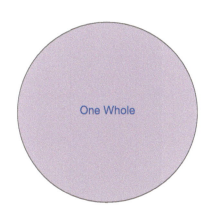

8 Book 5: *Fraction Sense*

CONTINUE THE PROBLEM SOLVING

Have students work individually to solve the problems on page 9. As they work, you may want to circulate and monitor their recorded answers. When students finish each problem, have them compare and discuss their answers with a partner. Then have each pair share their answers in a class discussion of the problem. Refer to the **Teacher Notes: Student Page 9** for more specific ideas about the problems on this page.

As students work and report their conclusions, focus on these issues:

Facilitate Students' Thinking – You may need to remind some students that if they are modeling 3/6, for example, they need to use 3 of the pieces marked 1/6.

Encourage Language Development – Continue to encourage students to use the correct fraction terminology as they discuss their models.

Allow Processing Time – Encourage students to take time to explore fraction circles and the fractional parts they represent.

TEACHER NOTES: STUDENT PAGE 9

Problems 1–12: Students will quickly develop facility with the fraction circle pieces as they compare the fractions in these problems. You may wish to challenge students to come up with a list of fraction pairs to compare on their own or to share with a peer. The equivalent fractions in problems 11 and 12 are precursors to the next problem, in which students will have to find different ways to represent equivalent fractions.

Forward Thinking: A Teaching Opportunity

In addition to using the parts of fraction circles to compare fractions, students can build on the physical comparison to compare fractions conceptually.

One way to compare fractions conceptually occurs when two fractions have the same denominator but different numerators, such as 4/5 and 2/5. Students can see from a model that 4/5 is greater because there are more fifths in 4/5 than in 2/5. A general rule to follow is that when two fractions have the same denominator, the fraction with the larger numerator is the greater fraction.

In another case, the numerators may be the same, but the denominators are different, such as 5/8 and 5/12. Through modeling, students see that the number of fractional parts are the same for each, but the size of those parts differs. Since eighths are larger than twelfths, 5/8 is larger than 5/12. So, when two fractions have the same numerator, the fraction with the smaller denominator is the greater fraction.

A third way to compare fractions involves using the benchmarks 0, 1/2, and 1. If students can determine that one fraction is greater than 1/2 and the other is less than 1/2, then they know which one is greater. If students can visualize how close a fraction is to 0, 1/2, or 1, then they can determine which is greater. When comparing the fractions 9/10 and 7/8, for example, students can see that both are one fractional part away from 1. Since 1/10 is smaller than 1/8, 9/10 must be closer to 1 and is therefore the greater fraction.

Equivalent Fractions: By now, students should have a solid understanding of fraction equivalence. Allow them plenty of time to explore fraction circle representations of equivalent fractions.

Student Page 9: Problems and Potential Answers

Section B: Fraction Circles — Set 2

Comparing Fractions

Which fraction in each pair is greater (covers more of the whole circle)? Use your fraction circles to help you decide. Then <u>draw a ring around the fraction that is greater</u>. If the two fractions cover the same part of the whole circle, then draw a ring around both fractions.

1. (½) or ¼
2. ⅔ or (6/8)
3. (¼) or ⅙
4. (⅜) or ¼
5. (⅔) or ½
6. (¾) or ⅔
7. (3/6) or (4/8)
8. (⅓) or ¼
9. (3/3) or ¾
10. ⅝ or (⅔)
11. (4/6) or (⅔)
12. (6/8) or (¾)

Equivalent Fractions

Use your fraction circles. Find as many ways as you can to model each fraction <u>with only one kind of fractional part</u>. Write the ways you find. For example, ½ could be modeled several different ways:

½ → ⬗ or ⬗ or ⬗ or ⬗

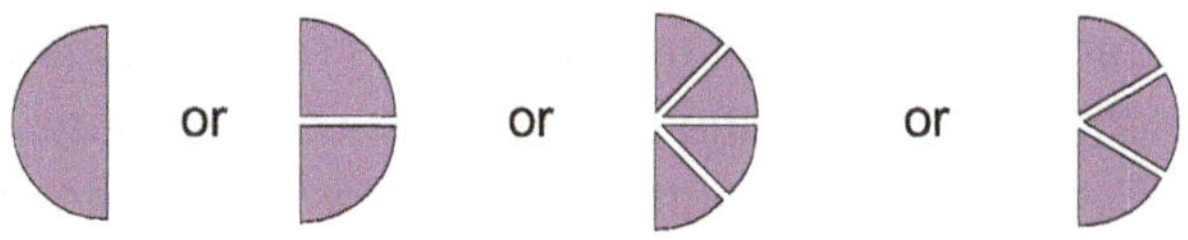

          ¼ + ¼   ⅛ + ⅛ + ⅛ + ⅛   ⅙ + ⅙ + ⅙

⅔ →   ⅓ + ⅓   ⅙ + ⅙ + ⅙ + ⅙   _____

¾ →   ¼ + ¼ + ¼   ⅛ + ⅛ + ⅛ + ⅛ + ⅛ + ⅛ _____

Book 5: *Fraction Sense*

CONTINUE THE PROBLEM SOLVING

Have students work individually to solve the problem on page 10. As they work, you may want to circulate and monitor their recorded answers. When students finish, have them compare and discuss their answers with a partner. Then have each pair share their answers in a class discussion of the problem. Refer to the **Teacher Notes: Student Page 10** for more specific ideas about the problems on this page.

As students work and report their conclusions, focus on these issues:

Allow Processing Time – The problem on page 10 requires that students think about multiple ways to cover 1 whole and then write the ways as addition expressions. Be sure to allow plenty of time for students to complete the problem.

Facilitate Students' Thinking – Some students may have trouble getting started on the problem. You might ask them to first think about the ways they can use their fraction circle pieces to cover 1/2.

Validate Representations – Some students may think of ways to cover 1 whole that do not occur to other students. Be sure to have all students share their results in a class discussion, and have the class decide whether all representations are valid.

TEACHER NOTES: STUDENT PAGE 10

This problem may appear to be tedious to students. However, it provides a great opportunity for students to find ways to decompose the number 1 in different ways that involve the system of thirds and the system of halves. The key is that the whole (number 1) can first be decomposed in terms of the half system or all the ways to make 1 with parts of 1/2, 1/4, and 1/8. Approaching this systematically makes sense. For example, start with the larger fractions, like 1/2 + 1/2, and decompose each of the addends into smaller addends. So the decomposition would begin with 1/2 + 1/4 + 1/4 and end with 1/8 + 1/8 + 1/8 + 1/8 + 1/8 + 1/8 + 1/8 + 1/8. The same strategy applies to the decomposition of the family of thirds: begin with 1/3 + 1/3 + 1/3 and move toward incorporating sixths. Finally, students may find a whole new set of solutions if they realize that the family of thirds can make 1/2 as can the family of halves. This will allow them to decompose one of the halves as combinations of thirds and sixths and the other half as combinations of halves, fourths, and eighths. *Watch for:* This is an excellent exercise not only for the repetition it provides, but also because it requires that students exhibit a certain amount of organization and pattern recognition. *Teaching Strategy:* Students may not find all of the possible solutions, but if they have an organized approach they are more likely to find most of the solutions. Be sure to discuss the patterns. For example, every 1/2 can be covered by two 1/4 pieces. Once this is established, a great many additional solutions can be found. This exercise will take some time to complete, but it is a valuable opportunity to solidify basic fraction sense in your students.

Section B: Fraction Circles — Set 2

Covering One Whole

Use your fraction circles. Find as many ways as you can to make a whole circle using different combinations of fractional parts. There are 21 in all. Record your solutions below. Be careful! A different arrangement of the same combination of pieces counts as the same solution. Think how to organize your investigation to help you keep track of all the combinations. One example has been done for you.

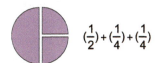 $(\frac{1}{2}) + (\frac{1}{4}) + (\frac{1}{4})$

$(\frac{1}{1})$

$(\frac{1}{2}) + (\frac{1}{2})$

$(\frac{1}{2}) + (\frac{1}{4}) + (\frac{1}{4})$

$(\frac{1}{2}) + (\frac{1}{4}) + (\frac{1}{8}) + (\frac{1}{8})$

$(\frac{1}{2}) + (\frac{1}{8}) + (\frac{1}{8}) + (\frac{1}{8}) + (\frac{1}{8})$

$(\frac{1}{4}) + (\frac{1}{4}) + (\frac{1}{4}) + (\frac{1}{4})$

$(\frac{1}{4}) + (\frac{1}{4}) + (\frac{1}{4}) + (\frac{1}{8}) + (\frac{1}{8})$

$(\frac{1}{4}) + (\frac{1}{4}) + (\frac{1}{8}) + (\frac{1}{8}) + (\frac{1}{8}) + (\frac{1}{8})$

$(\frac{1}{4}) + (\frac{1}{8}) + (\frac{1}{8}) + (\frac{1}{8}) + (\frac{1}{8}) + (\frac{1}{8}) + (\frac{1}{8})$

$(\frac{1}{8}) + (\frac{1}{8}) + (\frac{1}{8}) + (\frac{1}{8}) + (\frac{1}{8}) + (\frac{1}{8}) + (\frac{1}{8}) + (\frac{1}{8})$

$(\frac{1}{3}) + (\frac{1}{3}) + (\frac{1}{3})$

$(\frac{1}{3}) + (\frac{1}{6}) + (\frac{1}{6}) + (\frac{1}{6})$

$(\frac{1}{6}) + (\frac{1}{6}) + (\frac{1}{6}) + (\frac{1}{6}) + (\frac{1}{6}) + (\frac{1}{6})$

$(\frac{1}{6}) + (\frac{1}{6}) + (\frac{1}{6}) + (\frac{1}{2})$

$(\frac{1}{3}) + (\frac{1}{6}) + (\frac{1}{2})$

$(\frac{1}{6}) + (\frac{1}{6}) + (\frac{1}{6}) + (\frac{1}{4}) + (\frac{1}{4})$

$(\frac{1}{3}) + (\frac{1}{6}) + (\frac{1}{4}) + (\frac{1}{4})$

$(\frac{1}{6}) + (\frac{1}{6}) + (\frac{1}{6}) + (\frac{1}{4}) + (\frac{1}{8}) + (\frac{1}{8})$

$(\frac{1}{6}) + (\frac{1}{3}) + (\frac{1}{4}) + (\frac{1}{8}) + (\frac{1}{8})$

$(\frac{1}{6}) + (\frac{1}{6}) + (\frac{1}{6}) + (\frac{1}{8}) + (\frac{1}{8}) + (\frac{1}{8}) + (\frac{1}{8})$

$(\frac{1}{3}) + (\frac{1}{6}) + (\frac{1}{8}) + (\frac{1}{8}) + (\frac{1}{8}) + (\frac{1}{8})$

Section C: Fraction Strips

SECTION C PLANNER

THE MATHEMATICS CONTENT AND GOALS

GOALS
Students will:
- Be introduced to fraction strips as a model for illustrating fractional parts.
- Use fraction strips to "make a half" or to "make a whole," thereby informally exploring combinations of fractions.
- Use fraction strips to find equivalent fractions.
- Use fraction strips to compare fractions.

> **LANGUAGE DEVELOPMENT**
> **Mathematical language in this section includes:**
> **Unit Fraction:** A unit fraction is a fraction with a one in the numerator. For example, the unit fraction for fourths is: ¼. Students are introduced to fraction strips as a model for illustrating fractional parts.

PACING

The projected pacing for this unit is 2 class periods (based on a 45-minute period).

PROBLEM SETS: OVERVIEW

This section formalizes the intuitive work with fair shares completed in the first section of this book.

Set 1 (pp. 11–14; problems 1–20)
The intent of the problems in this set is to help students develop facility with a representational model for fractions and to use that model efficiently toward the goal of becoming fluent with fraction operations (explored in depth in Book 6). In these pages, students create their own fraction strips and then use them to compare fractions, find equivalent fractions, and combine fractions with an intended "target" in mind, such as 1/2 or 1 whole.

CONCEPT DEVELOPMENT (Pages 11–14)

INTRODUCE THE CONCEPT

ASSESS STUDENTS' PRIOR KNOWLEDGE
On the board, draw a rectangle separated into eighths by vertical line segments and a circle separated into eighths.

Ask:
Do these models show the same thing? How do you know?

Listen for:
- Yes. The models show the same thing because both are divided into eight equal parts.

MODEL MATHEMATICAL THINKING
Draw a rectangle on the board with the long side vertical. Model partitioning the rectangle by asking, *How can I separate this rectangle into fourths?* Partition the rectangle as you talk through the thinking.

Talk Through the Thinking:
Let me think about this for a minute. If I'm dividing the rectangle into fourths, that means I have to divide it into four equal parts. And equal parts means that the parts have to be the same size and shape. Well, one way to do it would be to draw a line 1/4 of the way from one side to the other, but I think it's hard to estimate where 1/4 of the way is. Another way I can divide it into fourths is to draw a horizontal line to divide the rectangle in half. Then I can separate each half into halves again. So I'll draw a horizontal line through the middle of the top half and a horizontal line through the middle of the bottom half. Is the rectangle now divided into four equal parts that all have the same size and shape? Yes.

Ask:
What other ways are there to divide the rectangle into fourths? You may wish to have students demonstrate on the board as they describe how to divide the rectangle.

Listen for:
- You can draw one vertical line through the middle of the rectangle to divide it in half. Then you can draw one horizontal line through the middle of the rectangle to divide each half into halves.
- You can draw one vertical line in the middle of the rectangle to divide it in half. Then you can draw two more vertical lines, one through the middle of the left half and the other through the middle of the right half.
- (Any method that separates the rectangle in half and then separates the halves into congruent parts.)

LAUNCH THE PROBLEM SOLVING

Provide each student with several strips of paper. Have students work individually to solve the problems on page 11. As they work, circulate and monitor their representations. When students finish each problem, have them compare and discuss their representations with a partner. Then have each pair share their answers in a class discussion of the problem. Refer to the **Teacher Notes: Student Page 11** for more specific ideas about the problems on this page.

As students work and report their conclusions, focus on these issues:

Validate Representations – Students may find creative ways to partition their strips of paper. Encourage these representations while motivating students toward a fraction strip model.

Validate Alternate Strategies – When students come up with different strategies for folding their strips of paper into thirds and fifths, have them share their strategies with the class.

Look for Misconceptions – Be sure students are aware that the partitions they create for each problem must all be the same size.

Encourage Language Development – By this point students should be comfortable with informal references to thirds, fourths, etc. Make sure that students see the connections between the word and the numerical representation. Fourths, for example, and 1/4 are the same.

Allow Processing Time – It may take some time for students to find a way to divide a fraction strip into five equal parts. Do not rush them toward a solution. Instead, encourage them to clarify their thinking and strategy.

Fraction Sense Teacher Edition

Student Page 11: Problems and Potential Answers

Section C: Fraction Strips Set 1

Paper Folding

Describe how you would fold each strip below into the given number of equal parts. Then draw lines on each strip to show how you folded it. For example, you would fold the strip of paper in half to fold it into two equal parts. Your teacher will give you strips of paper to help you as you experiment.

2 equal parts

fold in half

3 equal parts

fold in thirds

4 equal parts

fold in fourths

6 equal parts

fold in sixths

8 equal parts

fold in eighths

5 equal parts

fold in fifths

Book 5: *Fraction Sense* 11

TEACHER NOTES: STUDENT PAGE 11

Paper Folding: This exercise should be taken seriously. Embedded in it are some basic ideas for developing fraction sense. *Watch for:* Students should quickly recognize which fractions can be obtained by first using the fraction 1/2: 1/2, 1/4, 1/8, and so on. To create a strip with 4 equal parts, for example, students might fold the strip in half and then in half again. This method will not work with all fractions.

Watch for: Pay close attention to the strategies that students use to find fifths. Some students might start by folding the strip in half, which will not work unless they were able to fold the paper in half ten times. They might start by folding it into thirds, which again is fruitless. In the end, they may estimate through trial and error where the divisions would be. And some students may discover that if they "roll" the paper into a tube and count the number of revolutions they have made (depending on how tightly they roll the paper), they can count out five revolutions and then fold the paper along those creases. In any event, it is not a trivial exercise to divide a strip of paper into fifths.

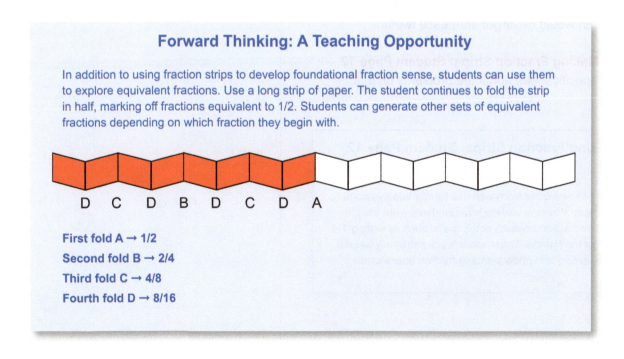

Forward Thinking: A Teaching Opportunity

In addition to using fraction strips to develop foundational fraction sense, students can use them to explore equivalent fractions. Use a long strip of paper. The student continues to fold the strip in half, marking off fractions equivalent to 1/2. Students can generate other sets of equivalent fractions depending on which fraction they begin with.

First fold A → 1/2
Second fold B → 2/4
Third fold C → 4/8
Fourth fold D → 8/16

CONTINUE THE PROBLEM SOLVING

Have students turn to page 12 and study the fraction strips. For each strip, ask, *What does each equal part of the strip represent?*

Listen for:
Students should recognize that each equal part represents a unit fraction, a fraction with a numerator of 1 and a denominator that is the number of equal parts in each strip.

Lead students in a discussion of the relative sizes of the fractional parts. Elicit that the more fractional parts there are in each strip, the smaller the size of each fractional part. Have students imagine a fraction strip for tenths.

Ask:
Would each tenth be larger or smaller than each eighth? Would each tenth be larger or smaller than each twelfth?

Listen for:
- Each tenth would be smaller than each eighth.
- Each tenth would be larger than each twelfth.

Refer to **Making Fraction Strips: Student Page 12** for more specific ideas about the problems on this page.

Making Fraction Strips: Student Page 12

Use heavy card stock for these fraction strip templates as they will become quite worn with use throughout this book and the next. You may wish to have students write the appropriate fraction on each of the parts, such as writing 1/4 on each of the fourths. These models are extremely helpful for representing and understanding fraction operations.

Student Page 12: Problems and Potential Answers

Section C: Fraction Strips — Set 1

Fraction Strips

Each fraction strip below models one of the benchmark fractions, such as halves, thirds, and fourths. Your teacher will give you a copy of the fraction strips. Write the correct fraction on each part of each strip. Cut apart the strips. Do not cut out each of the fractional parts.

Strip	Parts
One Whole	1
Halves	$\frac{1}{2}$ | $\frac{1}{2}$
3rds	$\frac{1}{3}$ | $\frac{1}{3}$ | $\frac{1}{3}$
4ths	$\frac{1}{4}$ | $\frac{1}{4}$ | $\frac{1}{4}$ | $\frac{1}{4}$
5ths	$\frac{1}{5}$ | $\frac{1}{5}$ | $\frac{1}{5}$ | $\frac{1}{5}$ | $\frac{1}{5}$
6ths	$\frac{1}{6}$ | $\frac{1}{6}$ | $\frac{1}{6}$ | $\frac{1}{6}$ | $\frac{1}{6}$ | $\frac{1}{6}$
8ths	$\frac{1}{8}$ | $\frac{1}{8}$ | $\frac{1}{8}$ | $\frac{1}{8}$ | $\frac{1}{8}$ | $\frac{1}{8}$ | $\frac{1}{8}$ | $\frac{1}{8}$
12ths	$\frac{1}{12}$ | $\frac{1}{12}$ | $\frac{1}{12}$ | $\frac{1}{12}$ | $\frac{1}{12}$ | $\frac{1}{12}$ | $\frac{1}{12}$ | $\frac{1}{12}$ | $\frac{1}{12}$ | $\frac{1}{12}$ | $\frac{1}{12}$ | $\frac{1}{12}$

Book 5: *Fraction Sense*

CONTINUE THE PROBLEM SOLVING

Have students work individually to solve the problems on page 13. As they work, you may want to circulate and monitor their recorded answers. When students finish each problem, have them compare and discuss their answers with a partner. Then have each pair share their answers in a class discussion of the problem. Refer to the **Teacher Notes: Student Page 13** for more specific ideas about the problems on this page.

As students work and report their conclusions, focus on these issues:

Allow Processing Time – Be sure to encourage students to use the fraction strips to complete this page. Although it may take some time, using the strips now will eventually enable students to do without them in the future.

Help Make Connections – Remind students that fraction strips, like the fraction circles they used before, are simply a way to model fractions. You may need to make explicit that the longer the strip, the greater the fraction.

Allow Waiting Time – When students struggle to explain their thinking, be sure to allow them ample time to organize their thoughts.

Use Technology – There are many mathematics education Web sites on the Internet that have applets for fraction strips that are quite engaging and helpful. Of course, there is great value in having students physically manipulate the fraction models themselves, but you will find excellent virtual manipulatives on the Internet as well that can be used with great effect as a complement to these homework problems.

TEACHER NOTES: STUDENT PAGE 13

Problems 1–20: These problems provide students with opportunities to compare fractions using fraction strip models. The more problems of this kind that students complete, the less they will have to depend on the fraction strips. *Teaching Strategy:* However, students should be encouraged to model as many of these problems as they can as they begin to recognize the utility of the fraction strips. The time investment with this tool will pay dividends in the next book when they use fraction strips to add and subtract fractions.

Equivalent Fractions: Once again, the idea of equivalence is presented. This time students are to use the fraction strips to find as many different ways to combine fractions to get 1/2. Again encourage them to use the fraction strips as they begin. With time, students will become less dependent on them.

Student Page 13: Problems and Potential Answers

Section C: Fraction Strips — Set 1

Comparing Fractions

Which fraction in each pair is greater (covers more of the one whole strip)? Use your fraction strips to help you decide. Then <u>draw a ring around the fraction that is greater</u>. If the two fractions cover the same part of the one whole strip, draw a ring around both fractions to show they are equal.

1. **($\frac{1}{2}$)** or $\frac{3}{8}$
2. $\frac{2}{3}$ or **($\frac{6}{8}$)**
3. **($\frac{1}{4}$)** or $\frac{1}{6}$
4. $\frac{3}{8}$ or **($\frac{2}{5}$)**
5. **($\frac{2}{3}$)** or $\frac{1}{2}$
6. **($\frac{2}{12}$)** or **($\frac{1}{6}$)**
7. $\frac{4}{5}$ or **($\frac{5}{6}$)**
8. **($\frac{1}{2}$)** or **($\frac{2}{4}$)**
9. **($\frac{3}{4}$)** or $\frac{3}{5}$
10. $\frac{7}{8}$ or **($\frac{11}{12}$)**
11. **($\frac{3}{6}$)** or **($\frac{4}{8}$)**
12. **($\frac{1}{3}$)** or $\frac{1}{4}$
13. $\frac{2}{3}$ or **($\frac{3}{4}$)**
14. $\frac{5}{8}$ or **($\frac{2}{3}$)**
15. **($\frac{4}{6}$)** or **($\frac{2}{3}$)**
16. **($\frac{5}{12}$)** or $\frac{2}{5}$
17. **($\frac{6}{8}$)** or **($\frac{3}{4}$)**
18. **($\frac{4}{12}$)** or **($\frac{1}{3}$)**
19. **($\frac{2}{4}$)** or $\frac{2}{5}$
20. **($\frac{9}{12}$)** or $\frac{4}{6}$

Equivalent Fractions

Use your fraction strips. What are all the possible combinations of fractions that add to $\frac{1}{2}$?

$(\frac{1}{4}) + (\frac{1}{4})$

$(\frac{1}{6}) + (\frac{1}{6}) + (\frac{1}{6})$

$(\frac{1}{8}) + (\frac{1}{8}) + (\frac{1}{8}) + (\frac{1}{8})$

$(\frac{1}{12}) + (\frac{1}{12}) + (\frac{1}{12}) + (\frac{1}{12}) + (\frac{1}{12}) + (\frac{1}{12})$

$(\frac{1}{4}) + (\frac{1}{8}) + (\frac{1}{8})$

$(\frac{1}{4}) + (\frac{1}{12}) + (\frac{1}{12}) + (\frac{1}{12})$

$(\frac{1}{6}) + (\frac{1}{3})$

$(\frac{1}{6}) + (\frac{1}{12}) + (\frac{1}{12}) + (\frac{1}{12}) + (\frac{1}{12})$

$(\frac{1}{8}) + (\frac{1}{8}) + (\frac{1}{12}) + (\frac{1}{12}) + (\frac{1}{12})$

Book 5: *Fraction Sense*

CONTINUE THE PROBLEM SOLVING

Have students work individually to solve the problems on page 14. As they work, you may want to circulate and monitor their recorded answers. When students finish each problem, have them compare and discuss their answers with a partner. Then have each pair share their answers in a class discussion of the problem. Refer to the **Teacher Notes: Student Page 14** for more specific ideas about the problems on this page.

As students work and report their conclusions, focus on these issues:

Allow Processing Time – The problem on page 14 requires that students think about multiple ways to cover the 1 whole strip and then write the ways as addition expressions. Be sure to allow plenty of time for students to complete the problem.

Facilitate Students' Thinking – Some students may have trouble getting started on the problem. You might ask them to first think about the ways they can make 1 whole using fraction parts with the same denominator. Then you might ask them to cover one or more fraction parts with other fraction parts, such as covering one 1/2 with two 1/4 parts or with four 1/8 parts. Suggest that students organize their lists of expressions.

Validate Representations – Some students may think of ways to cover 1 whole that do not occur to other students. Be sure to have all students share their results in a class discussion, and have the class decide whether all representations are valid.

Encourage Language Development – Remind students of the unit fractions, e.g., 1/2, 1/3, or 1/4.

TEACHER NOTES: STUDENT PAGE 14

This problem has many solutions. Students should be given enough time to try as many combinations as they desire. *Watch for:* Look for students to try to exhaust one particular starting point. For example, if students start with 1/2, they then need to find all the other possible combinations that total 1/2. Encourage students to develop patterns and efficiency in their solution attempts. This will help solidify their understanding of the benchmark fractions. Have students use only unit fractions (fractions with 1 in the numerator) for simplicity.

Student Page 14: Problems and Potential Answers

Section C: Fraction Strips

Making One Whole

Use your fraction strips. Find as many ways as you can to make one whole with different combinations of fractional parts. Record your solutions below. Be careful! A different arrangement of the same combination of parts counts as the same solution. Think how you could organize your investigation to help you keep track of all the combinations. An example has been done for you.

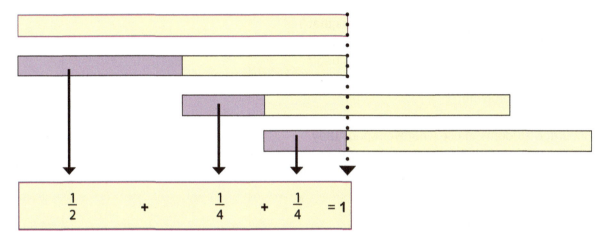

$\frac{1}{2} + \frac{1}{4} + \frac{1}{4} = 1$

How many combinations can you find?   Some possibilities are listed below

$\left(\frac{1}{1}\right)$

$\left(\frac{1}{2}\right) + \left(\frac{1}{2}\right)$

$\left(\frac{1}{2}\right) + \left(\frac{1}{4}\right) + \left(\frac{1}{4}\right)$

$\left(\frac{1}{2}\right) + \left(\frac{1}{4}\right) + \left(\frac{1}{8}\right) + \left(\frac{1}{8}\right)$

$\left(\frac{1}{2}\right) + \left(\frac{1}{8}\right) + \left(\frac{1}{8}\right) + \left(\frac{1}{8}\right) + \left(\frac{1}{8}\right)$

$\left(\frac{1}{2}\right) + \left(\frac{1}{12}\right) + \left(\frac{1}{12}\right) + \left(\frac{1}{12}\right) + \left(\frac{1}{12}\right) + \left(\frac{1}{12}\right) + \left(\frac{1}{12}\right)$

$\left(\frac{1}{4}\right) + \left(\frac{1}{4}\right) + \left(\frac{1}{4}\right) + \left(\frac{1}{4}\right)$

$\left(\frac{1}{4}\right) + \left(\frac{1}{4}\right) + \left(\frac{1}{4}\right) + \left(\frac{1}{8}\right) + \left(\frac{1}{8}\right)$

$\left(\frac{1}{4}\right) + \left(\frac{1}{4}\right) + \left(\frac{1}{8}\right) + \left(\frac{1}{8}\right) + \left(\frac{1}{8}\right) + \left(\frac{1}{8}\right)$

$\left(\frac{1}{4}\right) + \left(\frac{1}{8}\right) + \left(\frac{1}{8}\right) + \left(\frac{1}{8}\right) + \left(\frac{1}{8}\right) + \left(\frac{1}{8}\right) + \left(\frac{1}{8}\right)$

$\left(\frac{1}{8}\right) + \left(\frac{1}{8}\right) + \left(\frac{1}{8}\right) + \left(\frac{1}{8}\right) + \left(\frac{1}{8}\right) + \left(\frac{1}{8}\right) + \left(\frac{1}{8}\right) + \left(\frac{1}{8}\right)$

$\left(\frac{1}{3}\right) + \left(\frac{1}{3}\right) + \left(\frac{1}{3}\right)$

$\left(\frac{1}{3}\right) + \left(\frac{1}{3}\right) + \left(\frac{1}{6}\right) + \left(\frac{1}{6}\right)$

$\left(\frac{1}{3}\right) + \left(\frac{1}{6}\right) + \left(\frac{1}{6}\right) + \left(\frac{1}{6}\right) + \left(\frac{1}{6}\right)$

$\left(\frac{1}{6}\right) + \left(\frac{1}{6}\right) + \left(\frac{1}{6}\right) + \left(\frac{1}{6}\right) + \left(\frac{1}{6}\right) + \left(\frac{1}{6}\right)$

$\left(\frac{1}{6}\right) + \left(\frac{1}{6}\right) + \left(\frac{1}{6}\right) + \left(\frac{1}{2}\right)$

$\left(\frac{1}{6}\right) + \left(\frac{1}{6}\right) + \left(\frac{1}{6}\right) + \left(\frac{1}{4}\right) + \left(\frac{1}{4}\right)$

$\left(\frac{1}{6}\right) + \left(\frac{1}{6}\right) + \left(\frac{1}{6}\right) + \left(\frac{1}{4}\right) + \left(\frac{1}{8}\right) + \left(\frac{1}{8}\right)$

$\left(\frac{1}{6}\right) + \left(\frac{1}{6}\right) + \left(\frac{1}{6}\right) + \left(\frac{1}{8}\right) + \left(\frac{1}{8}\right) + \left(\frac{1}{8}\right) + \left(\frac{1}{8}\right)$

$\left(\frac{1}{5}\right) + \left(\frac{1}{5}\right) + \left(\frac{1}{5}\right) + \left(\frac{1}{5}\right) + \left(\frac{1}{5}\right)$

$\left(\frac{1}{12}\right) + \left(\frac{1}{12}\right) + \left(\frac{1}{12}\right) + \left(\frac{1}{12}\right) + \left(\frac{1}{12}\right) + \left(\frac{1}{12}\right) + \left(\frac{1}{12}\right) + \left(\frac{1}{12}\right) + \left(\frac{1}{12}\right) + \left(\frac{1}{12}\right) + \left(\frac{1}{12}\right) + \left(\frac{1}{12}\right)$

SECTIONS B AND C ASSESSMENT (PAGE 15)

LAUNCH THE ASSESSMENT

Have students turn to sections B and C assessment on page 15. An additional copy is found on page 81 of the Assessment Book. Have students work individually to solve the problems. As they work, circulate to be sure students understand what they need to do for each problem and that they are completing each part of the problem. For example, for problem 8, students must find all the combinations, with both like and unlike denominators, that are equivalent to 1/3. You may find it helpful to read through the directions before students begin, discussing the types of responses they will need to make for each problem.

Encourage students to use whatever space they need for problem 8. If the space on the page is inadequate, they should use an additional sheet of paper or the back of the page.

Refer to the **Teacher Notes: Assessment Problems for Sections B and C** for more specific ideas about the problems on this page.

Evaluate Student Responses

Use the assessment rubric on page 80 of the Assessment Book (pictured on page 46 of the Teacher Edition) to evaluate student responses. The Assessment Book has some general suggestions for using the rubric that you may find helpful.

TEACHER NOTES: ASSESSMENT PROBLEMS FOR SECTIONS B AND C

Problems 1–6: Each of these problems requires students to compare fractions to decide which is greater. *Watch for:* Students should use their fraction tools–fraction circles and fraction strips–to help them make the decision. Or, some students may have enough familiarity with these fractions based on their work in Sections A, B, and C that they may not need their fraction tools.

Problem 7: *Watch for:* Look for students to use their fraction tools to demonstrate their understanding of using the same fractional parts to build a larger fraction.

Problem 8: *Watch for:* Look for students to use their fraction tools to find as many combinations of fractions that add to 1/3 as they can. Some combinations, such as 1/6 + 1/6, are relatively easy to find. Other combinations, such as 1/8 + 1/8 +1/12, require more flexibility in their fraction sense. *Watch for:* Students should organize the information in a way that will help them find all the combinations.

Student Page 15: Problems and Potential Answers

Sections B and C: Problems for Assessment

Which fraction in each pair is greater? Use your fraction circles or fraction strips to help you decide. Draw a ring around the greater fraction. If the two fractions cover the same amount of the one whole circle or strip, then draw a ring around both fractions to show they are equal. For each pair, explain how you know which fraction is greater. *Explanations will vary.*

1. $\frac{1}{4}$ or $\boxed{\frac{1}{3}}$

2. $\boxed{\frac{1}{2}}$ or $\frac{2}{5}$

3. $\frac{3}{8}$ or $\boxed{\frac{3}{4}}$

4. $\boxed{\frac{4}{8}}$ or $\boxed{\frac{3}{6}}$

5. $\boxed{\frac{5}{12}}$ or $\frac{3}{8}$

6. $\boxed{\frac{5}{6}}$ or $\frac{4}{5}$

7. Use your fraction circles or fraction strips to find as many as ways as you can to express the given fraction as an addition problem with only one kind of fractional part. For example, two ways to express $\frac{1}{2}$ as an addition problem using only one kind of fractional part are $\frac{1}{4} + \frac{1}{4}$ and $\frac{1}{6} + \frac{1}{6} + \frac{1}{6}$.

   a) $\frac{1}{3}$ → $\left(\frac{1}{6}\right) + \left(\frac{1}{6}\right)$ or $\left(\frac{1}{12}\right) + \left(\frac{1}{12}\right) + \left(\frac{1}{12}\right) + \left(\frac{1}{12}\right)$

   b) $\frac{2}{4}$ → $\left(\frac{1}{4}\right) + \left(\frac{1}{4}\right)$ OR $\left(\frac{1}{8}\right) + \left(\frac{1}{8}\right) + \left(\frac{1}{8}\right) + \left(\frac{1}{8}\right)$ OR $\left(\frac{1}{6}\right) + \left(\frac{1}{6}\right) + \left(\frac{1}{6}\right)$ OR $\left(\frac{1}{12}\right) + \left(\frac{1}{12}\right) + \left(\frac{1}{12}\right) + \left(\frac{1}{12}\right) + \left(\frac{1}{12}\right) + \left(\frac{1}{12}\right)$

8. Use your fraction circles or fraction strips. What are all the possible combinations of fractions that add to $\frac{1}{3}$? (You may add with fractions that represent different fractional parts.)

   $\left(\frac{1}{6}\right) + \left(\frac{1}{6}\right)$ $\left(\frac{1}{6}\right) + \left(\frac{1}{12}\right) + \left(\frac{1}{12}\right)$ $\left(\frac{1}{12}\right) + \left(\frac{1}{12}\right) + \left(\frac{1}{12}\right) + \left(\frac{1}{12}\right)$

   $\left(\frac{1}{4}\right) + \left(\frac{1}{12}\right)$ $\left(\frac{1}{8}\right) + \left(\frac{1}{8}\right) + \left(\frac{1}{12}\right)$

SCORING GUIDE BOOK 5: FRACTION SENSE

Sections B and C Assessment
For Use With: Student Book Page 15

PROBLEM DESCRIPTION	SCORING: WHAT TO LOOK FOR	SCORE AND COMMENTS
Problems 1–6 Which fraction is bigger? Level 1: Comprehension and Knowledge Level 2: Tool use Level 4: Synthesis and Evaluation	Do students: • Understand visual representation of fractional pieces? • Compare fractions to determine which is greater? • Appropriately articulate strategies they use?	(#1) Points: ___ of 2 (#2) Points: ___ of 2 (#3) Points: ___ of 2 (#4) Points: ___ of 2 (#5) Points: ___ of 2 (#6) Points: ___ of 2
Problem 7 a–b Find as many equivalent fractions to 1/3 and 2/4. Level 1: Comprehension and Knowledge Level 2: Tool use	Do students: • Understand fractional amounts? • Recognize equivalent fractions (e.g., 1/3 = 2/6)? • Appropriately represent visuals?	(part a) Points: _____ of 3 (part b) Points: _____ of 3
Problem 8 Find as many ways to combine fractions to obtain a total sum of 1/3. Level 1: Comprehension and Knowledge Level 2: Tool use	Do students: • Understand fractional amounts? • Use informal strategies to add fractional pieces? • Understand fractional amounts? • Appropriately represent visuals?	Points: _____ of 5

TOTAL POINTS: _____ OF 23

Section D: Fraction Sense Applications

SECTION D PLANNER

THE MATHEMATICS CONTENT AND GOALS

GOALS
Students will:
- Recognize the usefulness of fractions in representing everyday situations.
- Recognize the value of having intuitive fraction strategies ready to apply to everyday situations.

> **LANGUAGE DEVELOPMENT**
> **Mathematical language in this section includes:**
> *A Fraction of:* The problem contexts in this section often require students to use fractions in realistic situations. In some of these cases, the notion of *a fraction of* becomes an important consideration. For example, "1/4 of the students in the class…" Prepare students to recognize this language as an indicator that they are to find a fractional part of a set.

PROBLEM SETS: OVERVIEW

Set 1 (p. 16; problems 1–4)
These problems ask students to use their fraction strips or other models to compare data between two soccer teams.

Set 2 (pp. 17–18; problems 1–6)
These problems are set in the context of a 120-mile relay race. Students use fraction models to help them answer questions about the various fractional parts of the race each participant will run and about the many possible combinations that could emerge as the teams divide up the miles in different ways.

Set 3 (pp. 19–20; problems 1–5)
The problems in this section ask students to use fraction models to help three brothers share the proceeds from their snow-shoveling business equitably. Various scenarios challenge students to represent, compare, and intuitively operate with fractions.

PACING
The projected pacing for this unit is 2 class periods (based on a 45-minute period).

CONCEPT DEVELOPMENT (Pages 16–20)

INTRODUCE THE CONCEPT

ASSESS STUDENTS' PRIOR KNOWLEDGE
Have students take out their fraction strips and use them to find the answer to the problem.

Ask:
Which fraction is greater, 4/6 or 5/8? How can you tell?

Listen for:
- 4/6 is the greater fraction.
- 4/6 covers more of 1 whole than 5/8 does.

MODEL MATHEMATICAL THINKING
Draw a rectangle on the board, and draw lines to separate it into tenths. Model the thinking for another example by saying, *Imagine that this rectangle represents a box that is 200 inches long. How many inches would 1/10 of the rectangle represent? How many inches would 7/10 of the rectangle represent?*

Talk Through the Thinking:
Let's try using simpler numbers to get a hint as to how we can find out. Let's suppose that the whole rectangle represents 10 inches instead of 200 inches. That's easy. Since each fractional part stands for 1/10, and there are 10 fractional parts, 1/10 would represent 1 inch. I could have gotten that by dividing 10 inches by 10 equal parts. Now if the whole rectangle represents 200 inches, I could find how many inches 1/10 represents by dividing 200 inches by 10 equal parts. 200 ÷ 10 = 20. So 1/10 represents 20 inches. To find how many inches 7/10 of the rectangle represents, I can add 20 inches 7 times, or I can multiply 7 × 20 inches. That's a total of 140 inches.

Ask:
Suppose I had divided the rectangle that stands for 200 inches into fifths instead of tenths. How many inches would 1/5 represent? How many inches would 3/5 represent?

Listen for:
- 1/5 would represent 40 inches.
- 3/5 would represent 120 inches.

LAUNCH THE PROBLEM SOLVING

Have students work individually to solve the problems on page 16. As they work, you may want to circulate to monitor their recorded answers. When students finish each problem, have them compare and discuss their answers with a partner. Then have each pair share their answers in a class discussion of the problem. Refer to the **Teacher Notes: Student Page 16** for more specific ideas about the problems on this page.

As students work and report their conclusions, focus on these issues:

Facilitate Students' Thinking – When students struggle with any of the problems on page 16, encourage them to model the fractions with either their fraction circles or their fractions strips.

Help Make Connections – These problems can be represented effectively with different models. Help students see the connections among the models by having students share their solution strategies with their classmates.

Encourage Language Development – The ability of students to apply appropriate mathematical terms to real-world situations is one of the goals of mathematics education. As part of this process, students should be able to use mathematical language to articulate their thinking. Encourage students to use the appropriate mathematical vocabulary as they describe their strategies and how they used their models.

Allow Waiting Time – As students struggle to explain their thinking, allow them ample time to organize their thoughts.

TEACHER NOTES: STUDENT PAGE 16

Problems 1–4: These problems are essentially a review of work done earlier in this book. Students can use fraction strips or other models to compare fractional parts to determine which fractions are greater. *Watch for:* Look for students to justify their answers. *Teaching Strategy:* As you do so, help them make the connections among the context of the problems, the fractional parts that emerge, and the way those fractions are represented pictorially, physically, and symbolically.

Student Page 16: Problems and Potential Answers

Section D: Fraction Sense Applications — Set 1

Comparing Two Teams

The players on two soccer teams were comparing last year's statistics. The data is listed below.

a) For each statistic, shade the bars to match the fraction for each team. Try to divide the bars into the same number of fractional parts so you can compare the fractions more easily.

b) For each statistic, write which team is represented by the greater fraction.

1. League Games Won

   Madison United: $\frac{2}{3}$ of the games

   F.C. Madison Gunners: $\frac{3}{4}$ of the games

   Gunners represents the greater fraction

2. Players who can juggle the ball more than 100 times

   Madison United: $\frac{5}{6}$ of the players

   F.C. Madison Gunners: $\frac{3}{4}$ of the players

   Madison United represents the greater fraction

3. Players who scored at least three goals in the season

   Madison United: $\frac{1}{2}$ of the players

   F.C. Madison Gunners: $\frac{5}{8}$ of the players

   Gunners represents the greater fraction

4. Players who have played soccer for at least 5 years

   Madison United: $\frac{2}{5}$ of the players

   F.C. Madison Gunners: $\frac{1}{4}$ of the players

   Madison United represents the greater fraction

CONTINUE THE PROBLEM SOLVING

Have students work individually to solve the problems on page 17. As students work, you may want to circulate and monitor their recorded answers. When students finish each problem, have them compare and discuss their answers with a partner. Then have each pair share their answers in a class discussion of the problem. Refer to the **Teacher Notes: Student Page 17** for more specific ideas about the problems on this page.

As students work and report their conclusions, focus on these issues:

Validate Representations – When several students use different drawings to represent each problem, have the class discuss whether all the representations are valid.

Allow Waiting Time – When students struggle to explain their thinking, be sure to allow them ample time to organize their thoughts.

Help Make Connections – If students draw rectangular models for each problem but are having difficulty finding the answer, remind them of the double number lines they worked with in Book 1. Help them understand that they can write the mileage below the rectangle and then figure out what number of miles each fractional part represents.

TEACHER NOTES: STUDENT PAGE 17

Problem 1a–1e: These problems are important not only because they review the use of the fraction models used previously, but also because they introduce an important tool that will be used repeatedly in the books ahead: the double number line (or double number bar). In a subtle movement forward, students are asked in these problems both to represent fractional parts with a number bar and to provide meaning for those fractional parts. That is, for each problem, students need to determine the fraction of the entire race that each runner will run as well as the number of miles that particular fraction represents. For example, a runner who has to run 1/3 of the race must run for 40 miles. This double-number-line model will be developed more fully in subsequent books, but it is important for the students to become familiar with it now. *Watch for:* Look for students to use various strategies (including formal division) to calculate the number of miles represented by each fractional part.

Forward Thinking: A Teaching Opportunity

A double number line is helpful for keeping track of information that can be categorized in two different ways. It is especially useful with percentages. Let's say a race is 20 miles long. The bottom row of numbers keeps track of the length in miles and the top row of numbers keeps track of the corresponding percent of the race. Future books will go into more detail about the double number line.

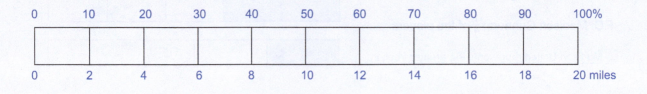

Student Page 17: Problems and Potential Answers

Section D: Fraction Sense Applications — Set 2

The Relay Race of the Rockies

Every year there is a 2-day relay race in the Colorado Rocky Mountains. The 120-mile race starts in Aspen and ends in Leadville, two historic mining towns. Teams of 2, 3, 4, 6, or 8 members can participate in the team competition.

1. For teams in the Recreational Division, each team member must run exactly the same number of miles before passing the relay baton to the next runner. How many miles will each member of the following teams have to run? Explain your answers in words or with a picture.

   a) two-person team

   _____60_____ miles

   b) three-person team

   _____40_____ miles

   c) four-person team

   _____30_____ miles

   d) six-person team

   _____20_____ miles

   e) eight-person team

   _____15_____ miles

Book 5: *Fraction Sense* 17

CONTINUE THE PROBLEM SOLVING

Have students work individually to solve the problems on page 18. As students work, you may want to circulate and monitor their recorded answers. When students finish each problem, have them compare and discuss their answers with a partner. Then have each pair share their answers in a class discussion of the problem. Refer to the **Teacher Notes: Student Page 18** for more specific ideas about the problems on this page.

As students work and report their conclusions, focus on these issues:

Validate Alternate Strategies – Have students discuss the strategies they used to solve the problems to determine which are more efficient.

Help Make Connections – These problems provide students with opportunities to express fractions in lower terms or simplest form. You may wish to review with the class how to rename fractions in lower terms.

Allow Waiting Time – When students struggle to explain their thinking, be sure to allow them ample time to organize their thoughts.

TEACHER NOTES: STUDENT PAGE 18

On this page, each question builds on the answers to the previous ones. *Teaching Strategy:* Be sure students are aware that the information they find in the first few problems will be used in the later problems. These problems make use of a double number bar because students must calculate both the fractions of the race and the number of miles each of the fractions represents. Note that the total number of miles is 120, making it possible for students to work with several benchmark fractions, including halves, thirds, fourths, sixths, tenths, and twelfths. You may wish students to work in small groups on this problem and represent their findings on a larger sheet of poster paper for clarity. The problems on page 18 are also designed to allow students to reduce several fractions. For example, in problem 5 students may determine that there is 1/3 of the race left to be run by using their fraction strips or by first calculating the number of miles already accounted for (80), subtracting the total from 120, and then determining that there are 40 out of 120 (40/120), or one third, of the total miles left to run. These problems offer excellent opportunities for students to engage in rich mathematical conversations about fractions.

Student Page 18: Problems and Potential Answers

Section D: Fraction Sense Applications Set 2

The Relay Race of the Rockies

In the Open Division of the 120-mile race, each team can decide how many miles each member will run. For example, the first person might run 20 miles, the second might run 10 miles, and so on. One team, The Crazy 8's, is trying to decide how many miles each of their 8 team members should run. Help them answer the following questions using your fraction strips or other helpful tools. Explain your answers.

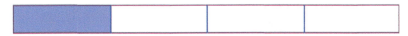
120 Mile Race

2. Paul runs marathons and is in excellent shape. He would like to run $\frac{1}{4}$ of the race himself. If the team agrees, how many miles will Paul run? _____30_____ miles.

3. The farthest Carol has ever run at one time is 10 miles. What fraction of the race is 10 miles? $\frac{10}{120}$ OR $\frac{1}{12}$

4. The first $\frac{1}{3}$ of the race is uphill and very difficult. The best hill runners of the group are Kevin, Darren, Andrew, and Joanie. If they split this uphill portion of the race equally, how many miles will each run? _____10_____ miles.

Uphill = 40 miles	40	40
10 | 10 | 10 | 10	40	40

5. So far, 6 team members have agreed to run these distances:
   - Paul will run $\frac{1}{4}$ of the race.
   - Carol will run 10 miles.
   - Kevin, Darren, Andrew and Joanie will equally share running $\frac{1}{3}$ of the race.

   a) How many miles are left for the final two runners to share? _____ miles.
   120 − (30 + 10 + 40) = 40
   b) What fraction represents the final number of miles left to be run? $\frac{40}{120}$ OR $\frac{1}{3}$

6. Kelli offers to run $\frac{1}{6}$ of the race, leaving the rest for Colleen to run.

   a) How many miles must Colleen run? __20 miles__ miles.
   b) What fraction of the race must Colleen run? $\frac{20}{120}$ or $\frac{1}{6}$

CONTINUE THE PROBLEM SOLVING

Have students work individually to solve the problems on page 19. As students work, you may want to circulate and monitor their recorded answers. When students finish each problem, have them compare and discuss their answers with a partner. Then have each pair share their answers in a class discussion of the problem. Refer to the **Teacher Notes: Student Page 19** for more specific ideas about the problems on this page.

As students work and report their conclusions, focus on these issues:

Validate Alternate Strategies – Students may use a variety of strategies to solve the problems on page 19. Have them share their strategies for each problem, and then have the class determine whether all are valid.

Validate Representations – Different models may be used to find the answers to problems 3 and 4.

Ask students to analyze these representations to determine which are correct.

Help Make Connections – You may wish to have a brief review of the meaning of fair shares and have students discuss how to determine fair shares.

Allow Waiting Time – It is important for students to discuss their strategies and solutions to the problems on this page. When some students struggle to explain their thinking, be sure to allow them ample time to organize their thoughts.

TEACHER NOTES: STUDENT PAGE 19

Problem 1: Students can make use of the double number line to solve this problem. In this case, the total amount of money needs to be divided among three boys. As students progress through the problems on this page, they will find that the problems become more complex because the money is to be shared not equally but by various fractional amounts.

Problem 2: This problem returns to one of the key strategies developed in the fair share problems in Section 1. *Teaching Strategy:* Be sure to encourage students to discuss their strategies.

Problem 3: *Watch for:* Students may use various strategies to attempt to divide $10 into three parts. One likely strategy is illustrated in the answer key. Have students discuss their solution strategies. Some students may choose to divide to solve this problem ($10 ÷ 3 = $3.33). That strategy is fine as long as they can explain how the division relates to the fraction concepts developed throughout this book. A fraction is a representation of division. This idea will be pursued in subsequent books.

Problem 4: There are many strategies students might use to illustrate that this plan is not feasible. Perhaps the easiest is to use fraction strips to show that 1/2 + 1/3 + 1/4 does not equal a whole unit. *Watch for:* Students will use a variety of strategies to solve this problem. *Teaching Strategy:* Be sure to allow them ample time to discuss their solution strategies.

Student Page 19: Problems and Potential Answers

Section D: Fraction Sense Applications — Set 3

Snow Busters, Inc.

Three brothers, Jon, Jeff, and Peter, shovel snow off driveways in winter. Depending on how big the driveway is and how much snow has fallen, they charge from $3 to $12.

1. One weekend, they earned $18 on Saturday and $36 on Sunday. They decide to share the money equally so that each boy receives $\frac{1}{3}$ of the total amount.

   How much did Peter earn on Saturday? __$6__

   How much did Jeff earn on Sunday? __$12__

   How much did Jon earn when he totaled his money for Saturday and Sunday? __$18__

2. One day they earn $22.20. Jeff doesn't think that the money can be shared equally. But Peter draws a picture like the one below and says that each brother should get $7.40. Explain Peter's thinking.

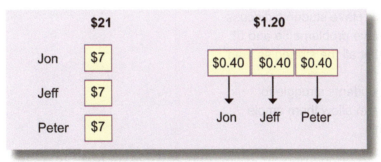

   Is Peter right? __yes__ Explain Peter's picture. ____

   $\frac{1}{3}$ of $21 is $7; $\frac{1}{3}$ of $1.20 is $0.40; $7 + $0.40 = $7.40

3. After the next snowstorm, they only earn $10. Jon says that it is impossible to share the money equally. Is he correct? Explain your thinking using words and/or pictures. ____
   He's correct. 1 penny is left over.

4. As the oldest, Jon feels that sharing the money equally is not fair because he is the strongest and does the most work. He proposes a new policy: Jon gets $\frac{1}{2}$ the money, Jeff gets $\frac{1}{3}$ of the money, and Peter–the youngest–gets $\frac{1}{4}$ of the money. Does this policy make sense? Why or why not? You may draw a picture to show your thinking. ____

   No. If Jon gets $\frac{1}{2}$ the money and Peter gets $\frac{1}{4}$ of the money, Jeff will only get $\frac{1}{4}$ of the money, not $\frac{1}{3}$.

Book 5: *Fraction Sense*

CONTINUE THE PROBLEM SOLVING

Have students work individually to solve the problems on page 20. As students work, you may want to circulate and monitor their recorded answers. When students finish each problem, have them compare and discuss their answers with a partner. Then have each pair share their answers in a class discussion of the problem. Refer to the **Teacher Notes: Student Page 20** for more specific ideas about the problems on this page.

As students work and report their conclusions, focus on these issues:

Validate Representations – When students use different models to illustrate concepts, have them analyze all the representations to determine which are valid.

Validate Alternate Strategies – Have students discuss the strategies they used to solve problems 5e and 5f. Ask them to determine whether all the strategies lead to the correct solution.

Allow Waiting Time – When students struggle to explain their thinking, be sure to allow them ample time to organize their thoughts.

TEACHER NOTES: STUDENT PAGE 20

Problem 5a: Students may choose to picture either fraction circles or fraction strips.

Problems 5b–5c: These problems are similar to the double-number-line problems on previous pages. Once students know the fractional amounts each boy earns, they must return to the total amount of money earned for a given work period to determine how each fractional amount translates into dollars. *Teaching Strategy:* These two problems again embody the idea that the value of the whole must be known (in this case, total dollars) before the fractional parts can be assigned a specific value. Without this starting point, the fractions simply represent proportions of potential earnings.

Problem 5d: This problem poses students with a different kind of challenge. They are given the value of a fraction of the money earned and need to find the total amount of money earned. *Watch for:* Knowing that $5 represents 1/6 of the total, students can use fraction strips or fraction circles, as shown in problem 5a, to find how much each of the other brothers earned.

Problem 5e: Students may use various formal and informal methods as they attempt to partition the $50 as the problem describes. *Teaching Strategy:* Be sure to allow students ample time to explain their solution strategies because students will use different strategies to solve the problem.

Problem 5f: *Watch for:* For this problem, different solutions will emerge. *Teaching Strategy:* Have students share their strategies. Be sure to have them illustrate their solutions with visual models when appropriate.

Student Page 20: Problems and Potential Answers

Section D: Fraction Sense Applications   Set 3

Snow Busters, Inc.

5. The three brothers finally agree to the following way to share the money they earn:

    - Jon gets $\frac{1}{2}$.
    - Jeff gets $\frac{1}{3}$.
    - Peter gets $\frac{1}{6}$.

    a) Is this agreement possible? __Yes__ Illustrate with your fraction circles or fraction strips.

    (circle illustration: Jon, Jeff, Peter)

    b) How much money would each boy receive if they earned $24 during one storm? Jon __$12__ Jeff __$8__ Peter __$4__ Illustrate.

    c) How much money would each boy receive if they earned $36? Jon __$18__ Jeff __$12__ Peter __$6__ Illustrate.

    d) If Peter earned $5 one storm, how much did the brothers earn in all? __$30 in all.__ Illustrate.
    Jon received $15,
    Jeff received $10,
    Peter received $5.

    e) If they earn $50 during a really big storm, can they share the money equally with no money left over using their new agreement? Explain. _____
    Jon would receive $25, Jeff would receive $16.67, and Peter would receive $8.33.
    No, there would be one cent left over.

    f) If the boys cannot share $50 according to their agreement, come up with a new policy that would allow them to share the money with no money left over. __Responses will vary__

20 Book 5: *Fraction Sense*

SECTION D ASSESSMENT (PAGE 21)

LAUNCH THE ASSESSMENT

Have students turn to the Section D Assessment on page 21. An additional copy is found on page 83 of the Assessment Book. Have students work individually to solve the problems and write their answers. As they work, circulate to be sure students understand what they need to do for each of the problems. Encourage students to focus on the visual models (fraction strips) as they complete their work, because the visual representations will be evaluated in the scoring rubric.

Encourage students to use whatever space they need to model their thinking. If the space on the page is inadequate, or if students need to create more than one fraction bar, they should use an additional sheet of paper or the back of the page.

Refer to the **Teacher Notes: Assessment Problems for Section D** for more specific ideas about the problems on this page.

Evaluate Student Responses

Use the assessment rubric on page 82 of the Assessment Book (pictured on page 60 of the Teacher Edition) to evaluate student responses. The Assessment Book has some general suggestions for using the rubric that you may find helpful.

TEACHER NOTES: ASSESSMENT PROBLEMS FOR SECTION D

The problems on this page are designed to give you an opportunity to assess the progress and the thinking of students about the use of the fraction models as they explore fraction equivalencies.

Problems 1a–d: In the first set of problems, students are asked to complete two fraction bars to determine which of the given amounts is the largest. Look for students to be able to divide the fraction strip in thirds, halves, etc., and subsequently make the connection to how the whole amount given (e.g., $24) might also be split accordingly.

Problems 2a–d: In these problems, students are asked to think through a context involving two identically sized pizzas that have been divided into different fractional parts (slices). Students need to compare the relative sizes of pizza slices while working with eighths and twelfths. Look for students to use either fraction circles or fraction strips to compare different fractional parts of the pizzas.

Student Page 21: Problems and Potential Answers

Section D: Problems for Assessment

1. Which is more? Are they equal? Circle the larger amount of money. If they are the same, circle both.

   a)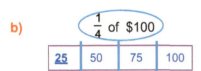

   b)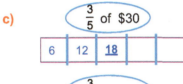

   c)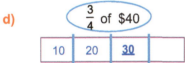

   d) $\frac{3}{4}$ of $40 *(circled)* — 10 | 20 | **30** | $\frac{2}{3}$ of $45 *(circled)* — 15 | **30** |

   a)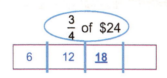

   b)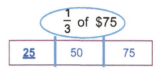

   c, d)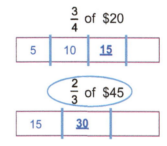

2. Juan and Jose order two large pizzas (same size). Pizza #1 is cut in **8ths**. Pizza #2 is cut in **12ths**.

   a) How many slices are there in Pizza #1? ___8___
   b) How many slices are there in Pizza #2? ___12___
   c) In which pizza are the slices the **biggest**? ___Pizza #1___
   d) Juan and Jose <u>eat the same amount of pizza</u>. Use fraction circles or fraction strips to illustrate.
   - Juan eats 4 slices of Pizza #1. How many slices of Pizza #2 does Jose eat? ___6___
   - Juan eats 2 slices of Pizza #1. How many slices of Pizza #2 does Jose eat? ___3___
   - Juan eats 6 slices of Pizza #1. How many slices of Pizza #2 does Jose eat? ___9___

   Check students' illustrations.

SCORING GUIDE BOOK 5: FRACTION SENSE

Section D Assessment
For Use With: Student Book Page 21

PROBLEM DESCRIPTION	SCORING: WHAT TO LOOK FOR	SCORE AND COMMENTS
Problem 1a–d Use fraction strip. Level 1: Comprehension and Knowledge Level 2: Tool use	Do students: • Understand how to partition a fraction strip into equal segments? • Understand how to divide the whole by the appropriate number of fractional pieces? • Have a general number sense?	Scoring scheme: 3 points total. One point for circling correct answer, one point for correct fraction strip and representation for each part. Points: _____ of 12
Problem 2a–b Understand division of the whole into fractional pieces. Level 1: Comprehension and Knowledge	Do students: • Understand the relationship between fractional name and fractional pieces?	Points: _____ of 2
Problem 2c Understand common fraction representations and fraction sense.	Do students: • Understand the meaning of a fraction?	Points: _____ of 1
Problem 2d Understand fraction equivalencies. Level 1: Comprehension and Knowledge Level 2: Tool use	Do students: • Understand the concept of fraction equivalence? • Have the ability to find equivalent fractions between the eighths and twelfths fraction families? • Use fraction models (strips or pie charts) to find equivalencies?	Points: _____ of 3

TOTAL POINTS: _____ OF 18

END-OF-BOOK ASSSESSMENT (PAGES 22–23)

LAUNCH THE ASSESSMENT

Have students turn to the End-of-Book Assessment on page 22. An additional copy is found on page 85 of the Assessment Book. Have students work individually to solve the problems and draw their pictures. As they work, circulate to be sure students understand what they need to do for each problem and that they are completing each part of the problem. For example, for problem 1, students need to illustrate two ways to show how 4 children can equally share 3 pieces of toast. You may find it helpful to read through the directions for all the problems before students begin, discussing the types of responses they will need to make for each problem.

Encourage students to use whatever space they need to make their drawings. If the space on the page is inadequate, they should use an additional sheet of paper or the back of the page. Refer to the **Teacher Notes: End-of-Book Assessment, Student Page 22**, for more specific ideas about the problems on this page.

Evaluate Student Responses

Use the assessment rubric on page 84 of the Assessment Book (pictured on page 65 of the Teacher Edition) to evaluate student responses. The Assessment Book has some general suggestions for using the rubric that you may find helpful.

TEACHER NOTES: END-OF-BOOK ASSSESSMENT, STUDENT PAGE 22

The assessment problems on this page provide you with several opportunities to determine whether students have acquired the fundamental conceptual knowledge targeted in this book. These assessment problems may be used as individual measures, or they may be used to generate broader discussion among your students as the concepts are reviewed in the final two pages of this book.

Student Page 22: Problems and Potential Answers

End-of-Book Assessment

1. Show two different ways that 4 children might share 3 slices of toast equally. Explain the differences between your two methods.

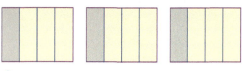 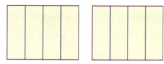

$\frac{1}{4}$ from each toast $\hspace{4cm}$ $\frac{3}{4}$ of 1 toast

Explain. __Answers will vary_____

_____

2. What fraction of each model is shaded?

a) $\frac{2}{4}$

b) $\frac{2}{3}$

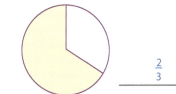

c) $\frac{2}{3}$

d) $\frac{4}{5}$

e) $\frac{6}{12}$

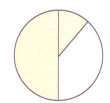

f) $\frac{5}{8}$

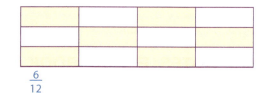

3. Find at least three ways to combine fractions to add to $\frac{3}{4}$. Illustrate your solutions with drawings of either fraction strips or fraction circles.

$\frac{1}{2} + \frac{1}{4}$ $\hspace{2cm}$ $\frac{1}{4} + \frac{1}{4} + \frac{1}{8} + \frac{1}{8}$ $\hspace{2cm}$ $\frac{1}{3} + \frac{1}{6} + \frac{1}{6} + \frac{1}{12}$

CONTINUE THE ASSESSMENT

Have students turn to the End-of-Book Assessment on page 23. An additional copy is found on page 86 of the Assessment Book. Have students work individually to solve the problems and write their explanations. As they work, circulate to be sure students understand what they need to do for each problem and that they are completing each part of the problem. For example, for each problem, students need to determine the fraction of the total number of votes that each category of votes represents. Then they have to compare that fraction to a given fraction. You may find it helpful to read through the directions for all the problems before students begin, discussing the types of responses they will need to make for each problem.

Encourage students to use whatever space they need to explain their thinking. If the space on the page is inadequate, they should use an additional sheet of paper or the back of the page. Refer to the **Teacher Notes: End-of-Book Assessment, Student Page 23**, for more specific ideas about the problems on this page.

Evaluate Student Responses

Use the assessment rubric on page 84 of the Assessment Book (pictured on page 65 of the Teacher Edition) to evaluate student responses. The Assessment Book has some general suggestions for using the rubric that you may find helpful.

TEACHER NOTES: END-OF-BOOK ASSESSMENT, STUDENT PAGE 23

Student page 23 contains additional assessment problems to be used at your discretion.

Fraction Sense *Teacher Edition*

Student Page 23: Problems and Potential Answers

End-of-Book Assessment

4. The Redcliff City Council surveyed residents to see how the city park should be improved. 300 people answered the survey. The results are shown in the table below.

Results: How to Improve Redcliff City Park	
Idea	Number of 1st Place Votes
New Playground	49
New Baseball/Softball Diamond	37
New Soccer Field	103
Update Swimming Pool	76
Walking Trails	35

Is each statement about the results true? Write *True* or *False*. Explain your answers.

a) About $\frac{1}{6}$ of the voters thought a new playground was the best idea.   Yes, $\frac{49}{300}$ is about $\frac{1}{6}$

b) More than $\frac{1}{3}$ voted for a new soccer field.   Yes, $\frac{103}{300}$ is more than $\frac{1}{3}$

c) Over $\frac{2}{3}$ of the voters wanted either new walking trails or an updated swimming pool.

76 + 35 is 111 but $\frac{111}{300}$ is not more than $\frac{2}{3}$

d) Fewer than $\frac{1}{12}$ wanted a new baseball field.

$\frac{37}{300}$ is not less than $\frac{1}{12}$

e) About $\frac{1}{4}$ wanted to update the swimming pool.   Yes, $\frac{76}{300}$ is about $\frac{1}{4}$

SCORING GUIDE BOOK 5: FRACTION SENSE

End-of-Book Assessment
For Use With: Student Book Pages 22–23

PROBLEM DESCRIPTION	SCORING: WHAT TO LOOK FOR	SCORE AND COMMENTS
Problem 1 Divide 3 squares into 4 equal parts. Level 1: Comprehension and Knowledge Level 3: Connection and Application	Do students: • Find equal partitions of squares? • Equally distribute pieces across 4 people? • Demonstrate fluency in combining fractional pieces? • Demonstrate articulation of thinking?	Points: _____ of 4
Problem 2 Recognize the fractional name for a shaded region. Level 1: Comprehension and Knowledge Level 2: Tool use	Do students: • Understand the relationship between visual representation and fractional name? • Understand fractional notation—parts shaded over total parts?	Points: _____ of 6
Problem 3 Find three ways to combine fractions to obtain a total sum of ¾. Level 1: Comprehension and Knowledge Level 2: Tool use	Do students: • Understand fractional amounts? • Use informal strategies for adding fractions? • Recognize the benchmark fraction of ¾? • Have an appropriate visual representation?	Points: _____ of 4
Problem 4a-e Convert raw data tallies into fractional amounts in real-world context. Level 3: Connection and Application Level 4: Synthesis and Evaluation	Do students: • Understand the definition of a fraction? • Represent fractions based on given data (category votes over total votes)? • Demonstrate general fraction sense by estimating fractional equivalencies based on data? • Demonstrate articulation of thinking?	(a) Points: _____ of 2 (b) Points: _____ of 2 (c) Points: _____ of 2 (d) Points: _____ of 2 (e) Points: _____ of 2

TOTAL POINTS: _____ OF 24

Book 6:
Fraction Operations

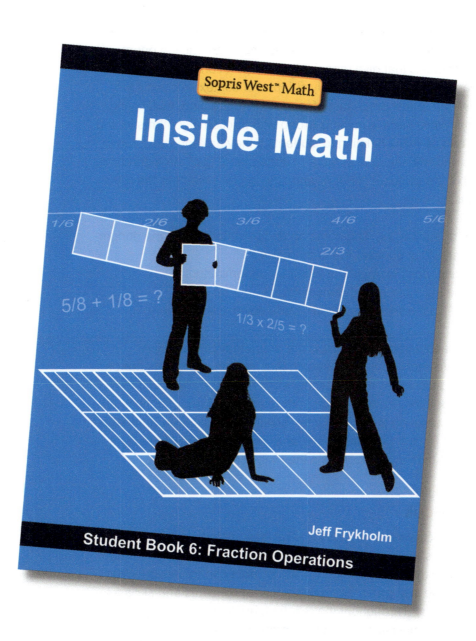

Book Six Overview: Fraction Operations

Introduction

This book is the sixth in a series of eight units that are geared toward helping middle-grades learners acquire both facility with, and understanding of, the basic mathematical procedures and concepts that lay the groundwork for more advanced mathematical study. In particular, this series cultivates understanding of a number of mathematical tools that children learn to use with facility in various mathematical and real-world contexts.

Book Focus

This book engages students in situations in which their informal, intuitive understanding of fractions will gradually lead them to proficiency with fraction operations. By drawing on contexts that give meaning to the operations–as opposed to the traditional problem sets that are frequently stripped of context–students will explore both informal and formal procedures for adding, subtracting, multiplying, and dividing fractions. While there is nothing wrong with fraction algorithms in and of themselves, they can be overwhelming to students if they are not presented in appropriate contexts and with the goal of student understanding of the algorithms. Imagine the thinking of the confused student who is trying to remember the rules for fraction operations:

- When adding or subtracting, find common denominators; keep the denominators and just add or subtract the numerators.
- When multiplying, don't worry about common denominators; just multiply the numerators and denominators.
- When dividing, flip the second fraction upside down; then multiply.

A large literature base about fractions exists in the mathematics education research community. We know from this research that fraction operations are one of the primary stumbling blocks for middle school students largely because they are never given the opportunity to develop an understanding of what fractions are and what it means to operate on them. This book builds on the intuitive approaches and visual models of Book 5 to enhance students' understanding of fractions and moves them toward the formal algorithms they will use in the future.

How To Use This Book

There are two primary sections in every lesson. The lesson starts with a discussion that helps you assess what students already know and a suggestion for how to model the type of mathematical thinking they will be doing on their own. What follows is a resource guide to support the development of concepts and skills as students solve the problems. Throughout the resource guide, you will be provided with insights into the mathematical content of the problems, pedagogical ideas to enhance teaching and learning, samples of anticipated student work, insights about student thinking related to the topics at hand, and ideas about assessment. You will also find a reproduction of the student page that includes answers. This program is meant to be flexible and relies on your craft and knowledge. Toward that end, the resource materials that accompany this text are not intended to be used as a script. Instead, the intention of this program is that you will have a chance to apply your knowledge of students, your own experiences with these mathematical tools, and your intuition about teaching to make this program as effective as possible.

Models Of Implementation

This program has been designed to be as flexible as possible. While this series of books may be used as the primary curriculum for the classroom, it was not designed as the full curriculum for any given grade level. Rather, it was crafted to support you as you help students understand the number operations and concepts that precede more advanced work in algebra. You may therefore choose to use this program either as a guide for whole-class explorations or as the text for smaller, pull-out groups of students. In both cases, it is important to note that this program is designed on the principle that students learn mathematics in large measure through interactions with one another. Throughout the books, you will find numerous questions that ask students to explain their thinking. These occasions should not be taken lightly. It is in the sharing and comparing of solution strategies that students begin to build a firm foundation of understanding. The social dynamic of learning mathematics is important to recognize. Participation in mathematical discourse may be the most powerful impetus for learning mathematics available to young learners, and you should take advantage of every opportunity to encourage students to talk about their mathematical thinking and processes. Given a commitment to this principle, this program is likely to be most successful when students are progressing through the problems with their peers.

Addressing Issues of Language

There is no question that one of the greatest challenges facing teachers today is to make instruction relevant and accessible for second language learners. *Inside Math* has been written with this concern in mind. Careful consideration was given to the language that appears in directions, contextually based problems, and other sections of the book where text is necessary. When possible, for example, we have limited new vocabulary to only what is essential to the concepts being presented, and we revisit new vocabulary words and concepts repeatedly throughout the text. To assist you in making instruction accessible for English language learners, as well as other students for whom reading presents particular challenges, several supporting features were added to the teacher's edition. First, within the section planner that introduces each new major mathematical concept contained in the book, there is a heading that reads: *Language Development.* In this section of the overview, new vocabulary words are introduced and defined. Later in the text, when these words and concepts are introduced in a specific lesson, the teacher notes include additional information about pertinent language considerations and vocabulary. These notes appear as Encouraging Language Development under the Concept Development and Continue the Problem Solving headings.

Explaining Thinking

Throughout this series, students will be instructed to explain their thinking. The ability to articulate mathematical ideas and solution strategies is a feature of mathematics education that continues to grow in its importance. We see numerous examples in state, national, and international achievement tests in which answers alone are not enough—students must also be able to express their thought processes, give rationale for answers, and articulate steps in any given strategy. In this book, there are opportunities for students to do likewise.

As this is often a new and challenging task for students, it is important for teachers to be able to model the process of making thinking explicit. At the beginning of each section in the book, there are suggestions for ways to introduce the content at hand, many of which are suitable for teachers to illustrate what it means to explain thinking in an intelligible way. Be aware of both the importance of this feature of the program and the challenge it might provide students as they practice this skill for what might be the first time.

Assessment

At the conclusion of each section, you will find several problems that may be used for formative assessments. These problems review key concepts discussed in the previous section. At the end of the book you will find additional assessment problems that cover the content of the entire book. These problems may be used as a cumulative assessment of student understanding of the key concepts in the book. The teachers' guide contains insights as to how the assessment problems might best be used and what they are intended to measure.

Assessment rubrics and scoring guides for every assessment may be found in *Assessment Teacher Edition*. Detailed instructions regarding assessment in general, and the use of the program rubrics in particular, are included in the introduction of *Assessment Teacher Edition*.

Professional Background

As noted in the overview for the previous book on fractions, there is no more difficult concept for young learners throughout the number strand landscape to grasp than the conceptual understanding of fraction operations. And yet, there are rather simple rules that can be followed to compute with fractions. Because these rules are not complicated, many students implement them efficiently with ample practice. This puts the teacher in an interesting place: Do I try to teach for conceptual understanding of fractions? Or do I instead spend the time helping my students develop competency with the fraction operation algorithms?

As has been the case throughout this series of textbooks, it is important to do both. We definitely want students to have a rich understanding of fraction operations for various reasons, not the least of which is so that they can determine which algorithm is necessary to use in a given situation and whether the answer they get is reasonable. Because of their familiarity with whole-number operations, for example, many students are surprised to learn that when multiplying by a fraction less than one, they end up with a smaller number for an answer than we began with. Something similar can be said for division—when we divide by a fraction less than one, we end up getting a larger number than what we started with, a result that is counterintuitive to what students know about whole-number division. It is important for students to understand these conceptual differences between operations with whole numbers and operations with fractions. On the other hand, we also want students to be able to use fraction algorithms effectively. When teaching fraction operations, therefore, we must use students' understanding of whole-number operations by building on what the operations mean. And we also must depend on a firm understanding of fraction sense in general. Without this critical foundation, young learners are likely to learn rules without understanding them, which is a situation we must try to avoid.

The Big Ideas

1. When we teach fraction operations, we must begin as we do with whole-number operations, by focusing on the meaning of the operation. In this way semantics becomes an important element of our teaching. For example, just as in whole-number multiplication, we might think of fraction multiplication as "so many groups of another number". In whole-number multiplication, two times three is stated as "Two groups of three." Similarly, we think of 2/3 × 3/4 as, "2/3 of a group of 3/4." In context, the statement might be "We need 2/3 of 3/4 of a cup of flour." So it is not surprising for students to see that our answer must be smaller than what we started with: we need 2/3 of some given amount. Similar steps can be taken with division as well. The point is that we must find words to help students develop understanding of the operation at hand. Language is crucial if students are to learn fraction operations with meaning.

2. For addition and subtraction, it is important for students to understand that the numerator is indicating the number of parts we are collecting (or subtracting), and the denominator indicates *what kind* of part is being collected. This is important to convey, as it provides a justification for the need to find a common denominator so that we are adding or subtracting the same size part.

3. Estimation of fraction computations becomes an important part of working with fractions. Making an estimate does not require the use of an algorithm, and in many cases estimates can be quite accurate, particularly if they are based upon fraction sense and models developed in the previous book. Combining an emphasis on fraction estimates along with the operations will also help students to be focused on the meanings of the operations and what they might expect for an answer.

4. Fraction models developed earlier (e.g., fraction strips) can be instrumental in developing understanding of fraction operations, for determining if answers are reasonable, and for completing the operations themselves.

5. Using contexts to provide meaning for fraction operations is essential. This is especially true when students are at the initial stages of developing understanding of fraction algorithms.

Teaching Ideas

Addition and Subtraction Based on the previous big ideas, this book begins by encouraging students to add and subtract fractions informally, through simple contexts, and with the use of fraction strips. In this way, the book begins by demystifying the myth that fractions can only be added or subtracted by finding a common denominator. To help in this process, the initial problem contexts are designed strategically with a target of one whole unit in mind. In the first problem set, for example, students are asked to determine whether various amounts of motor oil will fill up an oil reservoir. Students can use estimation strategies as part of this process, drawing on visual pictures they may have stored in their minds from repeated use of fraction models. Would, for example, 1/2 gallon of oil plus another 1/4 gallon fill up the tank completely? If not, how much would be left? In this example, although the question does not specifically ask for the addition algorithm, students are indeed adding two fractions. They can do so easily with fraction models. Gradually, as the problems grow in complexity, fractions from different families are included, such that the student may be asked to find the solution to a similar problem in which 1/2 gallon is being added to 1/3 gallon.

Using their own invented strategies and common fraction models, students can find many correct solutions without using the common-denominator strategy. Consider the following problems:

$$\frac{3}{4}+\frac{1}{8} \qquad \frac{1}{2}-\frac{1}{8} \qquad \frac{1}{2}+\frac{2}{3} \qquad 1\frac{1}{2}-\frac{3}{4} \qquad 1\frac{2}{3}+\frac{3}{4}$$

Even in these cases, informal strategies can be used quite effectively in advance of the formal common-denominator algorithm. Fraction families like halves, fourths, and eighths are easily related. Children who have used fraction circles extensively can also see the relationship between thirds, and halves, for example. Consider how much can be done in adding and subtracting benchmark fractions like those above with an understanding of the diagram. We can see a picture of 1/2, 1/3, 1/4, 1/6, 1/8 (half of 1/4), and 1/12. From these pictures, each of the problems above can be solved intuitively without explicit attention given at the onset to determining a common denominator.

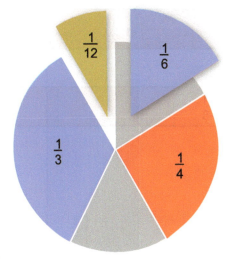

After these sorts of visual explorations, students are much more receptive to the idea of finding common denominators and adding/subtracting by following a procedure. The addition and subtraction procedures (finding common denominators) are carefully developed in the text, and your students will benefit greatly from that exploration if they have had this kind of intuitive experience prior to learning the algorithm.

Multiplication Similar to the approach taken with addition and subtraction, multiplication of fractions is first introduced with a contextual problem that allows students to multiply in a way that resonates with their intuitions based on their understanding of the problem. The context begins by suggesting that out of 24 children in a class, 1/2 are boys. Of the boys, 1/3 are on the same soccer team. How many boys are on the team? Intuitively, students can reason, "1/2 of 24 is 12. Now, of those 12, 1/3 play on the team. What is 1/3 of a group of 12? Four." You can also see how fraction strips might be very helpful in this context:

One half of the students are boys.

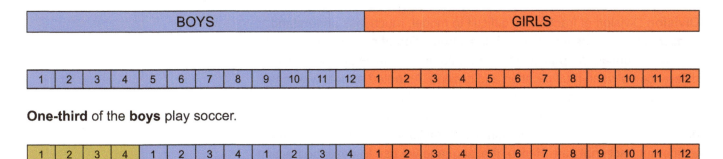

One-third of the **boys** play soccer.

From this intuitive basis, meaning behind the multiplication algorithm is developed with visual diagrams that reflect the language we use to describe fraction multiplication. It is crucial to help students use words to develop meaning for the multiplication they are doing. For example, 1/2 × 1/4 might be expressed in words as 1/4 of 1/2 equals 1/8. This kind of problem can be modeled visually quite nicely both with a fraction strip and an area model.

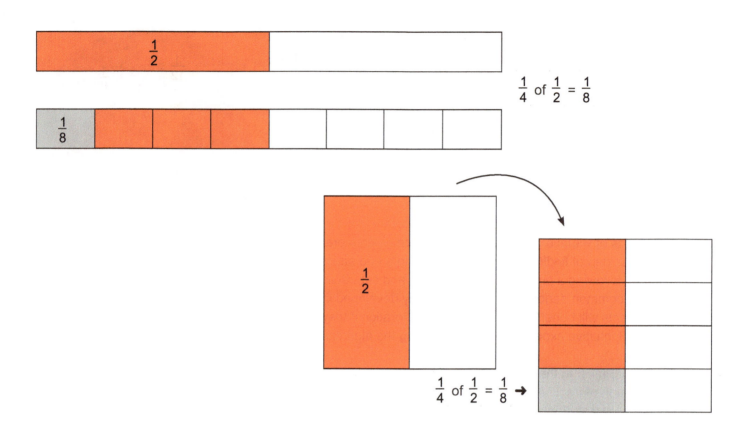

The second model an area or rectangle model is quite effective in representing more complicated multiplication problems that sometimes cannot be modeled easily with a fraction strip. The textbook elaborates this model in great detail, stressing the important distinction between fraction multiplication and division in the sense that while in division we are interested in counting fractional parts, with multiplication we are interested in a given fractional part with respect to the whole.

Division Division of fractions is difficult to model, much less understand, conceptually. As was the case with the introduction of multiplication, division is also introduced through context, and with an emphasis on the semantic difference between multiplication and division. As noted above, whereas multiplication is concerned with the size of a fractional part with respect to the whole, division is not concerned with the unit whole at all. Rather, fraction division is an effort to count the number of fractional parts that can fit into a different fractional part. Hence, the language we use to describe fraction division is important. With whole numbers we might express division as, "How many groups of size A are in size B?" Six divided by two, therefore, means: How many twos are there in six? Fraction division operates in the same way. The problem: $\frac{1}{2} \div \frac{1}{4}$ might be thought of as, "How many 1/4ths are there in 1/2?" In context we might say, "How many times could you dip a 1/4 measuring cup into 1/2 cup of flour?" When conceptualized in this way, students can see that the answer of 2, although counterintuitive perhaps to whole-number division, is entirely reasonable for the given problem, two 1/4 cup scoops of flour will equal 1/2 cup of flour.

Representing fraction division is somewhat more complicated than representing fraction multiplication, but the basic idea remains the same. We model the starting fraction and then see how many times the second fraction can fit within the first. As illustrated below with an example that comes from the text, one can recognize quickly that we are no longer concerned with the whole unit, but rather in counting how many 1/4s can be found in 1/2.

How many 1/4s are there in 1/2?

Start by representing 1/2.

How many 1/4 parts may be found in that 1/2 section?

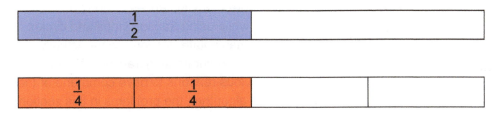

As noted, it becomes very difficult to model division of fractions once we leave the comfortable domain of the benchmark fractions. Hence, once students are comfortable with a conceptual explanation of fraction division, then they may be moved toward the algorithm. As a word of caution, however, do not rush students to the algorithm without first encouraging them to develop an intuitive understanding of fraction division.

Section A: Informal Addition and Subtraction of Fractions

SECTION A PLANNER

THE MATHEMATICS CONTENT AND GOALS

GOALS
Students will:
- Use fraction strips to complete one-step addition problems that require adding two fractions to make one whole.
- Compare fraction amounts using fractional strips or fraction circles to determine whether a fraction is greater than, less than, or equal to one whole.
- Combine benchmark fractions to find sums greater than one whole.
- Compare fractional distances on a map.
- Compare fractional quantities.

LANGUAGE DEVELOPMENT
Mathematical language in this section includes:

Fraction: A number in the form $\frac{a}{b}$ that names part of a whole, a region, or a set.

Fractional Part: Fractional parts might be thought of as equal-sized portions (fair shares) of a whole, a unit, or a collection of objects.

Numerator: The numerator of a fraction is a counter. It indicates the number of fractional parts (the size of which are determined by the denominator) that are presently under consideration.

Denominator: The denominator may be thought of as the number of equal-sized parts into which the whole has been divided.

Simplest Form: The form of a fraction when its numerator and denominator have no common factor other than 1.

PACING

The projected pacing for this unit is 3–4 class periods (based on a 45-minute period).

PROBLEM SETS: OVERVIEW

Contrary to past practices and common opinion, it is not always necessary to find the common denominator of two fractions in order to add them. This is particularly true with the benchmark fractions that students are expected to master in the elementary and middle grades. There were many instances in Book 5 in which students, while using fraction strips and circles to compare and manipulate fractions, were actually informally adding and subtracting fractions. While it is important for obvious reasons to have command of the fraction addition algorithm, the problems in this section begin this process by having students draw on their intuition and past informal work with fraction models.

Set 1 (pp. 1–2; problems 1–6)
These problems require students to compare fractional amounts with the intended goal of adding two fractions to make one whole. Using the context of an automobile oil change, students are asked to determine how much oil it will take to fill the engine, given a starting amount already in the reservoir.

Set 2 (pp. 3–4; problems 1–7)
Students will work with the set of fractions in the 1/8 family (1/8, 1/4, 1/2) as they try to determine various routes through a city to create road races of different lengths. This context is used throughout Section A.

Set 3 (pp. 5–6)
The problems in Set 3 reinforce the intuitive strategies and comparisons students used in Sets 1 and 2. Students are asked to combine distances and quantities, and in the process are exposed to a wider range of the benchmark fractions.

CONCEPT DEVELOPMENT (Pages 1–2)

INTRODUCE THE CONCEPT

ASSESS STUDENTS' PRIOR KNOWLEDGE

Ask:
Lorna needs 1 quart of white paint for the woodwork in her kitchen. She has three 1-quart cans of white paint in her garage, but she has used paint out of all those cans before. One can is 1/6 full, another can is 1/2 full, and a third can is 1/4 full. Can she make 1 quart of paint with the leftover paint in the three cans? Explain. You may use your fraction circles or fraction strips.

Listen for:
- No, she does not have enough paint.
- When I modeled 1/6 + 1/2 + 1/4 with my fraction strips (or circles), they did not make one whole. So, she does not have enough paint to make 1 quart.

MODEL MATHEMATICAL THINKING

Model the thinking for solving the above problem by asking, *Suppose you could not find your fraction circles or fraction strips. How could you solve this problem?*

Talk Through the Thinking:
If you had the same paint in the same cans as Lorna, you could pour all the paint into one 1-quart can. But since you don't have the paint, you can figure out the problem in another way. Let's start with the can of paint that is 1/2 full. We know that two halves make one whole. So we would need another 1/2 can to make 1 quart. Well, we know that a second 1-quart can is 1/4 full. Another thing we know is that 2/4 is equivalent to 1/2. So we would need one more fourth of a can of paint to make 1 quart. But the last can is only 1/6 full, and we know that 1/6 is less than 1/4. So, there is not enough paint to make 1 quart, and Lorna does not have enough paint.

Ask:
What if Lorna had only two 1-quart cans of paint in her garage and one was 1/2 full while the other was 5/8 full? Would she have enough paint to make 1 full quart? Why?

Listen for:
- Yes, she would have enough paint.
- She would need two half-cans. She has one 1, and one 5/8 can, and 5/8 is greater than 1/2.

LAUNCH THE PROBLEM SOLVING

Have students work individually to solve the problems on page 1. As they work, circulate to monitor their recorded answers. When students finish each problem, have them compare and discuss their answers with a partner. Then have each pair share their answers in a class discussion of the problem. Refer to the **Teacher Notes: Student Page 1** for more specific ideas about the problems on this page.

As students work and discuss their conclusions, focus on these issues:

Help Make Connections – Help students see and understand the connections between their fraction strips and the pictures on the page.

Allow Processing Time – The idea of informally combining fractions is a difficult step for some students. Time spent on these intuitive combinations will pay dividends later on when students are introduced to more formal fraction algorithms.

Facilitate Students' Thinking – Encourage students to use their fraction strips to enhance their thinking about the problems in this section.

Allow Waiting Time – When students struggle to explain their thinking, be sure to allow them at least 20 seconds to organize their thoughts. (This may seem like a long time.)

Student Page 1: Problems and Potential Answers

Addition and Subtraction of Fractions — Set 1

a local gas station. One of his jobs is to check the oil in the cars that stop at the ... do this, John uses a **key**, a tool that measures how much oil is left in the oil tank.

John makes sure that every car has one full gallon of oil in the tank. Because he cannot see inside the engine, he has to use a key. After putting the key into the tank, the oil leaves a mark on the key. When he takes the key out of the tank, the oil leaves a mark on the key. Then he knows how much oil is in the tank.

Here is a closeup of the key.

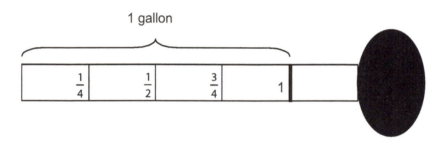

For each measurement below, indicate **about** how much of a gallon of oil John needs **to add** in order **to make 1 full gallon**.

1. 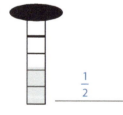 $\frac{1}{2}$

2. 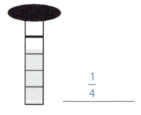 $\frac{1}{4}$

3. 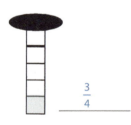 $\frac{3}{4}$

4.  0

5. 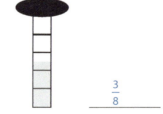 $\frac{3}{8}$

6. 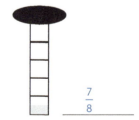 $\frac{7}{8}$

Book 6: *Fraction Operations*   1

TEACHER NOTES: STUDENT PAGE 1

The intent of page 1 is to provide a context that closely matches the way in which fraction strips will be used for understanding fraction operations throughout this book. *Watch for:* In these problems, students are to use visualization to estimate about how much oil is needed to fill the engine. The point here is to encourage students to think about the whole, represented by the one whole fraction strip, and the ways in which various fractions can be combined to make one whole.

Teaching Strategy: One point you may want to discuss with students is that these problems can most readily be solved by staying within one family of fractions as defined by the denominator. Once students determine the fractional amount of oil already in the engine, they can focus on only one fraction strip, such as fourths, halves, or thirds. Adding like fractions, or fractions with the same denominator, is the best way to introduce the concept because students can simply count the number of fractional parts that are being combined in the problem. Later on in this book students will begin to add fractions from different families, those with unlike denominators. For now, students need to become more comfortable using fraction strips because this work sets the stage for understanding the algorithms that will be developed throughout this book.

Forward Thinking: A Teaching Opportunity

It's important to remind students that the numerator (top number) of a fraction counts and that the denominator (bottom number) indicates what is being counted. For example, 3/8 means that there are three (3) parts, each of which is one eighth (1/8). So, 3/8 + 2/8 = 5/8, because that is how many 1/8 parts there are altogether. This is the reason that adding and subtracting fractions with like denominators is the same as adding and subtracting whole numbers–the numerators are simply counted and added together or counted and subtracted one from the other.

CONTINUE THE PROBLEM SOLVING

Have students work individually to solve the problems on page 2. As they work, circulate to monitor their recorded answers. When students finish each problem, have them compare and discuss their answers with a partner. Then have each pair share their answers in a class discussion of the problem. Refer to the **Teacher Notes: Student Page 2** for more specific ideas about the problems on this page.

As students work and discuss their conclusions, focus on these issues:

Validate Representations – Students may want to use their fraction strips to help them with the problems on this page. If they use different models, have them analyze which are correct.

Help Make Connections – Remind students how they combined different fractions to make one whole in the problems in Book 5. Ask them to think about fractions that combine to make more than one whole.

Validate Alternate Strategies – Have students compare and discuss their explanations to see whether they used different strategies to solve the problems. Then have them discuss whether all the strategies are valid.

Allow Waiting Time – When students struggle to explain their thinking, be sure to allow them ample time to organize their thoughts.

TEACHER NOTES: STUDENT PAGE 2

This page begins the steps students will find necessary to understand how to add fractions with different denominators. The point of this exercise is to help students build their informal and intuitive sense about how various fractions combine. *Watch for:* If students have completed Book 5, they should have a basic sense about the relative sizes of different fractions. For example, students with even a little informal experience thinking about fractions will quickly recognize that 3/4 + 3/4 is greater than 1.

Teaching Strategy: Before students begin, model the example problems with fraction strips for the class. The most direct and effective way to initiate solution strategies is to use the fraction strips that represent each of the fractions mentioned. For example, suppose we were trying to determine whether 3/4 and 1/2 will more than fill up the engine. We might begin by identifying the three fraction strips we need: 1 whole, 3/4, and 1/2.

We then can set the two fractions end to end and then compare the new length to the one whole to see if together they are longer, shorter, or exactly equal to the one whole strip.

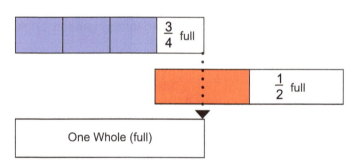

Through the models, it becomes obvious that 3/4 + 1/2 is going to be greater than one whole. You may choose to present this strategy to your students or to let them discover it on their own. In any event, be sure to allow students time to discuss this strategy with their peers. It will become important as the strategy is revisited in subsequent sections of this book.

Student Page 2: Problems and Potential Answers

Section A: Informal Addition and Subtraction of Fractions Set 1

Enough Oil?

John saves any leftover oil to use on the next car. And when he is adding oil to the cars, John always wants to fill the oil tank to exactly one gallon. He never wants to overfill the tank by pouring too much oil into it. So first he uses the key to see how much oil is in the tank. Then he looks at his leftover oil amounts to see if there is enough to fill it up. Help John decide whether the following combinations of oil amounts are just right (equal to 1 gallon), too much (more than 1 gallon), or too little (less than 1 gallon). Use your fraction strips to help. Explain how you know. Three examples have been done to help you get started.

Oil in the Reservoir	Leftover Oil Amounts	Too Little	Too Much	Just Right	How do you know?
$\frac{1}{2}$	$\frac{1}{4}$	✓			I know that $\frac{1}{2}+\frac{1}{2}=1$. I also know that $\frac{1}{4}$ is less than $\frac{1}{2}$. So $\frac{1}{2}+\frac{1}{4}$ has to be less than $\frac{1}{2}+\frac{1}{2}$, which means it is also less than 1 as well.
$\frac{3}{4}$	$\frac{1}{8}$ & $\frac{1}{8}$			✓	I know that $\frac{3}{4}+\frac{1}{4}=1$. Since $(\frac{1}{8}+\frac{1}{8})=\frac{1}{4}$, then I know we have the right amount because: $\frac{3}{4}+(\frac{1}{8}+\frac{1}{8})=1$
$\frac{1}{4}$	$\frac{5}{8}$ & $\frac{1}{4}$		✓		I know we need $\frac{3}{4}$ to fill up the tank since there is $\frac{1}{4}$ already in there. $\frac{5}{8}$ is more than a half. Since $\frac{1}{2}+\frac{1}{4}$ is $\frac{3}{4}$, then I know that $\frac{5}{8}+\frac{1}{4}$ is going to be more than $\frac{3}{4}$. So, there is too much oil.
$\frac{3}{4}$	$\frac{1}{2}$		✓		$\frac{3}{4}+\frac{1}{4}=1$. Since $\frac{1}{2}$ is more than $\frac{1}{4}$, I have too much.
$\frac{5}{8}$	$\frac{3}{8}$			✓	$\frac{5}{8}+\frac{3}{8}=\frac{8}{8}$ (or 1)
$\frac{3}{8}$	$\frac{1}{2}$	✓			$\frac{1}{2}+\frac{4}{8}=1$. Since $\frac{3}{8}$ is less than $\frac{4}{8}$, I have too little.
$\frac{1}{4}$	$\frac{1}{8}$ & $\frac{5}{8}$			✓	Since $\frac{1}{4}$ is the same amount as $\frac{2}{8}$, then I know that $\frac{2}{8}+\frac{1}{8}+\frac{5}{8}=\frac{8}{8}$, or 1. Therefore I have exactly the correct amount of oil.
$\frac{3}{4}$	$\frac{3}{8}$		✓		$\frac{3}{4}+\frac{1}{4}=1$. Since $\frac{3}{8}$ is more than $\frac{1}{4}$, I have too much.
$\frac{7}{8}$	$\frac{1}{4}$		✓		$\frac{7}{8}+\frac{1}{8}=1$. Since $\frac{1}{4}$ is more than $\frac{1}{8}$, I have too much.

CONCEPT DEVELOPMENT (PAGES 3–6)

INTRODUCE THE CONCEPT

ASSESS STUDENTS' PRIOR KNOWLEDGE

In this set of problems, students begin to think linearly about combining fractions. To help them, begin with an introduction that builds on the fractional parts of a customary ruler. Place a transparent customary ruler that is divided into sixteenths of an inch on the overhead projector.

Ask:
Look at the ruler. What are all the fractional parts into which each inch is divided? How many 1/2-inch parts are there in one inch? How many 1/4-inch parts? How many 1/8-inch parts? How many 1/16-inch parts? What is the name of the fraction mark you would land on if you started at 1/2 inch and moved 1/4 inch to the right? What are all the other names you could use to identify this fraction?

Listen for:
- Each inch is divided into halves, fourths, eighths, and sixteenths.
- In one inch there are two 1/2-inch parts, four 1/4-inch parts, eight 1/8-inch parts, and sixteen 1/16-inch parts.
- You would land on the 3/4-inch mark. You could use 6/8 and 12/16 to identify the same mark.

MODEL MATHEMATICAL THINKING

Model the thinking for another example. As you ask the question and talk through the thinking, work out each step at the overhead projector using the transparent ruler.

Ask:
Let's suppose I use the ruler to draw a line from the beginning of the ruler to the 3/4-inch mark. If I want to extend the line another 7/8 inch, how long will the line be?

Talk Through the Thinking:
First let me find the fourth-, or quarter-inch, marks. They are: 1/4, 2/4 or 1/2, 3/4. This is how long my line will be to start with. If I have to extend the line 7/8 inch, I need to find the eighth-inch marks. Each 1/8-inch mark is halfway between two quarter-inch marks. I know that 7/8 is the same as seven 1/8 parts. So, what I can do is count on seven 1/8-inch marks from the end of my 3/4-inch line.
- 3/4 plus 1/8 is 7/8
- 7/8 plus 1/8 is 8/8 or 1
- 1 plus 1/8 is 1 1/8
- 1 1/8 plus 1/8 is 1 2/8 or 1 1/4
- 1 2/8 plus 1/8 is 1 3/8
- 1 3/8 plus 1/8 is 1 4/8 or 1 1/2
- 1 4/8 plus 1/8 is 1 5/8

I added seven 1/8 parts, or 7/8 inch and wound up at the 1 5/8-inch mark. So my extended line is 1 5/8-inches long.

Ask:
How could you use the same strategy to extend a 1/2-inch line another 3/4 inch? How long would the extended line be?

Listen for:
- First I would draw a line from the beginning of the ruler to the 1/2-inch mark.
- Next, I would count on three 1/4-inch parts. 1/2 plus 1/4 is 3/4, plus 1/4 is 4/4 or 1 inch, plus 1/4 is 1 1/4 inches.
- The line would be 1 1/4 inches long.

LAUNCH THE PROBLEM SOLVING

Have students work individually to solve the problems on page 3. As they work, you may want to circulate and monitor their recorded answers. When students finish each problem, have them compare and discuss their answers with a partner. Then have each pair share their answers in a class discussion of the problem. Refer to the **Teacher Notes: Student Page 3** for more specific ideas about the problems on this page.

As students work and report their conclusions, focus on these issues:

Validate Alternate Strategies – Students will use different strategies to solve these problems. Some may use fraction strips, some may want to return to the ruler as in the example used to introduce this lesson, and others may be able to tally the combinations of fractions mentally.

Help Make Connections – You may need to remind some students that the fractions in these problems are all part of the same family, 1/8, 1/4, and 1/2.

Allow Waiting Time – When students struggle to explain their thinking, be sure to allow them ample time to organize their thoughts.

Student Page 3: Problems and Potential Answers

Section A: Informal Addition and Subtraction of Fractions Set 2

How Far?

Every year the town of Spring Canyon hosts a running/walking race. This year, the planners want to have three different races: a 1-mile race, a 3-mile race, and a 4-mile race. They want all the races to start at the county Courthouse and finish at the entrance to City Park. Below is a map of the downtown area. Each square represents one city block. **Each city block is exactly $\frac{1}{8}$ mile on each side**. Only the darkened roads are available for the race routes.

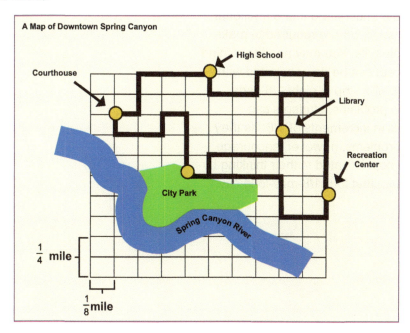

1. Is it possible to have a 1-mile race? What would the route be? _____
   Yes, from the Courthouse directly to the City Park along the darkened road.

2. Is it possible to have the 3-mile race? What would the route be? _____
   Yes, from the Courthouse to the High School, to the Library, to the City Park.

3. Is it possible to have the 4-mile race? What would the route be? _____
   Yes, from the Courthouse, to the High School, to the Library, to the Recreation Center, to the City Park.

4. Follow the darkened routes. What is the shortest distance between the locations below? Reduce your answers when you can. For example, $\frac{4}{8}$ mile = $\frac{1}{2}$ mile. So, use $\frac{1}{2}$.

   a) The Courthouse to the High School $\frac{3}{4}$ mile

   b) The Courthouse to City Park   1 mile

   c) The High School to the Library $1\frac{1}{2}$ mile

   d) The High School to the Recreation Center $2\frac{1}{8}$ miles

   e) The Recreation Center to the City Park $1\frac{1}{8}$ miles

Book 6: *Fraction Operations*

TEACHER NOTES: STUDENT PAGE 3

In these problems, students are encouraged to begin adding fractions using the context of a map. Here they are adding fractions that are part of only one fraction family, the least fraction being 1/8. Be sure that students understand this context. Some students may wonder why they cannot travel along other streets to find the shortest distance between two locations. Emphasize the race route, perhaps even asking students to trace the race route with their fingers or even another color pen or pencil. *Watch for:* For these problems, students must understand that 8 fractional parts that are each equal to 1/8 are required to make one whole, or one whole mile. You may need to remind students that this concept can be demonstrated with an eighths fraction strip–the strip is eight 1/8 parts long. For most of these problems, students can simply count city blocks in increments of 1/8. As they progress through the problems, however, encourage them to become more sophisticated in their thinking by recognizing, for example, that four 1/8-mile-long city blocks equal 1/2 mile.

CONTINUE THE PROBLEM SOLVING

Have students work individually to solve the problems on page 4. As they work, you may want to circulate and monitor their recorded answers. When students finish each problem, have them compare and discuss their answers with a partner. Then have each pair share their answers in a class discussion of the problem. Refer to the **Teacher Notes: Student Page 4** for more specific ideas about the problems on this page.

As students work and report their conclusions, focus on these issues:

Help Make Connections – You may need to remind students to think of how they determined the answers to the problems on page 3 in order to find the distances between two points on the map.

Facilitate Students' Thinking – When the opportunity presents itself, encourage students to name the distances they find in as many ways as they can. You may need to help them understand, for example, that 16/8 miles is equal to 2 miles and that 6/8 can be renamed as 3/4.

Allow Waiting Time – When students struggle to explain their thinking, be sure to allow them ample time to organize their thoughts.

TEACHER NOTES: STUDENT PAGE 4

These problems are an extension of those on page 3. In these problems students are asked to compare distances between various points on the map. By the end of the exercises, they should be developing confidence and comfort with the benchmark fractions used in these problems.

Teaching Strategy: When applicable, be sure to help students compare equivalent representations of the same distances. For example, in problem 7, students may simply count the number of 1/8-mile-long blocks, in which case one lap would consist of eighteen 1/8 parts. Be sure to take advantage of this opportunity to encourage students to find other ways to name that distance. *Watch for:* You might elicit at what point in the lap the runners would have traveled exactly 1 mile. At that point, students might retain the 1 mile and start over, counting 1/8-mile increments. At two miles (16 blocks) pause again to ask how students might represent this distance. Finally, be sure to point out that 18/8 miles is the same as 2 1/4 miles, which can also be represented as 2 2/8 miles.

Fraction Operations *Teacher Edition*

Student Page 4: Problems and Potential Answers

Section A: Informal Addition and Subtraction of Fractions — Set 2

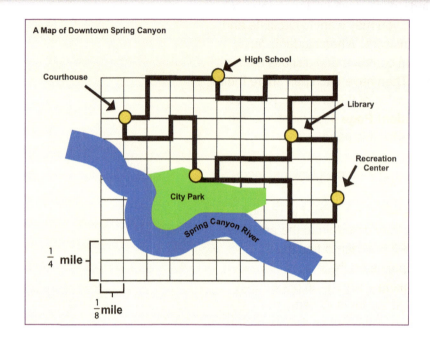

5. a) How far is it from the Courthouse to the Library if you go past the High School? $2\frac{1}{4}$ miles

   b) How far is it from the Courthouse to the Recreation Center if you go past the entrance to City Park?
   $2\frac{1}{8}$ miles

   c) What is the difference in the distances? $\frac{1}{8}$ mile

6. Which distance is greater:

   a) From City Park to the High School going past the Courthouse, **OR**

   b) From the Recreation Center to the City Park going past the Library?
   Distance (a) is greater

   What is the length of each distance?   Distance (a) is $1\frac{3}{4}$ miles. Distance (b) is $1\frac{3}{8}$ miles.
   What is the difference in the distances? $\frac{3}{8}$ mile

7. One loop starts at the Library, goes past the Recreation Center, and then goes back to the Library **without** going to the entrance to City Park. You run around this loop two times. How many miles do you run? _____

   Explain.   I run $4\frac{1}{2}$ miles. One time around is $\frac{18}{8}$ miles (or $2\frac{1}{4}$ miles). So two times around is $\frac{36}{8}$ miles (or $4\frac{1}{2}$ miles).

4   Book 6: *Fraction Operations*

CONTINUE THE PROBLEM SOLVING

Have students work individually to solve the problems on page 5. As they work, you may want to circulate and monitor their recorded answers. When students finish each problem, have them compare and discuss their answers with a partner. Then have each pair share their answers in a class discussion of the problem. Refer to the **Teacher Notes: Student Page 5** for more specific ideas about the problems on this page.

As students work and report their conclusions, focus on these issues:

Facilitate Students' Understanding – When students struggle to compare fractions, have them refer to the number line at the bottom of the page.

Validate Representations – Some students may need to model the fractions with fraction strips. Others may be able to visualize the fractions. Be sure to have students discuss their models to determine whether they are correct.

Help Make Connections – You may need to remind students that many fractions can be renamed in simpler terms by dividing their numerator and denominator by the same number and that a fraction is in simplest form when the numerator and denominator have no common factor other than 1.

Encourage Language Development – You may need to remind students of the concepts of halves and quarters and eighths, as they are used frequently to describe distances in these problems.

Student Page 5: Problems and Potential Answers

Section A: Informal Addition and Subtraction of Fractions Set 3

How Far Between Stops?

The city buses stop to pick up and drop off riders every few blocks. Below is a map of several bus stops.

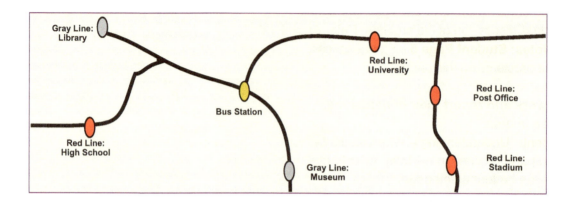

The distances from each bus stop to the bus station are shown in the table below. Complete the table by finding the distances between each of the stops. When you can, express the distances in halves and fourths instead of eighths. Use the number line below to help you.

	Bus Station	Library	Museum	High School	University	Post Office	Stadium
Bus Station	0	$1\frac{1}{2}$ miles	$\frac{5}{8}$ mile	$1\frac{3}{4}$ miles	1 mile	$1\frac{3}{8}$ miles	$1\frac{7}{8}$ miles
Library	$1\frac{1}{2}$ miles	0	$2\frac{1}{8}$ miles	$3\frac{1}{4}$ miles	$2\frac{1}{2}$ miles	$2\frac{7}{8}$ miles	$3\frac{3}{8}$ miles
Museum	$\frac{5}{8}$ mile	$2\frac{1}{8}$ miles	0	$2\frac{3}{8}$ miles	$1\frac{5}{8}$ miles	2 miles	$2\frac{1}{2}$ miles
High School	$1\frac{3}{4}$ miles	$3\frac{1}{4}$ miles	$2\frac{3}{8}$ miles	0	$2\frac{3}{4}$ miles	$3\frac{1}{8}$ miles	$3\frac{5}{8}$ miles
University	1 mile	$2\frac{1}{2}$ miles	$1\frac{5}{8}$ miles	$2\frac{3}{4}$ miles	0	$\frac{3}{8}$ mile	$\frac{7}{8}$ mile
Post Office	$1\frac{3}{8}$ miles	$2\frac{7}{8}$ miles	2 miles	$3\frac{1}{8}$ miles	$\frac{3}{8}$ mile	0	$\frac{1}{2}$ mile
Stadium	$1\frac{7}{8}$ miles	$3\frac{3}{8}$ miles	$2\frac{1}{2}$ miles	$3\frac{5}{8}$ miles	$\frac{7}{8}$ mile	$\frac{1}{2}$ mile	0

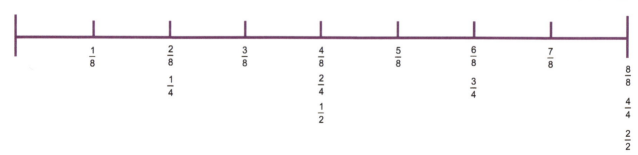

Book 6: *Fraction Operations*

TEACHER NOTES: STUDENT PAGE 5

This context, like the one before it, encourages the development of students' map-reading ability and it also moves them ahead in their comfort and ability to add fractions informally. Once again, the fractions in this problem are from one family: eighths, quarters, and halves. It is important that students understand this context. Take several minutes to discuss the setting of the problem and the connection between the map and the table.

Watch for: This context is slightly different in that students cannot simply count city blocks. Instead, they must either use visualization or fraction strips (one fraction model is provided below the problem) to represent the distances on the map. Another important distinction between these problems and the ones that preceded them is that students are asked to rename fractions in simplest form. *Teaching Strategy:* Be sure to emphasize to students that whenever possible, they should express the distances in halves or fourths instead of eighths.

While some students will be ready to make this step, others can be directed to the number line at the bottom of the page, which shows how eighths, fourths, and halves are related. *Teaching Strategy:* Help students understand this relationship as shown on the number line. You may ask them to create their own number lines at their work areas by aligning their eighths, fourths, and halves fraction strips as they may have done in the first set of problems in this book.

It cannot be emphasized too strongly how important this exercise is. Students will soon be introduced to the traditional fraction addition algorithm, in which they will need to find common denominators so that the fractions can be added together. Finding equivalent representations of the same fraction (e.g., 1/2 is the same as 3/6) is vital to this process. So as students are completing this page, they are being given opportunities to understand and practice this important concept. These informal exercises will help develop students' sense of fraction combinations and fraction equivalence. This fraction sense will be essential for later success with all the fraction operations.

Forward Thinking: A Teaching Opportunity

Students can write fractions in simplest form by using the number line. But they can also look for whole-number factors that are common to the numerator and denominator. When the numerator and denominator have no whole-number common factor other than 1, the fraction is said to be in simplest form, or lowest terms. By finding these common factors and dividing both the numerator and denominator by them, students can quickly simplify a fraction to rename it in simplest form.

CONTINUE THE PROBLEM SOLVING

Have students work individually to solve the problems on page 6. As they work, you may want to circulate and monitor their recorded answers. When students finish each problem, have them compare and discuss their answers with a partner. Then have each pair share their answers in a class discussion of the problem. Refer to the **Teacher Notes: Student Page 6** for more specific ideas about the problems on this page.

As students work and report their conclusions, focus on these issues:

Help Make Connections – You may need to remind students that, just as eighths, fourths, and halves are part of the same fraction family, so are sixths, thirds, and halves.

Facilitate Students' Thinking – Encourage students to complete page 6 using the same kind of thinking about fractions as they have used so far in this book.

Validate Representations – Some students may still need to use fraction strips to model the fractions as they work through this page. Have them check to be sure they are modeling correctly, but also encourage them to move away from modeling and try to work out the answers either mentally or with paper and pencil.

TEACHER NOTES: STUDENT PAGE 6

For this problem students are asked to complete the same kinds of intuitive steps they need to take to combine fractions as they have done in the past. This time, however, they are working with a new family of fractions. Rather than using eighths, fourths, and halves, they are now working with sixths, thirds, and halves. The same kinds of steps and thinking that they refined in the previous pages must now be transferred and applied to this new set of fractions. Continue to encourage students to use fraction strips as long as they need them. Gradually, you will find some students moving beyond the fraction strip models. This important cognitive leap is an indicator that they are getting ready for more abstract work with fractions, including the use of the formal addition and subtraction algorithms developed in the next set of pages.

Student Page 6: Problems and Potential Answers

Section A: Informal Addition and Subtraction of Fractions Set 3

How Much Gasoline?

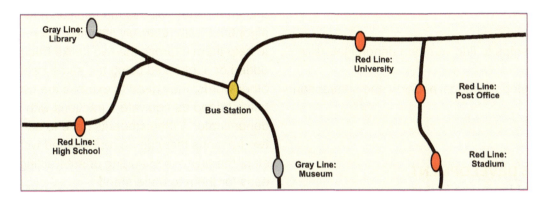

The table below shows how much gas is needed to get from the bus station to each of the stops. Complete the table by finding how much gas is needed to go between each of the stops. When you can, express the fractional parts of a gallon in halves and thirds instead of sixths. Use the number line below to help you.

	Bus Station	Library	Museum	High School	University	Post Office	Stadium
Bus Station	0	$\frac{1}{3}$ gallon	$\frac{1}{6}$ gallon	$\frac{1}{2}$ gallon	1 gallon	$1\frac{1}{3}$ gallons	$1\frac{5}{6}$ gallons
Library	$\frac{1}{3}$ gallon	0	$\frac{1}{2}$ gallon	$\frac{5}{6}$ gallon	$1\frac{1}{3}$ gallons	$1\frac{2}{3}$ gallons	$2\frac{1}{6}$ gallons
Museum	$\frac{1}{6}$ gallon	$\frac{1}{2}$ gallon	0	$\frac{2}{3}$ gallon	$1\frac{1}{6}$ gallons	$1\frac{1}{2}$ gallons	2 gallons
High School	$\frac{1}{2}$ gallon	$\frac{5}{6}$ gallon	$\frac{2}{3}$ gallon	0	$1\frac{1}{2}$ gallons	$1\frac{5}{6}$ gallons	$2\frac{1}{3}$ gallons
University	1 gallon	$1\frac{1}{3}$ gallons	$1\frac{1}{6}$ gallons	$1\frac{1}{2}$ gallons	0	$\frac{1}{3}$ gallon	$\frac{5}{6}$ gallon
Post Office	$1\frac{1}{3}$ gallons	$1\frac{2}{3}$ gallons	$1\frac{1}{2}$ gallons	$1\frac{5}{6}$ gallons	$\frac{1}{3}$ gallon	0	$\frac{1}{2}$ gallon
Stadium	$1\frac{5}{6}$ gallons	$2\frac{1}{6}$ gallons	2 gallons	$2\frac{1}{3}$ gallons	$\frac{5}{6}$ gallon	$\frac{1}{2}$ gallon	0

Section B: Adding and Subtracting Fractions Using Common Denominators

SECTION B PLANNER

THE MATHEMATICS CONTENT AND GOALS

GOALS
Students will:
- Use fraction strips to find common denominators of two fractions.
- Use fraction strips to model addition and subtraction of fractions.

LANGUAGE DEVELOPMENT
Mathematical language in this section includes:

Common Denominator: When adding and subtracting fractions, we often seek a common denominator, or a number that is a common multiple of the denominators of a set of fractions.

Diagram: In this section the word diagram is used to refer to a visual representation of a mathematical context.

Algorithm: An algorithm is a series of prescribed steps, rules, or procedures that can be followed to solve a given type of problem.

equivalence. Once students know that 1/2 can also be expressed in terms of fourths, sixths, eighths, and so on, they will use the addition and subtraction algorithms with relatively little hesitation. The idea is to help them express the two unlike fractions being added or subtracted using the same fraction strip. In other words, they need to express the two fractions being added as equivalent fractions with a common denominator. When students have to add or subtract two fractions that can be represented with the same strip, the process of adding or subtracting becomes easy for them to understand.

Set 1 (pp. 7–9; problems 1–10)
There is quite a bit of explanation, accompanied by diagrams, throughout this problem set. After studying and discussing the illustrations, students complete similar problems with the help of their fraction strips. As they become more comfortable with the problems, they will gradually depend less on their visual and physical models and more on abstract reasoning.

PACING

The projected pacing for this unit is 1–2 class periods (based on a 45-minute period).

PROBLEM SETS: OVERVIEW

The informal strategies developed in Section A have set the stage for an introduction of the traditional fraction addition and subtraction algorithms. The key mathematical principle that must be in place for this algorithm to have meaning has to do with fractional

CONCEPT DEVELOPMENT (PAGES 7–9)

INTRODUCE THE CONCEPT

ASSESS STUDENTS' PRIOR KNOWLEDGE
Examples of the kind shown on pages 7–9 are crucial to students' understanding of common denominators and the traditional algorithms for adding and subtracting fractions. With careful introduction, students will be able to use the algorithms with understanding and facility.

Ask:
What ways can you find to combine fourths and eighths to make 1/2? Explain how you know that each combination is equivalent to 1/2. You may use your fraction strips.

Listen for:
- There are three ways: 1/4 + 1/4; 1/4 + 1/8 + 1/8; 1/8 + 1/8 + 1/8 + 1/8.

Some students' explanations may reference their fraction strips and the physical modeling they have done. Others may already grasp how to combine these fractions without using models. In any case, their explanations should reflect understanding of fraction equivalence, for example that 2/4 = 1/2.

MODEL MATHEMATICAL THINKING
Write this incorrect example on the board:

$$\frac{5}{8} + \frac{3}{4} = \frac{8}{12}$$

Ask:
Do you think the person who added these fractions found the correct answer? How can we tell?

Talk Through the Thinking:
First let's look at all the fractions in this example: 5/8, 3/4, and the answer, 8/12. We know that 4/8 is equivalent to 1/2, so 5/8 must be greater than 1/2. We also know that 2/4 is equivalent to 1/2, so 3/4 must also be greater than 1/2. We know that 1/2 + 1/2 = 1. So, if we add two fractions that are each greater than 1/2, the answer must be greater than 1. Now let's look at 8/12. We know that 12/12 is equivalent to 1 and that 8/12 is less than 1. So the answer, 8/12, cannot be correct. The person must have added the numerators and then added the denominators. This is a common mistake when adding fractions with unlike denominators.

Ask:
What do you think you could do to get the correct answer to 5/8 + 3/4? What is the correct answer?

Listen for:
- First, I could rename 3/4 as the equivalent fraction 6/8.
- Once I renamed 3/4 as 6/8, I could combine the eighths: 5/8 + 6/8 = 11/8.
- Next, I can express 11/8 in simplest form: 1 3/8.

LAUNCH THE PROBLEM SOLVING

Have students read through page 7 and discuss the information with a partner. As they do so, you may want to circulate and monitor their discussions and answer any questions they may have. When everyone has finished the page, have pairs share their conclusions in a class discussion. Refer to the discussion **Adding Fractions with Unlike Denominators**.

As students work through page 7 and report their conclusions, focus on these issues:

Look for Misconceptions – Even though you may have used the examples in the concept introduction, many students will continue to add the numerators and then add the denominators. Find other counterexamples similar to the ones in the introduction. Encourage students to use their knowledge of fractions to find whether their answers make sense.

Facilitate Students' Thinking – When students struggle to understand the examples on page 7, have them replicate the diagrams with their fraction strips.

Allow Processing Time – It may take some students a while to grasp the ideas on page 7. Be sure to allow them time to discuss the examples with their peers and assimilate the given information.

Allow Waiting Time – When students struggle to explain their thinking, be sure to allow them ample time to organize their thoughts.

Encourage Language Development – Look for opportunities in this section to encourage language development around the ideas of fractions, such as common denominator, numerator, denominator, and fraction families.

Adding Fractions with Unlike Denominators

You may need to elaborate on the illustrations and presentation of the ideas on page 7.
Teaching Strategy: Although there are no problems or specific prompts for students, be sure to engage them in discussion about the concept developed on this page. The information presented here is the key to understanding and using the fraction addition algorithm.

On the Lookout for Misconceptions

A common error students make when adding fractions is to add the numerators together and add the denominators together. This mistake is understandable given students' understanding of addition of whole numbers. As an example, students might add in the following way: 1/2 + 1/3 = 2/5.

To correct this misconception, help students return to the meaning of addition itself. Help them recall that when they add two positive quantities, the sum should be greater than both addends. If students make the mistake of adding the numerators and then the denominators, as in the case above, you can help them use their intuitive understanding of addition to help them see the contradiction. For example, have students discuss whether it makes sense that the answer of 2/5 is actually *less* than one of the addends, 1/2. While students may still need help in understanding how to add fractions, they will at least not be as likely to make the mistake of adding both the numerators and the denominators.

Student Page 7: Problems and Potential Answers

Section B: Adding and Subtracting Fractions Using Common Denominators Set 1

To help make adding and subtracting fractions easier, you need to express one or both of the fractions as equivalent fractions **with the same denominator**. Fraction strips can help you. Think about this problem:

What is $\frac{1}{2} + \frac{1}{6}$?

We know $\frac{1}{2}$ looks like:

We know $\frac{1}{6}$ looks like:

Now we need to show $\frac{1}{2}$ and $\frac{1}{6}$ using the same fraction bar. First, we need to find another way to express $\frac{1}{2}$ using a fraction strip that is divided into 6 equal parts to show sixths.

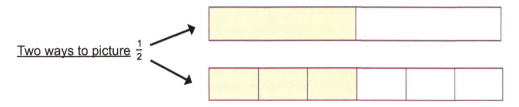

Two ways to picture $\frac{1}{2}$

The fraction strips show us that $\frac{1}{2}$ is equal to $\frac{3}{6}$. So, we can rename $\frac{1}{2}$ as $\frac{3}{6}$ and then rewrite the problem like this:

$$\frac{1}{2} + \frac{1}{6} \rightarrow \text{rewritten as} \rightarrow \frac{3}{6} + \frac{1}{6}$$

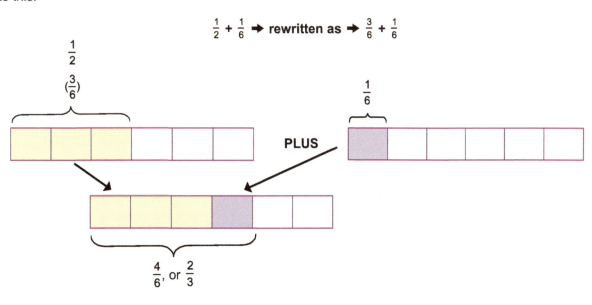

CONTINUE THE PROBLEM SOLVING

Have students work individually to solve the problems on page 8. As they work, you may want to circulate to monitor their recorded answers. When students finish each problem, have them compare and discuss their answers with a partner. Then have each pair share their answers in a class discussion of the problem. Refer to the **Teacher Notes: Student Page 8** for more specific ideas about the problems on this page.

As students work and report their conclusions, focus on these issues:

Validate Alternate Strategies – Ask students to share their strategies for finding common denominators, especially for problem 5. Have the class discuss whether these strategies result in the correct answer.

Facilitate Students' Thinking – You may need to remind students of the reasoning you used as you talked through the thinking in the concept introduction.

Validate Representations – Some students may need to continue to use their fraction strips to model the problems. Allow them to do so, and have them compare and discuss their representations with a partner to determine whether they are modeling correctly.

Student Page 8: Problems and Potential Answers

Section B: Adding and Subtracting Fractions Using Common Denominators Set 1

One More Example…

$\frac{3}{8} + \frac{1}{4}$ ➡ **Step 1:** Rename one or both fractions as equivalent fractions with the same denominator.

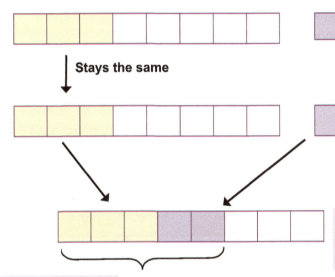

Stays the same

Changes to $\frac{2}{8}$

Step 2: Combine the fractional parts represented by the shaded amounts using **one** fraction strip that has 8 equal parts.

Step 3: So, $\frac{3}{8} + \frac{1}{4} = \frac{5}{8}$

Solve each problem. Use fraction strips or a diagram to help you find the common denominator.

1. $\frac{1}{4} + \frac{3}{4} = \frac{4}{4}$ or 1

2. $\frac{2}{3} + \frac{1}{6} = \frac{5}{6}$

3. $\frac{3}{8} + \frac{1}{8} = \frac{4}{8}$ or $\frac{1}{2}$

4. $\frac{1}{3} + \frac{1}{2} = \frac{5}{6}$

5. $\frac{1}{4} + \frac{1}{6} = \frac{5}{12}$

6. $\frac{2}{3} + \frac{1}{4} = \frac{11}{12}$

Book 6: *Fraction Operations*

TEACHER NOTES: STUDENT PAGE 8

If you find it necessary to do another example with your students before they begin the practice problems, one is illustrated at the top of page 8. In general, the problems increase in difficulty. The progression has to do with the steps needed to find common denominators.

Problem 1: The fractions have like denominators.
Watch for: The students can simply add the numerators.

Problem 2: In this problem, the fractions are compatible (the denominator of one is a factor of the denominator of the other). *Watch for:* Students must rename the first fraction, 2/3, as an equivalent fraction with a denominator of 6.

Problem 3: The fractions in this problem have like denominators.

Problem 4: *Watch for:* For this problem, students must rename **both** fractions as equivalent fractions with the same denominator, in this case, sixths. To model this problem, students will need to use three different fraction strips. This problem is slightly easier than the next one because the two denominators can simply be multiplied to find the least common denominator: 2 × 3 = 6. This is not the case with problem 5, discussed below.

Problem 5: This problem may be the most difficult for students to understand conceptually from an algebraic point of view, but it is still rather easy to demonstrate with visual models such as fraction strips. Students can always find a common denominator of two fractions by multiplying their denominators. But doing so may not result in the least common denominator. The least common denominators in problems 4 and 6 could be found by multiplying the denominators because in both cases the numbers are consecutive (2 and 3, and 3 and 4). When students multiply the two denominators in problem 5 (6 and 4), the resulting denominator is 24. Yet, a lesser common denominator can be found for these two fractions: 12. This can be explained because 6 and 4 share the common factor 2. The mathematical explanation of this phenomenon is fairly abstract for young students. That is why we must be careful to avoid rushing to abstract manipulations of fractions before students fully comprehend the mathematics at hand. If we wish to preserve and promote students' mathematical understanding, algorithms cannot be presented until after the presentation of the conceptual foundations that underlie them.

Problem 6: As with problem 4, students must rename both fractions as equivalent fractions with the same denominator.

Teaching Strategy: While the algebraic explanation for this problem is complex, finding the common denominator for these two fractions can still be illustrated with fraction strips. The key is to find a denominator greater than each of the two given denominators that can express, in this case, both sixths and fourths. We can try looking at the fraction strips for eighths and twelfths.

While the eighths strip **can** model fourths, it cannot do the same for sixths because it cannot be separated into 6 equal groups of eighths.

However, we see that the twelfths strip can be separated into 4 equal groups of twelfths and into 6 equal groups of twelfths.

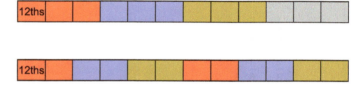

CONTINUE THE PROBLEM SOLVING

Have students work individually to solve the problems on page 9. As they work, you may want to circulate to monitor their recorded answers. When students finish each problem, have them compare and discuss their answers with a partner. Then have each pair share their answers in a class discussion of the problem. Refer to the **Teacher Notes: Student Page 9** for more specific ideas about the problems on this page.

As students work and report their conclusions, focus on these issues:

Help Make Connections – As students study the examples and work through the page, help them understand that they can find common denominators for the fractions in subtraction the same way they find them for the fractions in addition.

Encourage Language Development – When students discuss what they are doing on this page, encourage them to use the appropriate mathematical terms, such as numerator, denominator, and common denominator.

Allow Waiting Time – When students struggle to explain their thinking, be sure to allow them ample time to organize their thoughts.

Validate Representations – Again, help students make connections between the visual models (e.g., fraction strips) they find helpful, and symbolic representations of fractions, common denominators, etc.

TEACHER NOTES: STUDENT PAGE 9

The explanations provided for addition of fractions in the teacher notes of page 8 can be used as a basis for discussing the fraction subtraction problems on this page. *Teaching Strategy:* You might consider starting with the same two fractions and working them both as an addition and a subtraction problem to illustrate that the process of finding common denominators is key and is similar whether adding or subtracting. For example, you may wish to work through these two problems with the class:

$$\frac{1}{2} + \frac{1}{3}$$

$$\frac{1}{2} - \frac{1}{3}$$

Student Page 9: Problems and Potential Answers

Section B: Adding and Subtracting Fractions Using Common Denominators Set 1

Subtraction is like addition because you first need to find a common denominator.

Example: $\frac{3}{8} - \frac{1}{4}$

Step 1: Rename one or both fractions as equivalent fractions with the same denominator.

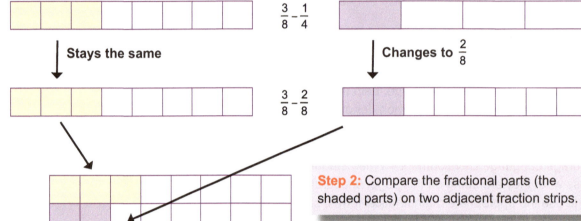

Step 2: Compare the fractional parts (the shaded parts) on two adjacent fraction strips.

Step 3: Subtract (take away) the two $\frac{1}{8}$-parts ($\frac{2}{8}$) from the original three $\frac{1}{8}$-parts ($\frac{3}{8}$).

Step 4: One $\frac{1}{8}$-part is left. So, $\frac{3}{8} - \frac{1}{4} = \frac{1}{8}$.

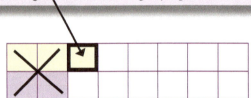

Complete each subtraction problem.

7. $\frac{5}{8} - \frac{2}{4} = \frac{1}{8}$

8. $\frac{2}{3} - \frac{1}{2} = \frac{1}{6}$

9. $\frac{1}{4} - \frac{1}{6} = \frac{1}{12}$

10. $\frac{3}{4} - \frac{1}{6} = \frac{7}{12}$

Book 6: *Fraction Operations*

SECTIONS A AND B ASSESSMENT (Page 10)

LAUNCH THE ASSESSMENT

Have students turn to the Sections A and B Assessment on page 10. An additional copy is found on page 93 of the Assessment Book. Have students work individually to solve the problems. As they work, circulate to be sure students understand what they need to do for each problem and that they are completing each part of the problem. For example, for problem 1, students must find three different points on the map that are the same distance from the City Park and the High School. You may find it helpful to read through the directions for all the problems before students begin, discussing the types of responses they will need to make for each problem. Refer to the **Teacher Notes: Assessment Problems for Sections A and B** for more specific ideas about the problems on this page.

Evaluate Student Responses
Use the assessment rubric on page 92 of the Assessment Book (pictured on page 102 of the Teacher Edition) to evaluate student responses. The Assessment Book has some general suggestions for using the rubric that you may find helpful.

TEACHER NOTES: ASSESSMENT PROBLEMS FOR SECTIONS A AND B

Problem 1: *Watch for:* Look for students to use the spaces in the grid to help them find the points that are the same distance from the two landmarks. Students may count the total distance from one landmark to the other, and then count off half the distance to make a mark. Alternatively, students may count off spaces from each landmark at the same time and continue this until they meet.

Problem 2: Allow students to use fraction strips to help them find a common denominator. *Watch for:* Some students may solve the problems without the need to find a common denominator.

SCORING GUIDE BOOK 6: FRACTION OPERATIONS

Sections A and B Assessment
For Use With: Student Book Page 10

PROBLEM DESCRIPTION	SCORING: WHAT TO LOOK FOR	SCORE AND COMMENTS
Problem 1 Find equal distances between points and informally add fractions. Level 1: Comprehension and Knowledge Level 3: Connection and Application	Do students: • Find equal distances from the labeled point to the given destinations? • Use informal strategies for adding fractions? • Demonstrate general fraction sense by calculating distances based on data?	(4 points for each student-generated mark and calculated distance) Points: _____ of 12
Problem 2a–d Addition and subtraction of fractions. Level 1: Comprehension and Knowledge Level 2: Tool use	Do students: • Demonstrate general fraction sense by finding a common denominator using appropriate tools? • Appropriately represent visuals?	(2 points each) Points: _____ of 8

TOTAL POINTS: _____ OF 20

Student Page 10: Problems and Potential Answers

Sections A and B: Problems for Assessment

How Far? Part 2
Let's go back to the map of the Spring Canyon race route. Remember **every city block is exactly** $\frac{1}{8}$ **mile** on each side, and you can only go along the darkened roads.

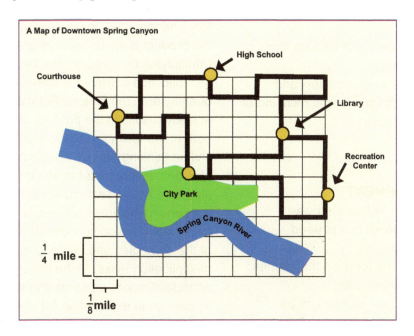

1. You are standing on the race route. You are the **same distance** from the City Park and from the High School. Draw three separate points on the map to show where you are standing. Label them A, B, and C. For each point, write how far is it is to the City Park or the High School.

   Point A: $\frac{7}{8}$ mile

   Point B: $\frac{9}{8}$ mile, or $1\frac{1}{8}$ miles

   Point C: $\frac{13}{8}$ mile, or $1\frac{5}{8}$ miles (via the Recreation Center)

2. Solve each problem. Use fraction strips or a diagram to help you find the common denominator.

   a) $\frac{1}{3} + \frac{1}{6}$ $\frac{3}{6}$ or $\frac{1}{2}$

   b) $\frac{5}{8} + \frac{1}{4}$ $\frac{7}{8}$

   c) $\frac{3}{4} - \frac{1}{2}$ $\frac{1}{4}$

   d) $\frac{2}{3} - \frac{1}{4}$ $\frac{5}{12}$

Book 6: *Fraction Operations*

Section C: Multiplying Fractions Informally

SECTION C PLANNER

THE MATHEMATICS CONTENT AND GOALS

GOALS
Students will:
- Be able to express in words the multiplicative relationship being explored.
- Model multiplication problems with fraction strips or other visual representations.
- Complete fraction multiplication problems and provide conceptual explanations for the meaning of both the problem and the answer.

LANGUAGE DEVELOPMENT
Mathematical language in this section includes many of the same terms used previously in the book:

Fraction: A number in the form *a/b* that names part of a whole, a region, or a set

Fractional Part: Fractional parts might be thought of as equal-sized portions, or *fair shares*, of a whole, a unit, or a collection of objects.

Numerator: The numerator of a fraction is a "counter." It indicates the number of fractional parts (the size of which are determined by the denominator) that are presently under consideration.

Denominator: The denominator may be thought of as the number of equal-sized parts into which the whole has been divided.

PACING

The projected pacing for this unit is 1–2 class periods (based on a 45-minute period).

PROBLEM SETS: OVERVIEW

The same approach that was followed with addition and subtraction, beginning with students' intuitive understanding, will again be used with multiplication of fractions. In order to understand fraction multiplication, students need to overcome one seemingly contradictory phenomenon. In whole-number multiplication the product is almost always greater than the factors (multiplying by zero and one being exceptions). Multiplication of fractions actually leads to a lesser quantity than the factors. For example, 1/2 × 3/4 actually results in the product, 3/8, that is less than both of the factors. Helping students understand this shift in thinking about multiplication is one of the key elements in teaching fraction multiplication with understanding. In this section, students will understand what it means to multiply fractions, which will then serve to help them develop confidence with and understanding of the strategies and procedures used to complete multiplication tasks. At the conclusion of the sections on multiplication, students should be able to provide a conceptual explanation for why the multiplication algorithm actually works.

Set 1 (pp. 11–14; problems 1–15)
There is quite a bit of explanation, accompanied by diagrams, throughout this problem set. After studying and discussing the illustrations, students complete similar problems with the help of their fraction strips. As they become more comfortable with the problems, they will gradually depend less on their visual and physical models. In the final set of problems on page 13, students are provided with several opportunities to develop proficiency with multiplication of fractions. Some students, by the end of those 15 problems, will have discovered the multiplication algorithm, which is explored in depth in a following section.

CONCEPT DEVELOPMENT (Pages 11–14)

INTRODUCE THE CONCEPT

ASSESS STUDENTS' PRIOR KNOWLEDGE
On the board write 2 × 3 and 12 × 10. You may wish to draw a picture of the first expression, for example drawing 2 sets of 3 squares each.

Ask:
Think in terms of groups. What does each of these multiplication expressions mean?

Listen for:
- 2 groups of 3
- 12 groups of 10

Expressing multiplication in terms of groups becomes crucial when multiplying fractions. Students should be led to see fraction multiplication as, for example, 1/2 of 1/4.

MODEL MATHEMATICAL THINKING
Write 1/4 × 1/2 on the board. Use measuring cups to illustrate the problem, or draw a measuring cup on the board or overhead projector. Use the cup(s) to illustrate as you talk through the thinking.

Ask:
What does each of these multiplication expressions mean? Will the product be greater or less than the factors?

Talk Through the Thinking:
Let's look at 1/4 × 1/2 and use the same reasoning we did for 2 × 3. If 2 × 3 means 2 groups of 3, then 1/4 × 1/2 means 1/4 of a group of 1/2. We can also express this as "1/4 of 1/2." Now let's look at the measuring cup and find the 1/2 cup mark. Here it is. Suppose we fill the cup with water to this mark. How much water would 1/4 of 1/2 cup be? I can draw a line to show 1/4 of 1/2 cup. This much water is less than either 1/4 or 1/2 cup. I think it is 1/8 cup. So the product of the two fractions is less than the factors.

Ask:
What does 1/2 × 2/3 mean? Will the product be greater or less than the factors?

Listen for:
- 1/2 of 2/3 is less than 2/3 because half of anything is less than the whole.
- The product will be less than the factors.

LAUNCH THE PROBLEM SOLVING

Have students work individually to read page 11 and answer the question at the bottom of the page. As they work, you may want to circulate and monitor their recorded answers. When students finish, have them discuss the information on the page with a partner. Then have each pair share their conclusions in a class discussion of the page. Refer to the **Teacher Notes: Student Page 11** for more specific ideas about the problems on this page.

As students work and report their conclusions, focus on these issues:

Look for Misconceptions – The most significant misconception students hold about fraction multiplication is that the product of two fractions or of a fraction and a whole number must be greater than both of the factors. This is a natural assumption, given students' prior experience with whole-number multiplication. Using grouping language, such as 1/2 × 4 being expressed as 1/2 of a group of 4, can help students understand that multiplying a whole number by a fraction results in a product that is less than the whole-number factor.

Facilitate Students' Thinking – Keep students focused on mentally restating these problems in terms of *groups of* to help them maintain conceptual understanding of the actions taken in these problems.

Allow Processing Time – It is essential that students be given ample time to think through the conceptualization of fraction multiplication.

Help Make Connections – Help students make the connection between the problem as written and their fraction models. They may want to use their fraction strips to replicate the models on the page.

Fraction Operations Teacher Edition

Student Page 11: Problems and Potential Answers

Section C: Multiplying Fractions Informally — Set 1

Think about this problem: Mr. Nelson has 24 students in his 6th grade class. One-half of the students are boys. Of the boys, $\frac{1}{3}$ play on the middle school soccer team. How many of Mr. Nelson's students play on the middle school soccer team?

Step 1: There are 24 students in Mr. Nelson's class.

Mr. Nelson's Class of 24 students

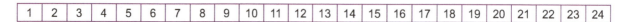

Step 2: One-half of the students are boys.

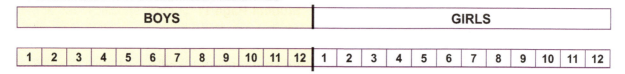

Step 3: One-third of the boys play soccer on the middle school team.

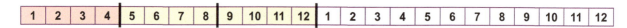

Step 4: One-third of the boys ➔ 4 boys. So, $\frac{1}{3}$ of $\frac{1}{2}$ of 24 = **4 boys on the soccer team.**

Diagrams like these can help us understand how to multiply fractions.

Problem 2: One-half of Mr. Nelson's 6th grade students are boys. Of the boys, $\frac{1}{3}$ play on the middle school soccer team. What **fraction** of all of Mr. Nelson's 6th grade students play on the middle school soccer team?

Write how you could solve this problem. Explain. _Responses will vary._

TEACHER NOTES: STUDENT PAGE 11

The key to developing conceptual understanding of both the multiplication and division algorithms lies in helping students create a sense of what these problem types actually mean. *Watch for:* Students may have heard earlier that the word *of* always means multiplication. While this is true most of the time, and while we are going to build on that notion to help understand operations with fractions, students must be told not to apply this rule indiscriminately. They must let the context dictate the way in which problems are represented and interpreted from a mathematical point of view. That being said, it is true that the word *of* becomes important when conceptualizing multiplication of fractions.

This idea can be emphasized in the introductory problem on this page. *Teaching Strategy:* Be sure to allow students plenty of time to articulate what the problem is asking. Representing this problem context with a fraction bar is important to help students understand what is meant by the multiplication of fractions.

For the question at the bottom of the page, encourage students to follow the same process that was outlined in the example problem. Here, instead of knowing that there are 24 students, students do not segment the bar that represents Mr. Nelson's students.

Teaching Strategy: Be sure to allow students ample time to articulate their thinking about the subtle difference between these two problem statements. *Watch for:* Look for insights similar to the one below, provided by a sixth-grade student. This problem will be fully elaborated on the next page. Nevertheless, the time invested now will pay dividends later.

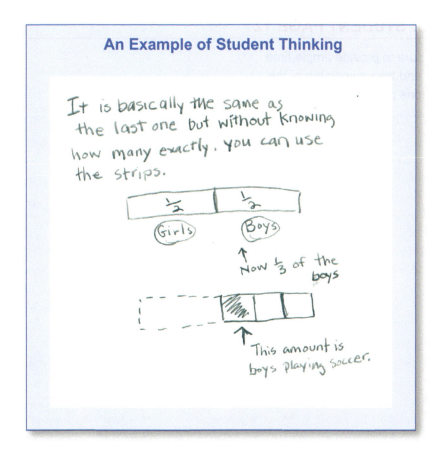

Fraction Operations *Teacher Edition*

CONTINUE THE PROBLEM SOLVING

Have students work individually to read through page 12. When they finish the page, have them compare and discuss their conclusions with a partner. Then have each pair share their conclusions in a class discussion of the page. Refer to the **Teacher Notes: Student Page 12** for more specific ideas about the problems on this page.

As students work and report their conclusions, focus on these issues:

Allow Waiting Time – When students struggle to explain their thinking, be sure to allow them ample time to organize their thoughts.

Allow Processing Time – The concepts on this page may be difficult for some students to grasp. Be sure to allow them ample time for study and discussion.

TEACHER NOTES: STUDENT PAGE 12

Teaching Strategy: Be sure to provide ample time for students to discuss and take ownership of the examples and descriptions presented on this page.

Student Page 12: Problems and Potential Answers

Section C: Multiplying Fractions Informally Set 1

You can use fraction strips to model this problem, even if you do not know how many 6th grade students Mr. Nelson has.

One-half of Mr. Nelson's 6th grade students are boys. Of the boys, $\frac{1}{3}$ play on the middle school soccer team. What fraction of Mr. Nelson's 6th grade students play on the middle school soccer team?

This problem can be expressed as the multiplication problem: What is $\frac{1}{3}$ of $\frac{1}{2}$?

Think about this for a moment. Can you picture one third of one half of a candy bar? An apple pie? How much is one third of one-half of a can of soda? Not too much!

It is important with multiplication and division of fractions <u>to be able to picture</u> what is taking place. So, let's picture $\frac{1}{3}$ of $\frac{1}{2}$.

We'll start with $\frac{1}{2}$.

Now, how can we picture $\frac{1}{3}$ of $\frac{1}{2}$?

This part shows $\frac{1}{3}$ of $\frac{1}{2}$. Now, we have to figure out the name of the fraction for this part of the whole.

The part is $\frac{1}{6}$ of the whole fraction strip. So, $\frac{1}{3}$ of $\frac{1}{2} = \frac{1}{6}$.

Another Example: What is $\frac{1}{2}$ of $\frac{2}{3}$?

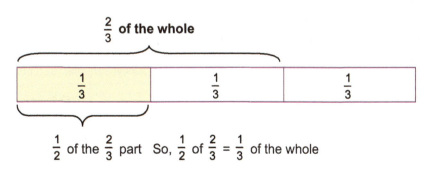

$\frac{1}{2}$ of the $\frac{2}{3}$ part   So, $\frac{1}{2}$ of $\frac{2}{3} = \frac{1}{3}$ of the whole

12   Book 6: *Fraction Operations*

Fraction Operations *Teacher Edition*   109

CONTINUE THE PROBLEM SOLVING

Have students work individually to solve the problems on page 13. As they work, you may want to circulate and monitor their recorded answers. When students finish each problem, have them compare and discuss their answers with a partner. Then have each pair share their answers in a class discussion of the problem. Refer to the **Teacher Notes: Student Page 13** for more specific ideas about the problems on this page.

As students work and report their conclusions, focus on these issues:

Look for Misconceptions – Students may need continual reminding, as in problem 6, that the answer refers to a part of the whole.

Help Make Connections – It is important that students make the connections among the problem itself, the verbal meaning, and the visual model. To help them do so, you may wish to have students write a sentence or two describing what each problem means.

Allow Waiting Time – When students struggle to explain their thinking, be sure to allow them ample time to organize their thoughts.

TEACHER NOTES: STUDENT PAGE 13

The key to successful completion and understanding of these problems is to represent them accurately with a visual model and then to be able express that visual model in words. *Teaching Strategy:* Be sure to encourage students to express in words what the particular problem is representing. You may wish to have them write in words what the problem means. Once students can make connections among the problem, its spoken meaning, and its visual representation, they are well on their way not only to understanding fraction multiplication, but also to understanding the multiplication algorithm soon to be introduced.

> ### On the Lookout for Misconceptions
>
> Problem 6 illustrates one of the primary areas of confusion students have as they try to understand fraction multiplication, particularly when multiplication is juxtaposed with division (as will be done later). Specifically, when multiplying fractions, the answer is always in reference to the whole unit. This is different from division, when the answer is an indication of how many fractional parts have been counted. Returning to the original problem we encountered when introducing multiplication *(How many of Mr. Nelson's students are on the soccer team?)* is helpful in demonstrating that with multiplication, we are always referring to some portion of the original whole.
>
> On the last problem of this page, for example, be sure to remind students that, although they are trying to determine 3/4 of 1/2, their final answer of 3/8 refers to the whole they started with. Stated in words: 3/4 of 1/2 is equal to 3/8 of the whole, and 3/4 of 1/2 of a candy bar is 3/8 of the whole candy bar.

Student Page 13: Problems and Potential Answers

Section C: Multiplying Fractions Informally

Solve each problem. Some diagrams have been provided to help you get started.

1. $\frac{1}{2}$ of $\frac{1}{4}$ = $\frac{1}{8}$

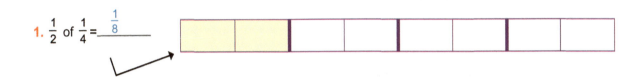

2. $\frac{1}{3}$ of $\frac{1}{2}$ = $\frac{1}{6}$

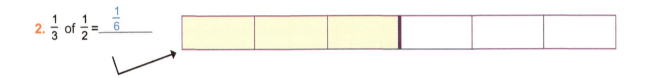

3. $\frac{1}{2}$ of $\frac{1}{3}$ = $\frac{1}{6}$

4. What do you notice about problems 2 and 3? *The answers are the same.*

5. $\frac{1}{2}$ of $\frac{1}{2}$ = $\frac{1}{4}$

6. $\frac{3}{4}$ of $\frac{1}{2}$ = $\frac{3}{8}$

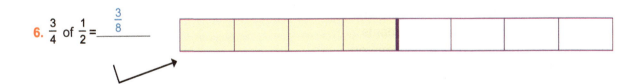

Book 6: *Fraction Operations* 13

CONTINUE THE PROBLEM SOLVING

Have students work individually to solve the problems on page 14. As they work, you may want to circulate and monitor their recorded answers. When students finish each problem, have them compare and discuss their answers with a partner. Then have each pair share their answers in a class discussion of the problem. Refer to the **Teacher Notes: Student Page 14** for more specific ideas about the problems on this page.

As students work and report their conclusions, focus on these issues:

Validate Representations – When students use their fraction strips or other models to represent the problems on this page, have them compare and discuss their representations to determine whether all are valid.

Allow Waiting Time – When students struggle to explain their thinking, be sure to allow them ample time to organize their thoughts.

Facilitate Students' Thinking – Encourage students who discover the fraction multiplication algorithm on their own. Ask them to explain their thinking and conclusions to their peers.

TEACHER NOTES: STUDENT PAGE 14

Teaching Strategy: Be sure to continue to encourage students to represent these problems with fraction strips. Do not rush them to the fraction multiplication algorithm. *Watch for:* Some students may discover the algorithm on their own, which is the most powerful form of learning possible. When students construct their own understandings of significant mathematics or reinvent mathematical procedures, they will make these procedures their own. So rather than explicitly telling students about the fraction multiplication shortcut, listen for conversations that suggest students may be on the brink of discovering the algorithm on their own. This will prepare them for the subsequent sections where the algorithm is introduced and developed.

Student Page 14: Problems and Potential Answers

Section C: Multiplying Fractions Informally — Set 1

Solve each problem.

7. $\frac{1}{4}$ of $\frac{1}{3}$ = $\frac{1}{12}$

8. $\frac{1}{4}$ of $\frac{1}{2}$ = $\frac{1}{8}$

9. $\frac{2}{3}$ of $\frac{1}{4}$ = $\frac{2}{12}$ (or $\frac{1}{6}$)

10. $\frac{1}{4}$ of $\frac{2}{3}$ = $\frac{2}{12}$ (or $\frac{1}{6}$)

11. $\frac{1}{3} \times \frac{1}{3}$ = $\frac{1}{9}$

12. $\frac{1}{3} \times \frac{1}{4}$ = $\frac{1}{12}$

13. $\frac{1}{2} \times \frac{2}{3}$ = $\frac{2}{6}$ (or $\frac{1}{3}$)

14. $\frac{1}{2} \times \frac{1}{5}$ = $\frac{1}{10}$

15. $\frac{2}{3} \times \frac{1}{3}$ = $\frac{2}{9}$

Section D: Multiplying Fractions in Context

SECTION D PLANNER

THE MATHEMATICS CONTENT AND GOALS

GOALS
Students will:
- Use various models and strategies to complete fraction multiplication problems as they arise in real-world contexts.

> **LANGUAGE DEVELOPMENT**
> **Mathematical language in this section includes many of the same terms used previously in the book:**
> *Fraction:* A number in the form *a/b* that names part of a whole, a region, or a set.
> *Fractional Part:* Fractional parts might be thought of as equal-sized portions, or fair shares, of a whole, a unit, or a collection of objects.
> *Numerator:* The numerator of a fraction is a "counter." It indicates the number of fractional parts (the size of which are determined by the denominator) that are presently under consideration.
> *Denominator:* The denominator may be thought of as the number of equal-sized parts into which the whole has been divided.
> *Algorithm:* An algorithm is a series of prescribed steps, rules, or procedures that can be followed to solve a given type of problem.

PROBLEM SETS: OVERVIEW

The problems in this section extend students' work with fraction multiplication by means of the presentation of various contexts in which multiplication is necessary and fruitful. Problems continue to direct students toward the traditional multiplication algorithm.

Set 1 (pp. 15–16; problems 1–5)
Various problem contexts are presented that will require students to approach multiplication of fractions from different starting points. The recipe context on page 15 provides many opportunities to practice multiplication and addition of fractions. Students should be encouraged to use both multiplication and addition for these problems, noting in particular how repeated addition is similar to multiplication.

PACING

The projected pacing for this unit is 1–2 class periods (based on a 45-minute period).

CONCEPT DEVELOPMENT (Pages 15–16)

INTRODUCE THE CONCEPT

ASSESS STUDENTS' PRIOR KNOWLEDGE
On the board write 1/4 × 12 and 1/3 of 1/2.

Ask:
In terms of groups, how would you express each of these problems? What is the answer to each problem? You may use your fraction strips.

Listen for:
- 1/4 of a group of 12; 1/3 of 1/2 of a group
- 1/4 × 12 = 3; 1/3 of 1/2 = 1/6

MODEL MATHEMATICAL THINKING
Model the thinking for another example by posing this problem to students: *There are 6 tuba players in a marching band. Two thirds of the tuba players are boys. How many of the tuba players are boys?* Draw the fraction bar on the board, and refer to it as you talk through the thinking:

Talk Through the Thinking:
To solve this problem, we need to find 2/3 of 6. How can we do this? Well, we can draw a picture. Because there are 6 tuba players in the band, we can draw a fraction strip for sixths. Then we can separate the sixths into 3 equal groups because the denominator of the fraction is 3. Finally, we can count how many sixths are in two of these equal groups. That's 4. So, 4 of the tuba players are boys.

Ask:
What if you had to find 3/4 of 12? How would you use fraction strips or a drawing to do it?

Listen for:
- I would draw a fraction strip for twelfths because that's how many there are in all.
- I would separate the twelfths into 4 equal groups because the denominator of the fraction is 4.
- I would count the number of twelfths in three of these equal groups. That's 9.

LAUNCH THE PROBLEM SOLVING

Have students work individually to solve the problems on page 15. As they work, you may want to circulate and monitor their recorded answers. When students finish each problem, have them compare and discuss their answers with a partner. Then have each pair share their answers in a class discussion of the problem. Refer to the **Teacher Notes: Student Page 15** for more specific ideas for each of the problems on the page.

As students work and report their conclusions, focus on these issues:

Allow Processing Time – Many students will struggle with these problems as they try to translate words into numeric symbols and expressions. Allow them enough time to decide how to do so and to discuss the process with their peers.

Validate Representations – Encourage students to model the problems with their fraction strips or to draw diagrams to represent the problems. Be sure to have students compare and discuss their diagrams with the class.

Allow Waiting Time – When students struggle to explain their thinking, be sure to allow them ample time to organize their thoughts.

TEACHER NOTES: STUDENT PAGE 15

Once again, encourage students to model these problems with fraction strips or drawings. As students become proficient and as their understanding of fraction multiplication increases, they will depend on the models less and less. *Teaching Strategy:* Be sure to let them spend as much time as they need to work with visual representations. Continue to have students express their answers in words, and be sure they are answering the question that each problem is asking.

Student Page 15: Problems and Potential Answers

Section D: Multiplying Fractions in Context Set 1

1. One-fourth of the animals at the pet store are puppies. Of the puppies, $\frac{1}{2}$ are golden retrievers. What fraction of the animals at the pet store are golden retrievers? $\frac{1}{8}$ of the animals; $\frac{1}{2}$ of $\frac{1}{4} = \frac{1}{8}$

2. Three-eighths of all children born in Europe have blonde hair. Of these blonde children, $\frac{1}{3}$ have blue eyes. What fraction of the children born in Europe have blonde hair and blue eyes?
$\frac{1}{8}$ of the children; $\frac{1}{3}$ of $\frac{3}{8} = \frac{3}{24}$ (or $\frac{1}{8}$)

3. A small motor scooter requires a mixture of oil and gasoline to run. For every gallon of gasoline, you need to mix in $\frac{3}{8}$ of a pint of oil. If you only have $\frac{1}{2}$ gallon of gas, how much oil do you need?
$\frac{3}{16}$ pint; $\frac{1}{2}$ of $\frac{3}{8} = \frac{3}{16}$

4. John loses $\frac{1}{4}$ point for every incorrect answer on Part One of his final exam in history. John answered 7 problems incorrectly on Part One. How many points did he lose?
$1\frac{3}{4}$ points; $\frac{1}{4}$ of $7 = 1\frac{3}{4}$

5. Two-thirds of the registered voters in Lake County are members of the Environmental Protection Coalition (EPC). In the last election, $\frac{3}{4}$ of the EPC members voted for the Democratic Party candidate. What fraction of the registered voters who are also EPC members **did not vote** for the Democratic Party Candidate? $\frac{1}{6}$ of the voters; $\frac{1}{4}$ of $\frac{2}{3} = \frac{2}{12}$ (or $\frac{1}{6}$)

CONTINUE THE PROBLEM SOLVING

The intent of page 16 is to use one context to provide several opportunities for students to combine, double, halve, and multiply fractions. The use of a recipe allows us to do this. Encourage students to think intuitively about this context and use whatever models they find helpful. It is a good idea to bring measuring cups and spoons to class for students to use to help them visualize the problem.

Have students work individually to solve the problems on page 16. As they work, you may want to circulate and monitor their recorded answers. When students finish the page, have them compare and discuss their answers with a partner. Then have each pair share their answers in a class discussion of the page. Refer to the **Teacher Notes: Student Page 16** for more specific ideas about the problems on this page.

As students work and report their conclusions, focus on these issues:

Help Make Connections – Encourage students to use what they have learned about adding and multiplying fractions to complete the table.

Validate Alternate Strategies – Several students may use different strategies to complete the page. Have these students share their strategies with the class. Then have them discuss whether the strategies are valid and efficient.

Facilitate Students' Thinking – Help students understand that the table on the page is similar to the ratio tables that they worked with in previous books. Remind them that they can use some of the same ratio-table strategies (e.g., doubling and halving) to complete this table.

Encourage Language Development – It might be helpful to remind students of the vocabulary and strategies commonly used with ratio tables in earlier books such as *doubling* and *halving*.

TEACHER NOTES: STUDENT PAGE 16

This problem is important for several reasons. First, there are multiple opportunities for practice with fraction operations that are embedded within the table. Second, this problem context extracts a different kind of thinking from students than simply presenting students with a list of fractions to multiply. Encourage students to use what they have learned from earlier steps to complete the table. Finally, this problem draws on various kinds of thinking and strategies. For example, some of the problems in the table can be solved by division, which students will do intuitively at this point, or by addition or multiplication. Let the context drive the students' strategies and explanations of their work.

> **Forward Thinking: A Teaching Opportunity**
>
> This type of problem elicits a kind of proportional reasoning that students will encounter in pre-algebra. Any type of ratio table, which is what this problem models, provides data that students can graph. You might wish to take this opportunity to have students graph some of the information from the table. The horizontal axis can correspond to the number of servings and the vertical axis can correspond to any one of the items in the table, such as cups of strawberries.
>
> A graph allows students another way to think proportionally and to see visually. All the equivalent ratios of strawberries (or any other item from the table) will line up to form a straight line through the origin, and its equation is in the form of $y = mx$. The slope, m, is equal to one of the equivalent ratios, and we normally express that ratio in its simplest form. This exploration is an excellent opportunity for advanced students to explore mathematical connections among representations.

Student Page 16: Problems and Potential Answers

Section D: Multiplying Fractions in Context — Set 1

Working with Recipes

Kevin runs a catering business. Below is his recipe for the filling of his famous Lemon Juice Cake.

Lemon Juice Cake: Ingredients for Filling
Makes 4 servings

- 8 lemons (squeezed to get fresh juice)
- 4 teaspoons vanilla
- $1\frac{1}{3}$ cups flour
- $\frac{2}{3}$ cup sugar
- $\frac{1}{4}$ cup sliced strawberries

Complete the table so that Kevin can easily tell how much of each ingredient he needs for different size servings of his cake. You may use your fraction strips or fraction circles to help.

SERVINGS	4	2	8	16	12	18	20	30
Sugar (Cups)	$\frac{2}{3}$	$\frac{1}{3}$	$1\frac{1}{3}$	$2\frac{2}{3}$	2	3	$3\frac{1}{3}$	5
Strawberries (Cups)	$\frac{1}{4}$	$\frac{1}{8}$	$\frac{1}{2}$	1	$\frac{3}{4}$	$1\frac{1}{8}$	$1\frac{1}{4}$	$1\frac{7}{8}$
Flour (Cups)	$1\frac{1}{3}$	$\frac{2}{3}$	$2\frac{2}{3}$	$5\frac{1}{3}$	4	6	$6\frac{2}{3}$	10
Vanilla (Teaspoons)	4	2	8	16	12	18	20	30
Lemons (Squeezed)	8	4	16	32	24	36	40	60

Explain your thinking. Which strategies were helpful in completing the table? _Responses will vary._

Section E: The Fraction Multiplication Algorithm

SECTION E PLANNER

THE MATHEMATICS CONTENT AND GOALS

GOALS
Students will:
- Use and explain the algorithm for traditional multiplication of fractions.

LANGUAGE DEVELOPMENT
Mathematical language in this section includes:
Product: The result (answer) of a given multiplication problem.
Algorithm: An algorithm is a series of prescribed steps, rules, or procedures that can be followed to solve a given type of problem.

PROBLEM SETS: OVERVIEW

In this section, a conceptual explanation for the traditional fraction multiplication algorithm is presented. This explanation is based on an area model of multiplication, developed in an earlier book in this series.

Set 1 (pp. 17–19; problems 1–6)
After two pages of explanation, students are asked to use the traditional algorithm to solve problems and to draw diagrams to illustrate the process.

PACING

The projected pacing for this unit is 1–2 class periods (based on a 45-minute period).

CONCEPT DEVELOPMENT (Pages 17–19)

INTRODUCE THE CONCEPT

ASSESS STUDENTS' PRIOR KNOWLEDGE
This section introduces a visual model for fraction multiplication. It depends largely on the grouping language of the previous sections, the fraction models developed earlier, and students' intuitive strategies.

Ask:
Seven-eighths of the 32 students in Mr. Marsh's class passed a math test. How many students passed the test? Explain your strategy.

Fraction Operations *Teacher Edition*   119

Listen for:
- The 32 is separated into 8 equal groups, and there are 7 of the equal groups.
- 7/8 of 32 = 28

MODEL MATHEMATICAL THINKING

Model the thinking for another example by posing this problem to students: *One half of a farmer's rectangular field was planted with wheat. The other half was planted with corn. The farmer decided to water 1/2 of the corn plants twice a day to see whether they would grow taller, while he watered the rest of the rectangular field only once a day. How can we draw a picture or diagram of this problem? What part of the whole rectangular field did he water twice a day?*
Draw the diagram as you talk through the thinking:

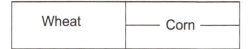

Talk Through the Thinking:
You learned when you multiplied whole numbers that one way to represent the multiplication was to use an area model. We can do the same when multiplying with fractions. Let's think about the problem. The field is rectangular, so we can draw a rectangle. One half is wheat and the other half is corn. We divide the rectangle in half and label the halves. The farmer waters 1/2 of the corn plants twice a day. We can draw a line to show that half the corn plants are watered twice a day while the rest of the corn plants are not. What does the diagram show? It shows that 1/2 of 1/2 of the whole field is watered twice a day. It also shows that this is 1/4 of the whole rectangular field.

Ask:
Suppose another farmer divided his rectangular field into thirds and he planted 1/3 with wheat, 1/3 with corn, and 1/3 with rye. Then he decided to water 1/2 the rye plants twice a day while he watered the rest of the field only once a day. What part of the whole rectangular field did he water twice a day?

Encourage students to draw a diagram to represent the problem.

Listen for:
- The part of the field that he watered twice a day can be expressed as 1/2 of 1/3.
- 1/2 of 1/3 = 1/6. He watered 1/6 of the whole rectangular field twice a day.

LAUNCH THE PROBLEM SOLVING

Have students read through page 17 on their own. When they finish, have them discuss the information on the page with a partner. Then have pairs share their insights and conclusions in a class discussion of the page. Refer to the **Teacher Notes: Student Page 17** for more specific ideas about the problems on this page. These notes are short because the explanation of the page occurs in the student book.

As students read and report their conclusions, focus on these issues:

Allow Processing Time – Be sure to allow students ample time for reading the information on page 17, discussing it with a partner, and then assimilating that information.

Facilitate Students' Thinking – Encourage students to think about the problem you modeled in the concept introduction as they work through the page. Suggest that they look for similarities between that problem and the one on page 17.

Allow Waiting Time – When students struggle to explain their thinking, be sure to allow them ample time to organize their thoughts.

Validate Representations – Encourage students to draw their own diagrams for the problem on the page. You might suggest that they model the first fraction and then represent the second fraction perpendicular to the first.

Student Page 17: Problems and Potential Answers

Section E: The Fraction Multiplication Algorithm Set 1

How can we multiply more complicated fractions when we have no fraction strips? A different kind of model and a different procedure can help us.

Remember that we can use an area model to represent multiplication. For example, we can model 3 × 2 (3 groups of 2) by drawing a rectangle that is 3 units long and 2 units wide.

3 × 2 = 6 (three groups of two)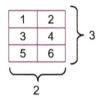

Can we use an area model for multiplying fractions? Yes! What if we wanted to multiply $\frac{1}{3} \times \frac{2}{5}$? Here is how to use an area-model diagram to help find the answer.

First, let's model $\frac{2}{5}$.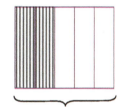

$\frac{2}{5}$ of the columns are shaded.

Next, remember that $\frac{1}{3} \times \frac{2}{5}$ means $\frac{1}{3}$ of $\frac{2}{5}$. So, we can divide the rectangle into thirds and then shade $\frac{1}{3}$.

$\frac{1}{3}$ of the rows are shaded.

To find $\frac{1}{3} \times \frac{2}{5}$, look for the overlap. This is $\frac{1}{3}$ of the originally shaded $\frac{2}{5}$.

Right Here!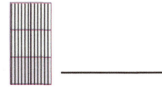

These 2 parts represent $\frac{2}{15}$ of the whole rectangle. So, $\frac{1}{3} \times \frac{2}{5} = \frac{2}{15}$.

Notice that we got the dimensions of our rectangle (**3** by **5**), and the total number of squares in the rectangle (**15**), by using the denominators, **3** and **5**, of the fractions we were multiplying.

Book 6: *Fraction Operations* 17

TEACHER NOTES: STUDENT PAGE 17

Although there are no problems on this page for students to solve, be sure to allow students ample time to discuss this introduction of the multiplication algorithm.

CONTINUE THE PROBLEM SOLVING

Page 18 is a continuation of page 17. Have students read through page 17 individually. When they finish, have students discuss the information with a partner. Then have pairs share their conclusions and insights in a class discussion of the page. Refer to the **Teacher Notes: Student Page 18** for more specific ideas about the problems on this page.

As students work and report their conclusions, focus on these issues:

Look for Misconceptions – Encourage students to rely on their fraction sense to solve problems, drawing diagrams when necessary, rather than on clue phrases or terms within the problems. See the discussion on misconceptions in the Teacher Notes.

Facilitate Students' Thinking – Remind students always to express the mathematics in words as a way to help them decide how to multiply.

Allow Waiting Time – When students struggle to explain their thinking, be sure to allow them ample time to organize their thoughts.

Student Page 18: Problems and Potential Answers

Section E: The Fraction Multiplication Algorithm Set 1

One more example: **What is $\frac{3}{4} \times \frac{2}{5}$, or, in words, $\frac{3}{4}$ of $\frac{2}{5}$?**

Step 1: Begin a diagram, starting with $\frac{2}{5}$.

Step 2: We need to show $\frac{3}{4}$ of that $\frac{2}{5}$. So, divide the rectangle into 4 equal rows. Shade **3** of these rows.

Step 3: Look at the overlap to find $\frac{3}{4}$ of $\frac{2}{5}$. These 6 parts!

That is $\frac{6}{20}$ of the rectangle. So, $\frac{3}{4} \times \frac{2}{5} = \frac{6}{20}$.

The **denominators** of the fractions, 4 and 5, tell us the length and width of the rectangle we used to solve the problem. So, we know there are 4 × 5, or **20** fractional parts in all.

 Remember: When multiplying fractions, multiplying the denominators gives us the total number of fractional parts in the whole.

Now, **for the numerators**. Go back to the two examples we have just looked at.

Example 1

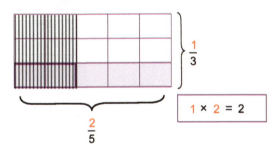

Example 2

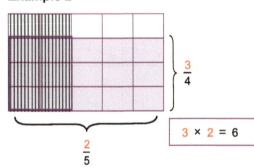

The **denominators** give us the total number of fractional parts of the whole. The **numerators** tell us **how many fractional parts** are in the overlapping area of the two original fractions.

 Remember: When we multiply fractions, we get the total number of fractional parts of the whole when we multiply the denominators. We get the number of fractional parts we are looking for when we multiply the numerators. So, the answer is <u>the product of the numerators over the product of the denominators</u>.

18   Book 6: *Fraction Operations*

TEACHER NOTES: STUDENT PAGE 18

Teaching Strategy: Have students discuss the examples on this page. Before moving on to page 19, give a similar example and allow students to take the lead in setting up and describing the visual model. Continue to have students articulate in words what these problems mean. Doing so will help them understand the area models used to represent the answers to these problems. It is important to take the time necessary to help students understand the models developed in these examples if they are to have a conceptual understanding of fraction multiplication.

On the Lookout for Misconceptions

Frequently in mathematics, students learn phrases or tricks to help them remember what to do to get the correct answer to a particular type of math problem. The problem is that when students tend to rely on such phrases, they often stop relying on their fraction sense. They are forced to remember which phrases go with which type of fraction problem. If they do not recall correctly, they usually miscalculate.

Many students are taught to cross multiply to determine whether two fractions are equivalent. Cross multiplication involves multiplying the numerator of one fraction and the denominator of the other fraction, and doing the same with the other numerator and denominator. If the products are the same, then the fractions are equivalent. While cross multiplying is a valid process for testing fraction equivalency, it is invalid for multiplying fractions. If students have an incomplete understanding of cross multiplication and multiplying fractions, they may confuse the two and inappropriately use cross multiplication to multiply.

Test for Equivalent Fractions	Multiplying Fractions
$\frac{2}{3} = \frac{4}{6}$ cross multiply $2 \times 6 = 3 \times 4$	$\frac{2}{3} \times \frac{1}{5}$ When students see this, they often think they have to cross multiply

When students are taught to remember these helpful phrases and terms, they also have to remember which phrase goes with which process. Rather than encouraging them to remember the tricks and clue terms, it is more helpful to encourage them to develop their fraction sense.

CONTINUE THE PROBLEM SOLVING

Have students work individually to solve the problems on page 19. As they work, you may want to circulate and monitor their recorded answers. When students finish, have them compare and discuss their answers with a partner. Then have each pair share their answers in a class discussion of the problem. Refer to the **Teacher Notes: Student Page 19** for more specific ideas about the problems on this page.

As students work and report their conclusions, focus on these issues:

Help Make Connections – Suggest that students draw diagrams or models of each problem to help them understand the problem and see what the answer should be.

Validate Representations – Have students share the models they draw for these problems with the class. Encourage discussion of the models and whether they represent the problems accurately.

Allow Waiting Time – When students struggle to explain their thinking, be sure to allow them ample time to organize their thoughts.

Student Page 19: Problems and Potential Answers

Section E: The Fraction Multiplication Algorithm — Set 1

Practice Problems

Draw a diagram and use the procedure you just learned to solve each problem.

1. $\frac{2}{3} \times \frac{3}{4} = \frac{6}{12}$ (or $\frac{1}{2}$)

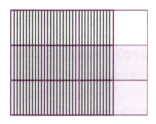

2. $\frac{1}{6} \times \frac{3}{4} = \frac{3}{24}$ (or $\frac{1}{8}$)

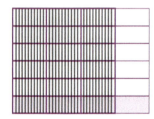

3. $\frac{4}{5} \times \frac{1}{3} = \frac{4}{15}$

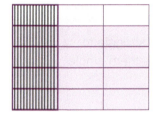

4. $\frac{3}{8} \times \frac{1}{2} = \frac{3}{16}$

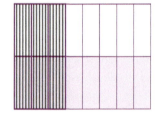

5. $\frac{6}{7} \times \frac{1}{2} = \frac{6}{14}$ (or $\frac{3}{7}$)

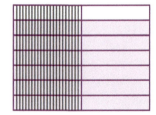

6. $\frac{1}{3} \times \frac{1}{6} = \frac{1}{18}$

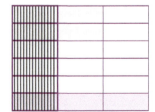

Book 6: *Fraction Operations*

TEACHER NOTES: STUDENT PAGE 19

Teaching Strategy: Be sure to encourage students to draw area models for these problems. As noted at the beginning of this book, middle-grade students tend to become confused and disillusioned with fraction computation as they are introduced to each of the different algorithms (addition, subtraction, multiplication, division). To help avoid this loss of understanding, encourage students to use visual models as long as they are helpful. Once students can meaningfully explain the steps in their solution strategies, they can be encouraged to decrease their dependence on the models. However, it is a mistake to rush students to that point even though they may realize the ease of using algorithms. Eventually, we want them to stop using the visual models, but there is no need to rush them.

Forward Thinking: A Teaching Opportunity

When the two factors are mixed numbers, such as $2\frac{2}{3} \times 4\frac{1}{4}$, you can show students how to think of this problem as having four partial products, which can be added to get the final product. This is an idea that students may have already encountered during multiplication of 2-digit numbers. It is an idea that will come up in algebra class when they are multiplying binomials, such as $(x + 2)(x + 5)$. In the case of the mixed numbers, here are the four partial products:

$2 \times 4 = 8$	$2 \times \frac{1}{4} = \frac{1}{2}$	$4 \times \frac{2}{3} = \frac{8}{3}$	$\frac{1}{4} \times \frac{2}{3} = \frac{2}{12}$

The partial products are added:

$8 + \frac{1}{2} + \frac{8}{3} + \frac{2}{12} = 10\frac{16}{12} = 11\frac{4}{12} = 11\frac{1}{3}$

In algebra, students will find partial products for $(x + 2)(x + 5)$.

$x \cdot x = x^2$	$x \cdot 5 = 5x$	$x \cdot 2 = 2x$	$2 \cdot 5 = 10$

Using this process, the answer is $x^2 + 5x + 2x + 10$, or $x^2 + 7x + 10$.

Fraction Operations *Teacher Edition*

Section F: Dividing Fractions

SECTION F PLANNER

THE MATHEMATICS CONTENT AND GOALS

GOALS
Students will:
- Express in words the relationship between two fractions in division of fractions.
- Model division problems with fraction strips or other visual representations.
- Complete division of fraction problems and provide conceptual explanations for what both the problem and the answer mean.

> **LANGUAGE DEVELOPMENT**
>
> **Mathematical language in this section includes:**
>
> *Dividend:* A number or quantity that is to be divided.
>
> *Divisor:* The number by which the dividend is divided.
>
> *Quotient:* The result of dividing a dividend by a divisor.
>
> *Reciprocal:* One of two numbers whose product is 1.

tion, students must recognize that division of whole numbers acts differently than division of fractions. While division of whole numbers almost always results in a quotient less than the dividend, division of fractions does the opposite. Helping students understand this shift in thinking about division is introduced intuitively and through verbal descriptions of division relationships.

Set 1 (pp. 20–21; problems 1–4)
There is an explanation with accompanying diagrams in this problem set. After discussing the illustrations, students complete similar problems with the help of their fraction strips. As they become more comfortable with the problems, they will gradually depend less on their visual models. On page 21 the traditional division algorithm is introduced (flip and multiply). A conceptual explanation is provided for this process. Although more complicated and richer explanations exist to explain why this algorithm works, they are beyond the scope of this text and the comprehension level of most students in the middle grades.

Set 2 (pp. 22–23; problems 1–2)
After a description and discussion of the division algorithm, students are given several problems to practice using it.

PACING

The projected pacing for this unit is 1–2 class periods (based on a 45-minute period).

PROBLEM SETS: OVERVIEW

As has been the case with other concepts throughout this series and this book, division of fractions is introduced intuitively prior to the presentation of the common algorithm. Just as with multiplica-

CONCEPT DEVELOPMENT (PAGES 20–23)

INTRODUCE THE CONCEPT

ASSESS STUDENTS' PRIOR KNOWLEDGE
This section introduces what many consider to be the most difficult mathematical topic prior to the study of algebra: division of fractions. It is important to begin this section by encouraging students to think about the nature of division and how division applies to fractions.

Write 10 ÷ 2 on the board.

Ask:
How can you use grouping language to express this division problem in words? What is the answer to 10 ÷ 2? How can you express in words the solution to this problem?

Listen for:
- How many groups of 2 are there in 10?
- 10 ÷ 2 = 5
- There are 5 groups of 2 in 10.

MODEL MATHEMATICAL THINKING
Model the thinking for an example of dividing by a fraction. Write 10 ÷ 1/2 on the board.

Ask:
How can you use grouping language to express this division problem in words? What is the answer to 10 ÷ 1/2? How can you express in words the solution to this problem?

Talk Through the Thinking:
Let's see. If we use the same kind of thinking that we did for the first problem, we can express this division by saying, "How many groups of 1/2 are there in 10?" That's really different than finding how many groups of 2 there are in 10, isn't it? To find how many groups of 1/2 there are in 10, we might use a ruler.

Place a transparent customary ruler on the overhead projector, and use it to demonstrate. *Let's use the ruler to find how many 1/2-inch segments there are in 10 inches. Each inch is made up of two 1/2-inch segments. We can count each inch by twos until we get to 10 inches: 2, 4, 6, 8, 10, 12, 14, 16, 18, 20. There are 20 1/2 inch segments in 10 inches, so there are 20 groups of 1/2 in 10. Now we know that 10 ÷ 1/2 = 20.*

Ask:
Using the same reasoning, what is the answer to 6 ÷ 1/4? Express the solution in words.

Listen for:
Students can use a ruler to count off 1/4-inch segments and to express the solution using grouping language. Some students may realize that they can multiply the denominator and the whole number to find the quotient.
- 6 ÷ 1/4 = 24
- There are 24 groups of 1/4 in 6.

LAUNCH THE PROBLEM SOLVING

Have students read through page 20 on their own. When they finish, have them discuss the page with a partner. Then have pairs share their insights and conclusions in a class discussion of the information on the page. Refer to the discussion **Dividing Fractions: Student Page 20** for more specific ideas about the problems on this page.

As students work and report their conclusions, focus on these issues:

Look for Misconceptions – Some students may find it difficult to understand that division of fractions results in a quotient that is greater than the dividend. This is because division of fractions is about **counting fractional parts.**

Facilitate Students' Thinking – Encourage students to think about fractional division in terms of grouping. For example, have them ask themselves, "How many groups of 1/2 are there in 10, or in 3/4?"

Allow Processing Time – It will take students a considerable amount of time to master and understand dividing fractions. Allow them as much time as they need.

Allow Waiting Time – When students struggle to explain their thinking, be sure to allow them ample time to organize their thoughts.

Encourage Language Development – Encourage students to use new language to describe division contexts, e.g., dividend, divisor, and quotient, and in subsequent lessons, reciprocal.

Student Page 20: Problems and Potential Answers

Section F: Dividing Fractions — Set 1

What does it mean to divide? Once we understand that question, division of fractions is not so hard! Think about this problem: 6 ÷ 2 = 3

We can restate this problem in words: "How many groups of 2 are there in 6?"

We use the same kind of thinking to divide fractions. For example, $\frac{1}{2} \div \frac{1}{4} = ?$

Step 1: Restate the problem in words: How many $\frac{1}{4}$'s are there in $\frac{1}{2}$?

Step 2: Use a picture to represent the problem. Start with $\frac{1}{2}$.

$\frac{1}{2}$	

Step 3: How many $\frac{1}{4}$'s are there in that $\frac{1}{2}$ part? Use your fraction strips to find out.

$\frac{1}{2}$	

$\frac{1}{4}$	$\frac{1}{4}$		

Step 4: Count. There are 2 of the $\frac{1}{4}$ parts in $\frac{1}{2}$. So, $\frac{1}{2} \div \frac{1}{4} = 2$

More Examples $\frac{3}{4} \div \frac{1}{2} = ?$

Step 1: Restate in words: How many $\frac{1}{2}$'s are there in $\frac{3}{4}$?

Step 2: Represent with a picture. Start with $\frac{3}{4}$. Use fraction strips.

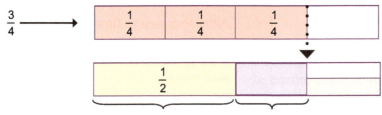

ONE $\frac{1}{2}$ fraction strip here... $\frac{1}{2}$ of another $\frac{1}{2}$ fraction strip here

Step 3: Count the number of $\frac{1}{2}$ parts in the diagram. There are ONE and $\frac{1}{2}$ of the $\frac{1}{2}$ fraction strips in $\frac{3}{4}$.

So, $\frac{3}{4} \div \frac{1}{2} = 1\frac{1}{2}$

TEACHER NOTES: STUDENT PAGE 20

Just as with multiplication of fractions, it is imperative that students be able to articulate the meaning of division problems that include fractions. As noted previously, it is important to help students distinguish between the verbal descriptions of multiplication and division and their connections to the ways in which we deal with the problems from a mathematical point of view. Consider these two number sentences:

$$\frac{1}{2} \times \frac{1}{4} = \frac{1}{8}$$

$$\frac{1}{2} \div \frac{1}{4} = 2$$

In multiplication, students are to find 1/2 of the quantity of 1/4 (which is 1/8). This is contrasted to division, for which they must count how many 1/4s there are 1/2 (2).

Be sure to encourage all students to articulate in words what these division problems are asking for. This is the key not only to representing the problems, but also to understanding the algorithm.

On the Lookout for Misconceptions

Students often have the misconception that a division problem will always result in a quotient that is less than the dividend.

This statement is true when dividing by numbers greater than 1. Let's look at the case of 10 ÷ 2. Here, the answer is 5 and it is less than the dividend, 10. You may wish to try other numbers to prove the statement.

However, in the case of dividing by a fraction less than 1, the quotient will be greater than the dividend. For example, for 10 ÷ 1/2, the quotient is 20. Students who have the above misconception will typically have trouble accepting the answer as 20. They may mistakenly think of 10 ÷ 1/2 as being the same as 10 ÷ 2 and arrive at a quotient of 5.

To help avoid this common misconception about division of fractions, it is important to encourage students to think of division in words. For example, "How many sets of 1/2 are in 10?" Stating these problems in words will help students understand the conceptual meaning of division of fractions and help them develop their number sense.

CONTINUE THE PROBLEM SOLVING

Have students work individually to study the example and solve the problems on page 21. As they work, you may want to circulate and monitor their recorded answers. When students finish each problem, have them compare and discuss their answers with a partner. Then have each pair share their answers in a class discussion of the problem. Refer to the **Teacher Notes: Student Page 21** for more specific ideas about the problems on this page.

As students work and report their conclusions, focus on these issues:

Validate Representations – Have students share their representations with the class. Encourage discussion about the representations to determine whether they are all valid.

Help Make Connections – Remind students to think in terms of grouping language as they did in the concept introduction activity.

Facilitate Students' Thinking – Encourage students to review page 20 and look at the size of the quotient as compared with the size of the dividend. Help students come to the conclusion that the quotient in fractional division is greater than the dividend.

Allow Waiting Time – When students struggle to explain their thinking, be sure to allow them ample time to organize their thoughts.

Encourage Language Development – Look for opportunities to use the mathematical language of division: divisor, dividend, and quotient.

TEACHER NOTES: STUDENT PAGE 21

Teaching Strategy: You might consider completing these problems as a whole-class activity. Again, the visual models and verbal interpretations of the problem are significant, so encourage students to use their fraction models and to explain their thinking.

Student Page 21: Problems and Potential Answers

Section F: Dividing Fractions — Set 1

One More Example . . .

What is $\frac{2}{3} \div \frac{1}{6}$? Or, how many $\frac{1}{6}$s are there in $\frac{2}{3}$?

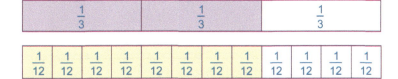

There are 4 of the $\frac{1}{6}$ fraction parts in $\frac{2}{3}$.

So, $\frac{2}{3} \div \frac{1}{6} = 4$.

Your Turn. Use a diagram to complete each problem.

1. $\frac{3}{4} \div \frac{1}{4}$ (How many $\frac{1}{4}$s are there in $\frac{3}{4}$?) _____ 3

2. $\frac{2}{3} \div \frac{1}{12}$ (How many $\frac{1}{12}$s are there in $\frac{2}{3}$?) _____ 8

3. $\frac{5}{6} \div \frac{1}{3}$ (How many $\frac{1}{3}$s are there in $\frac{5}{6}$?) _____ $2\frac{1}{2}$

4. $\frac{1}{3} \div \frac{2}{3}$ (How many $\frac{2}{3}$s are there in $\frac{1}{3}$?) _____ $\frac{1}{2}$

Book 6: *Fraction Operations* 21

CONTINUE THE PROBLEM SOLVING

Have students read through page 22 on their own. When they finish, have them discuss the information on the page with a partner. Then have each pair share their insights and conclusions in a class discussion of the page. Refer to the discussion **The Division Algorithm: Student Page 22** for more specific ideas about the problems on this page.

As students work and report their conclusions, focus on these issues:

Allow Processing Time – Be sure to allow students ample time to assimilate the information on page 22.

Validate Representations – As students model the examples at the bottom of the page, have them share their representations and explanations of those representations with the class.

Allow Waiting Time – When students struggle to explain their thinking, be sure to allow them ample time to organize their thoughts.

Encourage Language Development – Remind students of the definition of an *algorithm:* A prescribed series of steps that can be taken to solve a given problem. Also, in this section, use the word *reciprocal* when appropriate to continue to build the mathematical vocabulary of the students.

The Division Algorithm: Student Page 22

The division algorithm for fractions is by far the most difficult to explain and describe from a conceptual point of view. Because of this, perhaps more than any other rule in mathematics, the invert and multiply procedure has become legendary both for its widespread use, as well as the lack of meaning for students that accompanies it.

Explaining the invert and multiply algorithm in the same way that the area model was used to explain the multiplication algorithm is beyond learners in the middle grades. Yet, as developed on this page, we can still present a conceptual foundation for the algorithm. However, this explanation relies more on number theory (multiplying a number is the same as dividing by its reciprocal) than on the geometry models used with multiplication.

At some point it is inevitable that students will simply invert and multiply. Hopefully, this explanation will give them the beginnings of understanding why inverting and then multiplying is a mathematically valid step. This explanation is not a conceptual model for division of fractions. It is rather an explanation about the nature of the relationship between multiplication and division. In any event, students should be exposed to this rationale, and more advanced students can be challenged to link this explanation to visual models.

Student Page 22: Problems and Potential Answers

Section F: Dividing Fractions   Set 1

Dividing Fractions

Just as with multiplying fractions, there is a procedure, or algorithm, that can be used to quickly find the answer when dividing fractions. In fact, when we divide fractions, we actually **use** the multiplication algorithm (multiply the numerators, then multiply the denominators).

First, we need to understand that division and multiplication are related. So, if we could turn every division problem into a multiplication problem, we would be fine, because we already know how to multiply fractions.

Think about this problem: $4 \times 2 = ?$

In words, we could say, "**How much is 4 groups of 2?**"

4 groups of 2 is 8

Now, compare that to this problem: $4 \div \frac{1}{2} = ?$

In words, we could say, "**How many $\frac{1}{2}$'s are there in 4?**"

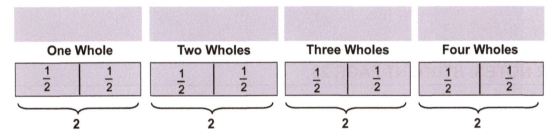

There are **eight $\frac{1}{2}$'s in 4 wholes**, or $4 \div \frac{1}{2} = 8$.

So... $4 \div \frac{1}{2} = 8$ **gives us the same answer as** $4 \times 2 = 8$

What do you notice about these two numbers in red? They are called **reciprocals**. $\frac{1}{2}$ and 2, or $\frac{2}{1}$, are reciprocals of each other. In this case, multiplying by two gives the same answer as dividing by the reciprocal of 2, which is $\frac{1}{2}$.

Will that always work? Try out a few of these yourself.

Does... $6 \div \frac{1}{2}$ equal $6 \times 2?$
(How many $\frac{1}{2}$'s in 6?)   (6 groups of 2)

Does ... $2 \div \frac{1}{4}$ equal 2×4
(How many $\frac{1}{4}$ in 2?)   (2 groups of 4)

22   Book 6: *Fraction Operations*

CONTINUE THE PROBLEM SOLVING

Have students work individually to study the example and solve the problems on page 23. As they work, you may want to circulate and monitor their recorded answers. When students finish each problem, have them compare and discuss their answers with a partner. Then have each pair share their answers in a class discussion of the problem. Refer to the **Teacher Notes: Student Page 23** for more specific ideas about the problems on this page.

As students work and report their conclusions, focus on these issues:

Facilitate Students' Thinking – Encourage students to express each problem in grouping terms to help them decide whether their answers are sensible.

Validate Representations – Some students may still need to use visual models. Have these students share their representations with the class. Have the class discuss how the models and the algorithm are related.

Allow Waiting Time – When students struggle to explain their thinking, be sure to allow them ample time to organize their thoughts.

Encourage Language Development – Continue to emphasize appropriate vocabulary for work with the division of fractions.

TEACHER NOTES: STUDENT PAGE 23

Page 23 gives students the opportunity to practice division of fractions. *Teaching Strategy:* Encourage students to express each of these problems in words. For some problems, students may find visual representations helpful.

**Forward Thinking:
A Teaching Opportunity**

Another algorithm for division of fractions may be less familiar to students than the invert-and-multiply algorithm. It's called the common-denominator algorithm. When two fractions have a common denominator, the problem simply involves dividing their numerators.

Let's look at 4/5 ÷ 1/3. By renaming these fractions as equivalent fractions with the least common denominator, namely 12/15 ÷ 5/15, the problem becomes 12 ÷ 5, or 2 2/5.

Why does this work? 4/5 ÷ 1/3 means "How many sets of 1/3 are in 4/5?" After renaming the fractions and changing the problem to 12/15 ÷ 5/15, the new expression means "How many sets of 5/15 are in 12/15?" Since the fractional parts (denominators) are the same, there is no need to consider them to answer the question. The new question is "How many sets of 5 are in 12?" The answer is 2 2/5.

Student Page 23: Problems and Potential Answers

Section F: Dividing Fractions — Set 1

Yes, it is true. <u>Dividing by a number always results in the same answer as multiplying by its reciprocal.</u> We can use this fact to make dividing fractions like multiplying fractions.

For example, $\frac{1}{4} \div \frac{2}{3}$ (How many $\frac{2}{3}$'s are in $\frac{1}{4}$?) is the same as multiplying the reciprocal of $\frac{2}{3}$ by $\frac{1}{4}$.

Or, $\frac{1}{4} \div \frac{2}{3} \rightarrow \frac{1}{4} \times \frac{3}{2} = \frac{3}{8}$

 So, when dividing fractions, you can (1) find the reciprocal of the second fraction and (2) multiply the two fractions.

1. What is the reciprocal of each fraction?

   a) $\frac{2}{3}$ $\frac{3}{2}$ b) $\frac{3}{4}$ $\frac{4}{3}$ c) $\frac{1}{5}$ $\frac{5}{1}$ d) $\frac{5}{3}$ $\frac{3}{5}$ e) $\frac{1}{2}$ $\frac{2}{1}$

2. Divide using the division algorithm. (Find the reciprocal; then multiply.)

   a) $\frac{3}{4} \div \frac{4}{5} = \frac{15}{16}$ b) $\frac{2}{3} \div \frac{2}{3} = 1$ c) $\frac{4}{5} \div \frac{2}{3} = \frac{12}{10}$ (or $\frac{6}{5}$)

   d) $2 \div \frac{1}{2} = 4$ e) $\frac{4}{3} \div \frac{3}{4} = \frac{16}{9}$ (or $1\frac{7}{9}$)   f) $\frac{1}{2} \div \frac{1}{3} = \frac{3}{2}$ (or $1\frac{1}{2}$)

Book 6: *Fraction Operations*   23

SECTIONS C–F ASSESSMENT (PAGE 24)

LAUNCH THE ASSESSMENT

Have students turn to the Sections C–F Assessment on page 24. An additional copy is found on page 95 of the Assessment Book. Have students work individually to solve the problems and write their explanations. As they work, circulate to be sure students understand what they need to do for each problem and that they are completing each part of the problem. For example, for problem 3, students are to explain what the problem means, draw a diagram, and then find the answer. You may find it helpful to read the directions for all the problems before students begin, discussing the types of responses they will need to make for each problem.

Encourage students to use whatever space they need to make their drawings and explain their thinking. If the space on the page is inadequate, students should use an additional sheet of paper or the back of the page. Refer to the **Teacher Notes: Assessment Problems for Sections C–F** for more specific ideas about the problems on this page.

Evaluate Student Responses

Use the assessment rubric on page 94 of the Assessment Book (pictured on page 139 of the Teacher Edition) to evaluate student responses. The Assessment Book has some general suggestions for using the rubric that you may find helpful.

TEACHER NOTES: ASSESSMENT PROBLEMS FOR SECTIONS C–F

Problem 1: *Watch for:* Make sure students correctly shade the rectangles and to focus on the portion of the rectangle that is shaded in from both factors.

Problem 2: *Watch for:* Make sure students' written context is mathematically appropriate for the given multiplication problems.

Problem 3: *Watch for:* Make sure students explain that division can mean, "How many 1/4's are in 3/4?"

SCORING GUIDE BOOK 6: FRACTION OPERATIONS

Sections C–F Assessment
For Use With: Student Book Page 24

PROBLEM DESCRIPTION	SCORING: WHAT TO LOOK FOR	SCORE AND COMMENTS
Problem 1 a–b Solve multiplication of fractions problems with rectangle diagrams. Level 1: Comprehension and Knowledge Level 2: Tool use	Do students: • Have a conceptual understanding of fraction multiplication? • Represent multiplication with visual drawings? • Find the correct result?	(4 points each) Points: _____ of 8
Problem 2 a–b Create stories for fractional multiplication problems. Level 3: Connection and Application Level 4: Synthesis and Evaluation	Do students: • Have an understanding of multiplication? • Have an understanding of fraction multiplication? • Tie the context of the story to the multiplication problem?	(4 points each) Points: _____ of 8
Problem 3 a–b Understand meaning of division of fractions and solve a problem. Level 1: Comprehension and Knowledge Level 2: Tool use Level 4: Synthesis and evaluation	Do students: • Have an understanding of division? • Have a conceptual understanding of fraction division? • Represent division with visual drawings? • Find the correct result?	(4 points each) Points: _____ of 8

TOTAL POINTS: _____ OF 24

Student Page 24: Problems and Potential Answers

Sections C–F: Problems for Assessment

1. Draw rectangles for each multiplication problem. Use your rectangles to help you solve each problem.

   a) $\frac{2}{3} \times \frac{3}{5} = \frac{6}{15}$ or $\frac{2}{5}$

   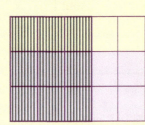

   b) $\frac{1}{6} \times \frac{3}{4} = \frac{3}{24}$ or $\frac{1}{8}$

   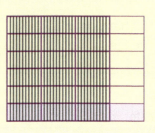

2. Write a short word problem to go with each multiplication problem. *Responses will vary.*

   a) $\frac{4}{5} \times \frac{1}{3}$ _____

   b) $\frac{3}{8} \times \frac{1}{2}$ _____

3. Explain one possible meaning for each division problem. Use diagrams to help you with your explanations. Then solve the problems using your diagrams. *Responses will vary. Check students' diagrams.*

   a) $\frac{3}{4} \div \frac{1}{4} = 3$

   Explain. _____

   b) $\frac{5}{6} \div \frac{1}{3} = 2\frac{1}{2}$

   Explain. _____

24 Book 6: *Fraction Operations*

END-OF-BOOK ASSESSMENT, STUDENT PAGES 25–28

LAUNCH THE ASSESSMENT

Have students turn to the End-of-Book Assessment on page 25. An additional copy is found on page 99 of the Assessment Book. Have students work individually to solve the problems. As they work, circulate to be sure students understand what they need to do for each problem and that they are completing each part of the problem. For example, for problem 1a, students need to draw a picture or use their fraction strips and then determine how many fractional cups of flour are needed to make 1 cup. You may find it helpful to read the directions before students begin, discussing the types of responses they will need to make for each problem.

Encourage students to use whatever space they need to make their drawings. If the space on the page is inadequate, they should use an additional sheet of paper or the back of the page.

Refer to the **Teacher Notes: End-of-Book Assessment Problems, Student Page 25**, for more specific ideas about the problems on this page.

Evaluate Student Responses

Use the assessment rubric on page 96 of the Assessment Book (pictured on page 149 of the Teacher Edition) to evaluate student responses. The Assessment Book has some general suggestions for using the rubric that you may find helpful.

TEACHER NOTES: END-OF-BOOK ASSESSMENT, STUDENT PAGE 25

The contexts used in these assessment problems may be used and pursued at your discretion. They require students to recognize instances in which each of the fraction operations may be necessary to complete a given step of a problem. The opportunity for you to assess the depth of your students' understanding and thinking (beyond simply applying the algorithms) will depend on how much you ask students to elaborate on their strategies and explain their thinking.

Fraction Operations *Teacher Edition*

Student Page 25: Problems and Potential Answers

End-of-Book Assessment

1. Your friend is baking cookies for the school fundraiser. But she does not have all the measuring cups she needs. Here is what she has:

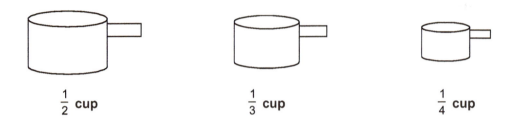

$\frac{1}{2}$ cup $\frac{1}{3}$ cup $\frac{1}{4}$ cup

Describe how she would get the following quantities of ingredients using the tools she has. You may draw a picture and/or use fraction strips to help you. *Responses may vary. Sample responses are given.*

a) 1 cup of flour   *two $\frac{1}{2}$ cups*

b) $\frac{3}{4}$ cup sugar   *one $\frac{1}{2}$ cup and one $\frac{1}{4}$ cup*

c) $1\frac{2}{3}$ cups of brown sugar   *two $\frac{1}{2}$ cups and two $\frac{1}{3}$ cups.*

d) $\frac{1}{8}$ cup of baking powder   *$\frac{1}{2}$ of $\frac{1}{4}$ cup*

e) $\frac{3}{8}$ cup of oil   *one $\frac{1}{4}$ cup and $\frac{1}{2}$ of $\frac{1}{4}$ cup*

f) $\frac{1}{12}$ cup of water   *$\frac{1}{3}$ of $\frac{1}{4}$ cup*

g) $2\frac{3}{4}$ cups of chocolate chips   *five $\frac{1}{2}$ cups and one $\frac{1}{4}$ cup*

h) $\frac{5}{6}$ cup of melted butter   *two $\frac{1}{3}$ cups and $\frac{1}{2}$ of $\frac{1}{3}$ cup*

Book 6: *Fraction Operations*   25

CONTINUE THE ASSESSMENT

Have students turn to the End-of-Book Assessment on page 26. An additional copy is found on page 100 of the Assessment Book. Have students work individually to solve the problems and write their explanations. As they work, circulate to be sure students understand what they need to do for each problem and that they are completing each part of the problem. For example, for problem 3, students will need to mark on the map the locations of both the trash cans and the park benches. You may find it helpful to read through the directions before students begin, discussing the types of responses they will need to make for each problem.

Encourage students to use whatever space they need to explain their thinking. If the space on the page is inadequate, they should use an additional sheet of paper or the back of the page.

Refer to the **Teacher Notes: End-of-Book Assessment, Student Page 26**, for more specific ideas about the problems on this page.

Evaluate Student Responses

Use the assessment rubric on pages 96–97 of the Assessment Book (pictured on pages 149–150 of the Teacher Edition) to evaluate student responses. The Assessment Book has some general suggestions for using the rubric that you may find helpful.

TEACHER NOTES: END-OF-BOOK ASSESSMENT, STUDENT PAGE 26

The contexts used in these assessment problems may be used at your discretion. They require students to recognize instances in which each of the fraction operations may be necessary to complete a given step of a problem. The opportunity for you to assess the depth of understanding and thinking of your students, beyond simply applying the algorithms, will depend on how much you ask students to elaborate on their strategies and express their thinking.

Student Page 26: Problems and Potential Answers

End-of-Book Assessment

The people of Springville want to put a bicycle path around the town. They will put park benches every $\frac{1}{3}$ mile and trash barrels every $\frac{3}{4}$ mile along the path.

2. If the trail is 6 miles long, how many park benches will they need? __18__ How many trash barrels will they need? __8__

Explain your thinking. __Responses will vary__

3. Are there any places where there will be both a trash barrel and a park bench at the same spot?
__Yes__ Where? __At the 3-mile and 6-mile marks__

4. On the map below, show about where each of the trash barrels and park benches will be located. Use **T** for the trash barrels and **B** for the park benches.

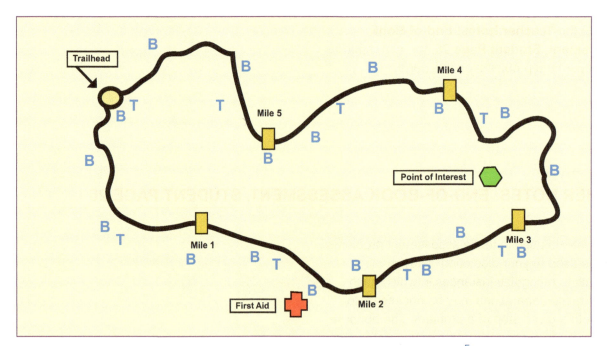

5. After the trailhead, how far is the first trash can from the first park bench? __$\frac{5}{12}$ mile__

6. How far is it between the first-aid station (at $1\frac{5}{8}$ miles) and the point of interest (at $3\frac{3}{4}$ miles)? __$2\frac{1}{8}$ miles__

CONTINUE THE ASSESSMENT

Have students turn to the End-of-Book Assessment on page 27. An additional copy is found on page 101 of the Assessment Book. Have students work individually to solve the problems and write their explanations. As they work, circulate to be sure students understand what they need to do for each problem and that they are completing each part of the problem. For example, for problem 8, students will need to complete a diagram, find an answer, and write an explanation. You may find it helpful to read through the directions before students begin, discussing the types of responses they will need to make for each problem.

Encourage students to use whatever space they need to explain their thinking. If the space on the page is inadequate, they should use an additional sheet of paper or the back of the page.

Refer to the **Teacher Notes: End-of-Book Assessment, Student Page 27**, for more specific ideas about the problems on this page.

Evaluate Student Responses

Use the assessment rubric on pages 97–98 of the Assessment Book (pictured on pages 150–151 of the Teacher Edition) to evaluate student responses. The Assessment Book has some general suggestions for using the rubric that you may find helpful.

TEACHER NOTES: END-OF-BOOK ASSESSMENT, STUDENT PAGE 27

The contexts used in these assessment problems may be used at your discretion. They require students to recognize instances in which each of the fraction operations may be necessary to complete a given step of a problem. The opportunity for you to assess the depth of understanding and thinking of your students, beyond simply applying the algorithms, will depend on how much you ask students to elaborate on their strategies and express their thinking.

Student Page 27: Problems and Potential Answers

End-of-Book Assessment

7. How could you express this multiplication problem in words: $\frac{2}{3} \times \frac{3}{4}$? _____
   What is two thirds of three fourths?

8. Solve the problem by using a diagram. Provide an explanation for your diagram.

   $\frac{2}{3} \times \frac{3}{4} = \frac{6}{12}$ (or $\frac{1}{2}$)

   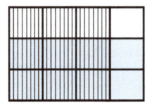

   Explain your diagram. $\frac{3}{4}$ of the columns are shaded. $\frac{2}{3}$ of the bars are shaded. The overlap is $\frac{6}{12}$ (or $\frac{1}{2}$) of the total number of squares.

   _____
   _____

9. Use the following diagram to explain why the multiplication algorithm (multiply the numerators, multiply the denominators) works.

   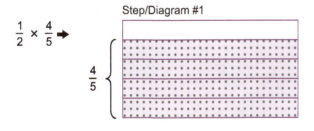 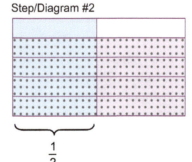

   Explanation.
   Step 1: $\frac{4}{5}$ of the bars are shaded. **Step 2:** $\frac{1}{2}$ of the columns are shaded. The overlap is $\frac{4}{10}$ of the total number of parts. Multiplying the numerators gives the number of overlapping parts. Multiplying the denominators gives the total number of parts.

   Book 6: *Fraction Operations*

CONTINUE THE ASSESSMENT

Have students turn to the End-of-Book Assessment on page 28. An additional copy is found on page 102 of the Assessment Book. Have students work individually to solve the problems and write their explanations. As they work, circulate to be sure students understand what they need to do for each problem and that they are completing each part of the problem. For example, for problem 11, students will need to explain how and why the division algorithm works. You may find it helpful to read the directions before students begin, discussing the types of responses they need to make for each problem.

Encourage students to use whatever space they need to explain their thinking. If the space on the page is inadequate, they should use an additional sheet of paper or the back of the page.

Refer to the **Teacher Notes: End-of-Book Assessment, Student Page 28**, for more specific ideas about the problems on this page.

Evaluate Student Responses

Use the assessment rubric on page 98 of the Assessment Book (pictured on page 151 of the Teacher Edition) to evaluate student responses. The Assessment Book has some general suggestions for using the rubric that you may find helpful.

TEACHER NOTES: END-OF-BOOK ASSESSMENT, STUDENT PAGE 28

The strategies that students use to solve the problems in problem 10 will indicate their understanding of the main concepts and procedures presented in this book.

Problem 11 may be particularly challenging and time consuming for many students.

Fraction Operations *Teacher Edition*

Student Page 28: Problems and Potential Answers

End-of-Book Assessment

10. Solve the following problems any way you choose.

a) $\dfrac{1}{2} \div \dfrac{4}{5} =$ $\dfrac{5}{8}$

b) $\dfrac{3}{4} \div \dfrac{4}{5} =$ $\dfrac{15}{16}$

c) $\dfrac{3}{2} \div \dfrac{1}{2} =$ 3

d) $\dfrac{5}{6} \div \dfrac{1}{3} =$ $\dfrac{15}{6}$ (or $2\dfrac{1}{2}$)

e) $\dfrac{3}{5} \div \dfrac{3}{5} =$ 1

f) $\dfrac{1}{3} \div \dfrac{2}{3} =$ $\dfrac{3}{6}$ (or $\dfrac{1}{2}$)

g) $\dfrac{2}{5} \div \dfrac{2}{5} =$ $\dfrac{10}{10}$ (or 1)

h) $\dfrac{4}{3} \div \dfrac{2}{3} =$ $\dfrac{12}{6}$ (or 2)

11. Explain the division of fractions algorithm. What is it, and why does it work? Responses will vary.

28   Book 6: *Fraction Operations*

148   **Fraction Operations** *Teacher Edition*

SCORING GUIDE BOOK 6: FRACTION OPERATIONS

End of Book Assessment
For Use With: Student Book Pages 25–28

PROBLEM DESCRIPTION	SCORING: WHAT TO LOOK FOR	SCORE AND COMMENTS
Problem 1a–h Determine how to acquire various amounts of ingredients by combining quantities from three different measuring cups. Level 1: Comprehension and Knowledge Level 2: Tool use Level 3: Connection and Application	Do students: • Use their intuitive understanding of fractional amounts and fraction sense? • Combine fractions to obtain other amounts? • Use informal (and formal) strategies for addition and subtraction of fractions? • Use pictures as visual representations of fractions?	(2 points per problem) Points: _____ of 16
Problem 2 Understand and use fractions in real-world context. Level 2: Tool use Level 3: Connection and Application	Do students: • Understand problem context? • Add in 1/3-units? • Multiply (or divide) to calculate the number of 1/3-mile intervals in 6 miles? • Add in 3/4-units? • Multiply (or divide) to calculate the number of 3/4-mile intervals in 6 miles? • Articulate their thinking?	Points: _____ of 4
Problem 3 Compare 1/3 and 3/4 to look for common denominators and equivalent fractions. Level 1: Comprehension and Knowledge Level 2: Tool use	Do students: • Understand equivalent fractions? • Understand common denominators to compare different fractions? • Articulate their thinking?	Points: _____ of 3
Problem 4 Use fraction sense to locate fractional increments on a trail map. Level 3: Connection and application	Do students: • Have an understanding of context? • Use appropriate placement of 1/3- and 3/4-mile increments along number line?	Points: _____ of 4

PROBLEMS 1–4: TOTAL POINTS: _____ OF 27

SCORING GUIDE BOOK 6: FRACTION OPERATIONS

End-of-Book Assessment (Cont.)
For Use With: Student Book Pages 25–28

PROBLEM DESCRIPTION	SCORING: WHAT TO LOOK FOR	SCORE AND COMMENTS
Problem 5 (p. 26) Determine relative distance between two locations expressed by benchmark fractions. Level 1: Comprehension and Knowledge Level 3: Connection and Application	Do students: • Have an intuitive understanding of fractional amounts and fraction sense? • Compare fractions to determine relative distance apart? • Articulate their thinking?	Points: _____ of 2
Problem 6 (p. 26) Determine relative distance between two locations expressed by benchmark fractions. Level 1: Comprehension and Knowledge Level 3: Connection and Application	Do students: • Have an intuitive understanding of fractional amounts and fraction sense? • Compare fractions to determine relative distance apart? • Articulate their thinking?	Points: _____ of 2
Problem 7 (p. 27) Conceptual understanding of fraction multiplication. Level 3: Connection and Application Level 4: Synthesis and Evaluation	Do students: • Understand multiplication? • Understand fraction multiplication? • Have the ability to translate into their own words?	Points: _____ of 2
Problem 8 (p. 27) Solve a fraction multiplication problem using a diagram. Level 2: Tool use Level 3: Connection and Application	Do students: • Have a conceptual understanding of fraction multiplication? • Represent multiplication with visual drawing? • Find the correct result?	Points: _____ of 2

PROBLEMS 5–8: TOTAL POINTS: _____ of 8

SCORING GUIDE BOOK 6: FRACTION OPERATIONS

End-of-Book Assessment (Cont.)
For Use With: Student Book Pages 25–28

PROBLEM DESCRIPTION	SCORING: WHAT TO LOOK FOR	SCORE AND COMMENTS
Problem 9 (p. 27) Explain a diagram that models fraction multiplication. Level 3: Connection and Application Level 4: Synthesis and Evaluation	Do students: • Have a conceptual understanding of fraction multiplication? • Understand representation of multiplication with visual drawings? • Articulate their thinking?	Points: _____ of 4
Problem 10a–h (p. 28) Solve fraction operation problems (multiplication). Level 2: Tool use	Do students: • Have a conceptual understanding of fraction multiplication? • Represent multiplication with visual drawings? • Find the correct result?	(2 points per problem) Points: _____ of 16
Problem 11 (p. 28) Explain fraction division. Level 4: Synthesis and Evaluation	Do students: • Understand division? • Understand fraction division? • Have an ability to translate understanding into their own words? • Use models or visual diagrams to support concept development?	Points: _____ of 4

PROBLEMS 9–11: TOTAL POINTS: _____ of 24

Fraction Strips: Template

One Whole
Halves
3rds
4ths
5ths
6ths
8ths
12ths

Book 7:
Decimals

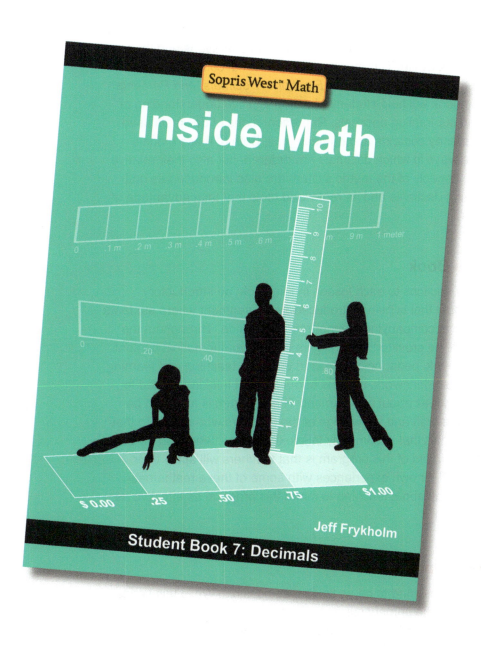

Book Seven Overview: Decimals

Introduction

This book is the seventh in a series of eight that are geared toward helping middle-grades learners acquire both facility with, and understanding of, the basic mathematical procedures and concepts that lay the groundwork for more advanced mathematical study. In particular, this series cultivates understanding of a number of mathematical tools that children learn to use with facility in various mathematical and real-world contexts

Book Focus

Book 7 engages students in contexts in which their informal, intuitive understanding of decimals will strengthen their comfort with decimal operations and their use of decimals in everyday life. This introduction to decimal concepts provides a foundation for the final book of this series: *Fractions, Decimals, and Percents.* The exercises in this book will help students develop intuitive understanding of ordering, adding, and subtracting decimals. Representations of decimals used in this book include money contexts and number lines. Both of these models reinforce not only the ways in which decimals are ordered, but also their relative sizes or magnitudes. Aspects of the metric system are also introduced as both models for representing decimals and as real-world tools that take advantage of decimal relationships.

How To Use This Book

There are two primary sections to each lesson in this book: an introductory discussion of the concept that is being introduced and a segment where students work problems with an accompanying teacher resource guide. Throughout the resource guide, you will be provided with insights into the mathematical content of each section of the book, pedagogical ideas to enhance teaching and learning, samples of anticipated student work, insights about student thinking related to the topics at hand, and ideas about assessment. This program is meant to be flexible and relies on the craft and knowledge of the teachers who use it. To that end, the resource materials that accompany this text are not intended to be used as a script. Instead, the intent of this program is that teachers will apply their knowledge of students, their own experiences with some of these mathematical tools, and their intuition about teaching to make this program as effective as possible.

Models Of Implementation

This program has been designed to be as flexible as possible. While this series of books may be used as the primary curriculum for the classroom, it was not designed as the full curriculum for any given grade level. Rather, it was crafted to support you as you help students understand the number operations and concepts that precede more advanced work in algebra. You may choose to use this program either as a guide for whole-class explorations or as the text for smaller, pull-out groups of students. In both cases, it is important to note that this program is designed on the principle that students learn mathematics in large measure through interactions with one another. Throughout the books, you will find numerous questions that ask students to explain their thinking. These occasions should not be taken lightly. It is in the sharing and comparing of solution strategies that students begin to build a firm foundation of understanding. The social dynamic of learning mathematics is important to recognize. Participation in mathematical discourse may be the most powerful impetus for learning mathematics available to young learners, and you should take advantage of every opportunity to encourage students to talk about their mathematical thinking and processes. Given a commitment to this principle, this program is likely to be most successful when students are progressing through the problems with their peers.

Addressing Issues of Language

There is no question that one of the greatest challenges facing teachers today is to make instruction relevant and accessible for second language learners. *Inside Math* has been written with this concern in mind. Careful consideration was given to the language that appears in directions, contextually based problems, and other sections of the book where text is necessary. When possible, for example, we have limited new vocabulary to only what is essential to the concepts being presented, and we revisit new vocabulary words and concepts repeatedly throughout the text. To assist you in making instruction accessible for English language learners, as well as other students for whom reading presents particular challenges, several supporting features were added to the teacher's edition. First, within the section planner that introduces each new major mathematical concept contained in the book, there is a heading that reads: Language Development. In this section of the overview, new vocabulary words are introduced and defined. Later in the text, when these words and concepts are introduced in a specific lesson, the teacher notes include additional information about pertinent language considerations and vocabulary. These notes appear as Encouraging Language Development under the Concept Development and Continue the Problem Solving headings.

Explaining Thinking

Throughout this series, and specifically in this book, students will be instructed, "Explain your thinking." The ability to articulate mathematical ideas and solution strategies is a feature of mathematics education that continues to grow in its importance. We see numerous examples in state, national, and international achievement tests in which answers alone are not enough. Students must also be able to express their thought processes, give rationales for answers, and articulate steps in any given strategy. As noted, in this book there are numerous opportunities for students to do likewise.

As this is often a new and challenging task for students, it is important for you to be able to model the process of making thinking explicit. At the beginning of each section in the book, there are suggestions for ways to introduce the content at hand, many of which are suitable candidates for you to illustrate what it means to explain thinking in an intelligible way. Be aware of both the importance of this feature of the program as well as the challenge it might provide students as they practice this skill for what might be the first time.

Assessment

At the conclusion of each section, you will find several problems that may be used for formative assessments. These problems review the key concepts discussed in the section. At the end of the book you will find additional assessment problems that cover the content of the entire book. These problems may be used as a cumulative assessment of student understanding of the key concepts in the book. The teachers' guide contains insights as to how the assessment problems might best be used and what they are intended to measure.

Assessment rubrics and scoring guides for every assessment may be found in *Assessment Teacher Edition*. Detailed instructions regarding assessment in general, and the use of the program rubrics in particular, are included in the introduction of *Assessment Teacher Edition*.

Professional Background

Overview

It is common practice in the United States to introduce decimals only after students have had good exposure to fractions—both in fraction sense and fraction operations. The same sequencing is followed in this series. While this approach is arguably the most sound pedagogically, it is unfortunate when fractions and decimals are taught independently of each other. Much of the teaching in this book on decimals rests on the foundation developed earlier with fractions. You may want to look for opportunities to point out the tools, representations, and models students may already understand (number bars, fraction strips, etc.) in conjunction with fractions throughout this book. These models can also serve in the development of decimal sense.

The Big Ideas

Big Idea #1: Different Forms of the Same Number Decimals, fractions, and percents can all be used to represent the same number. Each notation has relevance and value in a given context. Understanding how these representations are related to each other is fundamental in understanding how to work with decimals.

Big Idea #2: Base-10 Connections Decimals are intimately connected to our base-10 number system. Our base-10 system extends indefinitely both to the left and to the right of zero, and each place value is related to those on either side of the decimal by a 10-to-1 ratio. While young learners are normally comfortable with this 10-to-1 relationship with whole, or counting, numbers due to the extensive practice they have counting on from zero, they are much less comfortable representing values between zero and one, or between any two whole numbers, with this base-10 idea. Developing understanding of decimals is largely about familiarizing students with a 10-to-1 ratio as values get smaller and smaller.

Big Idea #3: Marking the Units Place Value The decimal point is a convention that is used to indicate the units position. The position immediately to the left of the decimal point indicates that the unit being counted is ones or single units. We might see a number like $1.1 million, which means that we are counting in millions. The same number would be represented as $1,100,000.00 if we were counting by ones. This is a fundamental element in understanding decimals.

Big Idea #4: Addition and Subtraction Addition and subtraction with decimals are operations that are based on the idea of adding or subtracting like units. For example, we would not add 1.1 million to 2.5 without first renaming 1.1 million in standard form and then lining up the decimals. In other words, 1.1 million + 2.5 is not equal to 3.6 million. Rather, 1,100,000 + 2.5 = 1,100,002.5. The use of base-10 models is essential for developing students' understanding of decimal addition and subtraction.

Big Idea #5: Multiplication and Division Multiplication and division of decimals do not receive extensive emphasis in this book because these operations are fundamentally the same as multiplication and division of whole numbers. Compare 2.4 × 1.9 = 4.56 to 24 × 19 = 456. In both cases, the sequence of digits is identical. The only difference is the placement of the decimal. For the most part, multiplication and division of decimals do not require new rules. Operations with decimals can be taught using knowledge of number relationships developed throughout this series, common sense, and estimation strategies to determine the placement of the decimal point in the final answer. For example, for the problem 2.4 × 1.9, students should be encouraged to think: "The number 2.4 is very close to 2.5. The number 1.9 is very close to 2. The answer is going to be very close to 2.5 × 2 = 5." Once the computation is completed, students can place the decimal point appropriately. To supplement these informal strategies and intuitions, many students are taught to multiply decimals by counting the number of decimal places in both factors, compute the product as if there were no decimal point, and then move the decimal point to the left to match the same number of places they counted in the factors. While this method works, students should first be encouraged to use estimation and their intuition to place the decimal point in the final answer.

Teaching Ideas

The treatment of decimals in this book depends heavily on a couple of visual and contextual models that are commonly understood by young learners. It is not surprising that our monetary system is the first context used to promote basic understanding of decimals. Connecting decimals to money cannot be stressed enough. The book begins by having students informally examine the hundredths place through the use of a double number bar that counts pennies on one side, and value (hundredths) on the other side. This roll of pennies provides an intuitive anchor for students to begin exploring decimals.

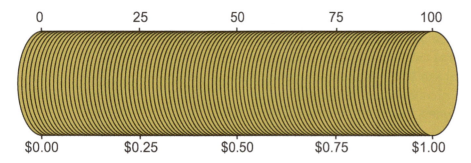

Students are given a blank double number line like the one above and asked to place various amounts of money on the number line: $0.22, $0.90, $0.05, $0.15. Beginning with this money context enables students to be comfortable in both representing dollar amounts and indicating the value of a given decimal. However, when the money context is replaced by a different context, or no context at all, students' proficiency declines. Because money contexts serve us only to the hundredths place, other models and tools are necessary in understanding decimals. But before turning to other contexts, this text takes advantage of students' familiarity with money to include instruction on estimates and basic addition and subtraction of decimals through hundredths.

Although money is a powerful context for teaching decimals, other ideas may be used effectively as well, perhaps with more difficulty. A second concept used to develop student's decimal sense is that of measurement. The use of metric measuring tools is a common model for helping students understand decimals. The metric system is based on a 10-to-1 ratio. For example, 10 millimeters = 1 centimeter, 10 centimeters = 1 decimeter, and 10 decimeters = 1 meter. This book takes advantage of this context to enhance work in the hundredths (100 centimeters in one meter is the most common comparison), and it also considers comparisons between units that have a difference of two, three, or more powers of ten. For example, students explore fractions and their decimal equivalents:

1 millimeter = 1/1000 meter
1 millimeter = 1/100 decimeter
1 millimeter = 1/10 centimeter

1 centimeter = 1/100 meter
1 centimeter = 1/10 decimeter

1 decimeter = 1/10 meter

Based on these fractions, students are asked to find decimal equivalents in problems such as:

2 cm = _____ meters
2 cm = _____ decimeters
2 mm = _____ centimeters
4 dm = _____ meters
50 cm = _____ meters

These problems may seem difficult at first, but with proper models and visuals (metersticks or other number lines), students can rename these measurements with conceptual understanding. The key is to help students recognize that our decimal system is built upon powers of ten, or the 10-to-1 relationship between adjacent place values.

Throughout the latter half of the book, decimal multiplication and division are introduced in an informal way. Questions such as, "How many 0.5s are there in 4?" are modeled with the number line. By using the number line in this way, students are using informal strategies to complete a problem for which they might otherwise have used a rather awkward algorithm. With a number line, the problem is rather easy to solve.

How many 0.5s are there in 4?

If students have a basic decimal sense of 0.5 (which should be in place at this point in the text), this problem simply becomes one of counting. There are 4 lengths of 0.5 between 0 and 2. There must be 8 lengths of 0.5 between 0 and 4.

Compare this method to the long division algorithm that many students use for all division problems:

$$0.5 \overline{\smash{)}4}$$

For this problem, according to the decimal division algorithm, we move the decimal point in the divisor one place to the right. Then make the corresponding move with the decimal point in the dividend. Next, the decimal point in the quotient is written directly above the decimal point in the dividend. Finally, the student divides as with whole numbers. While this process might be efficient, it is very difficult for students to understand the reasoning behind these manipulations. The solution using the number line provides students with a much better opportunity to understand the problem from a conceptual point of view, and there are likely to be fewer computational errors with the number line than with the traditional method. However, the number line is not a practical model in all cases. Students do need to know other methods. The most important goal from a teaching point of view is to help students develop proficiency with algorithms while at the same time allowing them opportunities to see and use intuitive models that will cultivate a rich conceptual understanding to support of the algorithms. Finding this balance has been a central premise for the development of the progression of ideas in this book on decimals.

Section A: Introduction to Decimals

SECTION A PLANNER

THE MATHEMATICS CONTENT AND GOALS

GOALS
Students will:
- Make connections between a number and the monetary value of pennies.
- Find decimal equivalents for various amounts of pennies.
- Locate decimals on a number line.
- Extend number lines by decimal intervals.

LANGUAGE DEVELOPMENT
Mathematical language in this section includes:

Decimal: A base-10 number that uses place value and a decimal point to express tenths, hundredths, and so on.

Decimal Point: The point between the ones place and the tenths place in a decimal.

Tenths: The first place value to the right of the decimal point.

Hundredths: The second place value to the right of the decimal point.

Penny: The smallest denomination of American currency, worth 0.01 of a dollar.

Nickel: A denomination of American currency worth 0.05 of a dollar.

Dime: A denomination of American currency worth 0.10 of a dollar.

Quarter: A denomination of American currency worth 0.25 of a dollar.

Value: The monetary worth of a denomination of money.

PROBLEM SETS: OVERVIEW

Because it is familiar to students, perhaps the most powerful model/manipulative to help students acquire understanding of decimals is our monetary system. Pennies are especially helpful models because of the simple connection between the number of pennies and the numeric representation of the value of those pennies. For example, 15 pennies represents 15/100 of a dollar. We can represent this amount as the decimal equivalent 0.15. This one-to-one relationship between number and value can be used to great advantage when exposing students to decimal notation and meaning. Much of Section A will require students to count and represent pennies.

The second teaching tool introduced in this section is the double number line. A transition is provided in the text to help students move from counting and organizing pennies to the use of a number line to represent decimals. Students will explore decimals on the number line by locating decimals on the line, extending number lines in given intervals, and so on.

Set 1 (pp. 1–4; problems 1–11)
There is only one set of problems in Section A. Students begin their exploration of decimals by counting pennies in a penny roll. Then, beginning with problem 3, students begin to explore decimals on the number line. Taking advantage of students' informal knowledge of common denominations of coins in our monetary system and their experiences with money, students begin to add decimals intuitively. This intuitive work is gradually formalized as the problems progress.

PACING

The projected pacing for this unit is 2 class periods (based on a 45-minute period).

CONCEPT DEVELOPMENT (Pages 1–4)

INTRODUCE THE CONCEPT

ASSESS STUDENTS' PRIOR KNOWLEDGE

Ask:
How many nickels are in one dollar? How many pennies? How many dimes? How many quarters?

Listen for:
(Students should understand that certain combinations of any one type of coin are equal to $1.)
- There are 20 nickels in one dollar.
- There are 100 pennies in one dollar.
- There are 10 dimes in one dollar.
- There are 4 quarters in one dollar.

MODEL MATHEMATICAL THINKING

Provide copies of the quiz below to students. Ask them to match the amounts by writing the letter of the correct answer next to the amount in the column on the left. Correct answers are given in blue.

1. 9 cents **d**		a. $0.03
2. 119 cents **h**		b. $0.40
3. 3 pennies **a**		c. $4.09
4. 3 dimes **l**		d. $0.09
5. 10 dimes and 3 pennies **k**		e. $0.90
6. 3 dimes and 10 pennies **b**		f. $0.33
7. 49 cents **g**		g. $0.49
8. 4 dollars and 9 cents **c**		h. $1.19
		i. $3.10
		j. $4.90
		k. $1.03
		l. $0.30

Ask:
Look at the amount of coins presented in problems 3 and 4. How can we tell which answer matches each amount? In other words, how can we tell which decimal in the second column represents the amount in the first column?

Talk Through the Thinking:
First, let's rename each amount as cents. Three pennies is the same as 3 cents, and 3 dimes is the same as 30 cents. Does that help us to find the correct answers? Maybe. Look at the dot in each answer. The dots are called decimal points and we read the decimal point as "and." Now, remember that the decimal point separates the dollars from the cents. Both 3 cents and 30 cents are less than one dollar. So, we are looking for amounts that have a zero in the dollars place and a 3 somewhere to the right of the decimal point. I see that answers a, f, and l have a 0 in the dollars place and a 3 somewhere to the right of the decimal point. We can eliminate $0.33 as an answer because that uses the digit 3 twice, and is 33 cents. That leaves us with answers a and l. 30 cents is greater than 3 cents, so that means that the answer to number 3 is a and the answer to number 4 is l.

Ask:
Look at the amounts for 7 and 8. How do you know which answer matches each amount?

Listen for:
(Students should go through similar reasoning and, in their explanations, refer to place value.)
- 49 cents is less than one dollar, so there will be a 0 in the dollars place. The answer is g.
- There should be a 4 in the dollars place for 4 dollars and 9 cents. There are no dimes, so the answer cannot be j. The answer is c.

LAUNCH THE PROBLEM SOLVING

Have students read through page 1. When they finish, have them discuss the information on the page with a partner. Then have each pair share their insights and conclusions with the class. Refer to the discussion **The Penny Roll and the Double Number Line: Student Page 1**.

As students work and report their conclusions, focus on these issues:

Facilitate Students' Thinking – It is important to help students understand the function of the decimal point. The decimal point separates whole units or dollars–to the left of the point–and fractional parts of a dollar, or cents.

Allow Processing Time – Just as with every topic area, the introduction of the key ideas and models on this page requires that students be allowed to spend time studying the models and digesting their embedded meanings.

Help Make Connections – Remind students to draw on their experience with the many presentations of number lines in Book 1. Students will be more comfortable using double number lines in this unit if they can connect them with what they have previously learned.

Allow Waiting Time – When students struggle to explain their thinking, be sure to allow them at least 20 seconds to organize their thoughts. (This may seem like a long time.)

Encourage Language Development – Do not take for granted that students know the monetary values of each of the coins presented in these exercises. Review the coins in our money system showing the penny, nickel, dime, and quarter and naming their values.

The Penny Roll and the Double Number Line: Student Page 1

This page introduces one of the primary teaching tools in this book: the use of pennies as a representation for decimals. You may wish to bring a penny tube counter into class. In essence, the penny roll is a double number line. As shown on page 1, two number lines can be affixed to the penny roll. One number line counts the actual number of pennies, while the second assigns a monetary value (using decimals) to that number of pennies. *Watch for:* Be sure that students are comfortable with this double number line representation before moving ahead because it will be revisited throughout this book.

Student Page 1: Problems and Potential Answers

Section A: Introduction to Decimals Set 1

Collecting Pennies

Jerry decided that for one month, he would pick up and keep every penny he found. At the end of a month, he was surprised at how many pennies he had found. He took his pennies to the bank to exchange them for larger coins and even dollar bills. The bank sorted the pennies into trays that each held 100 pennies. Each stack of 100 pennies was put into a paper roll. Jerry ended up with 275 pennies.

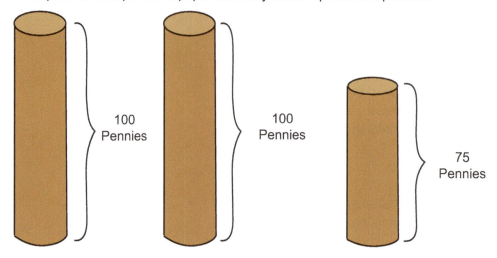

Let's look at one roll of 100 pennies.

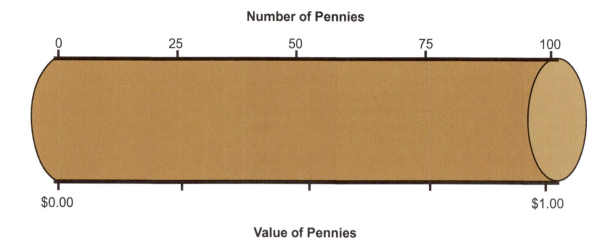

100 pennies **have a value** of $1.00

Book 7: *Decimals* 1

164 Decimals *Teacher Edition*

CONTINUE THE PROBLEM SOLVING

The intent of Student Pages 2–4 is to develop the double number line as a tool for understanding decimals and decimal notation.

Have students work individually to solve the problems on page 2. As they work, you may want to circulate and monitor their recorded answers. When students finish each problem, have them compare and discuss their answers with a partner. Then have each pair share their answers in a class discussion. Refer to the **Teacher Notes: Student Page 2** for more specific ideas about each problem on the page.

As students work and report their conclusions, focus on these issues:

Help Make Connections – Help students make the connections between fractions and decimals. For example, 1/10 and 0.1 name the same part, as do 1/100 and 0.01. You may wish to do the same for 2/100, 25/100, and so on.

Encourage Language Development – When students explain their thinking, encourage them to use mathematical language such as *decimal*, *decimal point*, and *tenths place*.

Validate Alternate Strategies – Have students share their strategies for solving the problems with the class. Ask the class to analyze the strategies to determine whether they are valid.

Allow Waiting Time – When students struggle to explain their thinking, be sure to allow them ample time to organize their thoughts.

TEACHER NOTES: STUDENT PAGE 2

The key to understanding this model is for students to recognize that 100 pennies can be represented numerically in different ways. The value of 100 pennies is 1 dollar because each penny represents 1/100 of a dollar. One-hundred pennies is 100/100 = 1 dollar. *Teaching Strategy:* It might be helpful to use a calculator here to stress the connection between the fractional representation of one penny (1/100) and its decimal equivalent (0.01), reminding students that a calculator does not display the dollar sign. To help make this connection concrete, you might ask students to name the fraction 1/100 as "one hundredth." The same verbal connection can be made for the equivalent decimal representation of one hundredth, or 0.01. Once students are comfortable with this language and representation, they will be much more likely to engage positively in the subsequent problems throughout the book. You may wish to extend this example with another one: two pennies would be represented as 2/100, or $0.02. The following progression of questions may be helpful in this regard:
- Show me 13 pennies on the penny roll.
- How can you describe these thirteen pennies as a fraction of one dollar? (13/100)
- How can you use words to express this fraction? (13 hundredths)
- How can you represent 13 hundredths as a decimal? (0.13)

Problem 1: This problem extends the previous discussion by asking students to come up with the decimal equivalents of 25 pennies, 50 pennies, and 75 pennies. *Teaching Strategy:* Remind students of the relationship between the fractional representations of these pennies as parts of one dollar and their decimal equivalents.

Problem 2: Students should be making the connection between the number of coins at hand and their decimal representation. You might encourage students to think specifically of their knowledge of monetary values as they place these values on the number line. For example, you might ask, "Suppose you have $0.05. How close is that to one dollar on the number line?"

Problem 3: *Watch for:* Make sure students are adding appropriately in increments of $0.05. *Teaching Strategy:* Encourage students who are struggling to think in terms of adding nickels. You may wish to have coins available as manipulatives to help students solve these problems.

Student Page 2: Problems and Potential Answers

Section A: Introduction to Decimals — Set 1

Looking at the penny roll, we can see that there is a one-to-one relationship between the number of pennies and the value of the pennies. 100 pennies have a <u>value of $1.00</u>. So, 100 pennies has the same value as a one-dollar bill. Let's explore this penny roll a bit more. How do we represent the value of a certain number of pennies? We do it by using *decimals*.

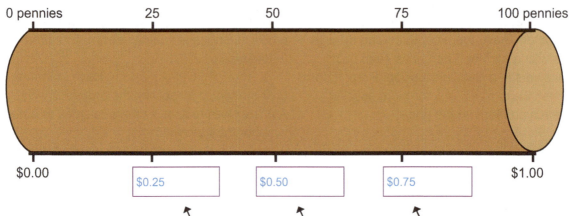

1. What is the value of 25 pennies? ...of 50 pennies? ...of 75 pennies?

2. Label each amount on the penny roll number line below.

   a) $0.50   b) $0.10   c) $0.80   d) $0.05   e) $0.95   f) $0.65   g) $0.25

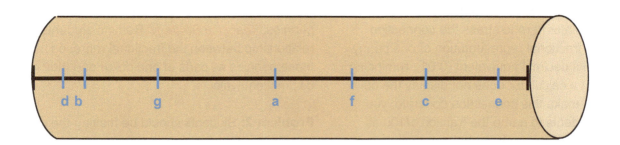

3. Start with zero pennies. Use increments of $0.05. Extend the number line to $0.50 (50 pennies).

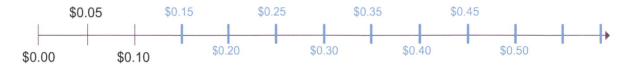

2   Book 7: *Decimals*

CONTINUE THE PROBLEM SOLVING

Have students work individually to solve the problems on page 3. As they work, you may want to circulate and monitor their recorded answers. When students finish each problem, have them compare and discuss their answers with a partner. Then have each pair share their answers in a class discussion of the problem. Refer to the **Teacher Notes: Student Page 3** for more specific ideas about each problem on the page.

As students work and report their conclusions, focus on these issues:

Validate Representations – Some students will want to use coins to help them solve these problems. Have them discuss with a partner whether their representations reflect the problems.

Help Make Connections – For problem 5, you may wish to remind students that they have completed similar tasks with whole numbers in earlier books.

Facilitate Students' Thinking – You may need to remind some students to recall the concept introduction activity when they determined how many of each kind of coin were equal to one dollar.

Allow Waiting Time – When students struggle to explain their thinking, be sure to allow them ample time to organize their thoughts.

TEACHER NOTES: STUDENT PAGE 3

Problem 4: The use of play quarters as manipulatives might be helpful for this sequence of problems. *Teaching Strategy:* If they are not already making that connection, help students understand that there are 4 quarters in one dollar.

Problem 5: Problem 5 asks students to start with a point on the number line and then determine its decimal representation. Students have done similar tasks in earlier books, but not with decimals. *Teaching Strategy:* Encourage students to draw on this previous knowledge of number relationships.

Problem 6: This problem is similar to problem 4, but here students make increments of 10 cents rather than 25 cents. This is an important problem in that it emphasizes our base-10 number system, upon which decimals are based.

Problem 7: Problem 7 provides students with more practice identifying decimal values on the number line.

Student Page 3: Problems and Potential Answers

Section A: Introduction to Decimals — Set 1

4. Start with zero and use increments of 25 pennies. Extend the number line to $3.00.

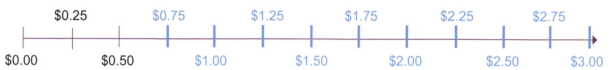

   a) What is the name of the coin that is worth $0.25? __quarter__

   b) How many $0.25's are there in $3.00? __12__   How many $0.25's are there in $2.25? __9__

   c) How many $0.25's are there in $1.00? __4__   Given this answer, why do you think that "quarter" is the name of the coin that represents $0.25? __The value of a quarter is ¼ the value of a dollar.__

5. Write the amount that matches each letter on the number line below.

   a) __$0.25__   b) __$0.70__   c) __$0.80__   d) __$0.40__   e) __$0.10__

6. Start with zero and use increments of $0.10. Extend the number line to $1.50.

   a) What is the name of the coin that has a value of $0.10? __dime__

   b) How many $0.10's are there in $1.00? __10__   In $1.50? __15__

7. Graph each amount on the number line below.

   a) $1.10   b) $0.75   c) $0.15   d) $0.10   e) $1.50   f) $1.80

Book 7: *Decimals*   3

CONTINUE THE PROBLEM SOLVING

Have students work individually to solve the problems on page 4. As they work, you may want to circulate and monitor their recorded answers. When students finish each problem, have them compare and discuss their answers with a partner. Then have each pair share their answers in a class discussion of the problem. Refer to the **Teacher Notes: Student Page 4** for more specific ideas about each problem on the page.

As students work and report their conclusions, focus on these issues:

Look for Misconceptions – When working with decimals, as in problem 9, students may confuse tenths and hundredths. For example, 0.1 and 0.01 are often confused. Using money notation can help them understand the difference between one dime, $0.10, and one penny, $0.01.

Allow Waiting Time – When students struggle to explain their thinking, be sure to allow them ample time to organize their thoughts.

Help Make Connections – You may need to remind students that the processes for ordering decimals and money amounts are the same as for ordering whole numbers.

Facilitate Students' Thinking – Encourage students to use what they already know about how many of a certain type of coin are in one dollar. For example, because there are 10 dimes in one dollar, 1/10 or 0.1, of one dollar can be represented by 1 dime.

TEACHER NOTES: STUDENT PAGE 4

If you choose to do so, you can use these problems as a formative assessment for the concepts covered thus far in the text. All the problems on page 4 serve to both review and extend students' knowledge.

Problem 8: Problem 8 is similar to others done previously in this text series. Only one of the items requires consideration of decimals. The purpose of the problem is to emphasize the consistencies that can be found when examining both whole and decimal numbers.
Watch for: Students should be developing an intuitive sense of the relative magnitude of decimals similar to the ways in which they do so with whole numbers.

Problem 9: This problem focuses on the difference between one hundredth (0.01) and ten hundredths (0.10). This distinction is one that is commonly misunderstood by students. Students may be tempted, for example, to write eight hundredths as 0.8. One way to challenge this common misconception is to juxtapose tenths and hundredths. This can be done effectively in this problem because students have to recognize what happens when moving from nine hundredths (0.09) to ten hundredths (one tenth, 0.10).

Problem 10: This problem reinforces concepts developed earlier.

Problem 11: Problem 11 helps students solidify connections between particular coins, their monetary values, and their decimal representations.

Student Page 4: Problems and Potential Answers

Section A: Introduction to Decimals — Set 1

8. Graph each amount on the number line below.

a) $5.00   b) $1.00   c) $12.00   d) $12.50   e) $19.00   f) $15.00

9. Start with zero and use increments of $0.01. Extend the number line to $0.13.

a) How many $0.01's (pennies) are there in $0.10? __10__

b) How many pennies are there in $0.13? __13__

c) How many pennies are there in $1.00? __100__

10. What is the value of each?

Example: one penny ➡ $0.01

a) one dime ➡ __$0.10__

b) one quarter ➡ __$0.25__

c) 10 pennies ➡ __$0.10__

d) 3 quarters ➡ __$0.75__

e) one nickel ➡ __$0.05__

11. Graph each on the number line below.

a) 2 dimes   b) 1 quarter   c) 3 nickels   d) 5 dimes   e) 3 quarters   f) 50 pennies

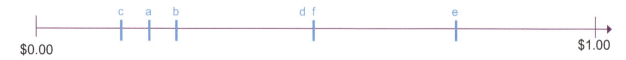

4   Book 7: *Decimals*

Section B: Formalizing Decimals and Beginning Operations

SECTION B PLANNER

THE MATHEMATICS CONTENT AND GOALS

GOALS
Students will:
- Solidify their understanding of decimal representations of monetary values.
- Experience contexts in which addition of decimals is necessary.
- Practice addition, subtraction, and estimation with decimals.

LANGUAGE DEVELOPMENT
Mathematical language in this section includes:

Estimate: A reasonable approximation or educated guess.

PROBLEM SETS: OVERVIEW

The purpose of this section is to formalize some of the concepts presented in Section A. Section B introduces students to simple addition and subtraction of decimals, as well as multiplication of decimals and whole numbers, by again capitalizing on students' familiarity with the decimal use in contexts involving money.

Set 1 (pp. 5–7; problems 1–5)

There is only one set of problems in Section B. The first several problems formalize the use of decimals presented in Section A. The final problems emphasize beginning addition and subtraction of decimals using the context of money.

PACING

The projected pacing for this unit is 2 class periods (based on a 45-minute period).

Decimals Teacher Edition   **171**

CONCEPT DEVELOPMENT (PAGES 5–7)

INTRODUCE THE CONCEPT

ASSESS STUDENTS' PRIOR KNOWLEDGE

Write the following on the board: 5 dimes and 3 nickels; 1 quarter, 2 nickels, and 4 pennies; 4 nickels and 12 pennies; 2 quarters, 6 dimes, 1 nickel, and 3 pennies.

Ask:
What is the value of each of these sets of coins? How did you find out?

Listen for:
Students may use several different strategies to find the value of each set, including counting on and adding.
- The value of 5 dimes and 3 nickels is $0.53.
- The value of 1 quarter, 2 nickels, and 4 pennies is $0.39.
- The value of 4 nickels and 12 pennies is $0.32.
- The value of 2 quarters, 6 dimes, 1 nickel, and 3 pennies is $1.18.

MODEL MATHEMATICAL THINKING

Display this table.

Rainfall in Inches							
City	Sun.	Mon.	Tues.	Wed.	Thurs.	Fri.	Sat.
Denver	0.25	0.10	0.05	0.05	0.25	0.35	0.05
Dallas	0.25	0.00	0.05	0.15	0.05	0.00	0.45
Detroit	0.10	0.05	0.05	0.28	0.38	0.02	0.40

Tell students that rainfall is measured in inches. Explain that the table shows what part of an inch of rain fell in three cities each day over a one-week period. Take some time to be sure students can read the information in the table. For students who may have difficulty with this problem, the script below connects coins as representations of decimals to the given problem.

Ask:
Which cities received more than 1 inch of rain that week? How can we find out?

Talk Through the Thinking:
Let's start with Denver. As we look through the amounts of rain for Denver, we can find amounts that are easy to add mentally. From working with money, I know I like to

work with quarters, dimes, and nickels. Remember that 1 quarter has a value of 25 cents, and we write its value as $0.25; 1 dime has a value of 10 cents and we write its value as $0.10; 1 nickel has a value of 5 cents and we write this value as $0.05. Write these values on the board. *I see if I remove the dollar sign from each value, I get some of the same numbers that are in the row for Denver.* Erase the dollar sign from each value on the board. *Now, to find how much rain fell in Denver that week, I can combine these amounts just like I would combine money amounts.* Write each addition step on the board. *First, I can combine the amounts for Sunday and Thursday. If $0.25 + $0.25 = $0.50, which is half of one dollar, then 0.25 + 0.25 = 0.50, which is half of 1. Now let's add on the decimals that could represent 10 cents. The amount for Monday is 0.10. So if we add that to 0.50, we get 0.60. We can get another 0.10 by combining the amounts for Tuesday, and Wednesday, which would be like adding nickels. So 0.05 + 0.05 = 0.10. Now we have 0.60 + 0.10 = 0.70. Let's look at the amounts for Friday and Saturday. We know that $0.35 + $0.05 = $0.40 and that if we add it to $0.70 we get $1.10. We read this amount as one and ten hundredths. This is more than 1 inch. Denver received more than one inch of rain that week.*

Ask:
What other city received more than one inch of rain that week? How much rain did it receive? How much rain did the third city receive? Explain your reasoning.

Listen for:
(Students to use similar reasoning in finding the answer.)
- Detroit received more than 1 inch of rain. It received 1.28 inches of rain.
- Dallas received less than 1 inch of rain. It received 0.95 inch of rain.

LAUNCH THE PROBLEM SOLVING

Have students work individually to solve the problems on page 5. As they work, you may want to circulate and monitor their recorded answers. When students finish each problem, have them compare and discuss their answers with a partner. Then have each pair share their answers in a class discussion of the problem. Refer to the **Teacher Notes: Student Page 5** for more specific ideas about each problem on the page.

As students work and report their conclusions, focus on these issues:

Facilitate Students' Thinking – Remind students to use what they have already learned about equivalent values of coins and placing money amounts on a number line to solve these problems.

Encourage Language Development – You may need to help students read decimal names properly. In problem 2 for example, 2.25 is read as 2 and 25 hundredths; 1.5 is read as 1 and 5 tenths; and 0.66 is read as 66 hundredths.

Allow Waiting Time – When students struggle to explain their thinking, be sure to allow them ample time to organize their thoughts.

TEACHER NOTES: STUDENT PAGE 5

Problem 1: Problem 1 is designed to encourage flexibility in student thought about various decimal amounts as they refer to different coins. It also provides opportunities for exploring informal methods of multiplication of decimals. For example, by asking students to think of the value of 3 quarters, students must multiply or use repeated addition to find 3 groups of $0.25.

Problem 2: This problem uses a new context with the familiar number-line representation to stimulate students to think more deeply about decimals. It introduces the approximate decimal equivalents of 1/3 and 2/3 and requires students to place these amounts on a number line in reference to previously used decimals such as 0.25, 0.5, and so on.

Student Page 5: Problems and Potential Answers

Section B: Formalizing Decimals and Beginning Operations   **Set 1**

1. Circle every value in the right column that has the same value as the decimal in the left column. An example has been done for you.

Example		5 dimes
		⭕ 5 pennies
a) $0.05		50 cents
		⭕ 5 cents
b) $0.50		⭕ 5 dimes
		5 pennies
		⭕ 50 pennies
		⭕ 2 quarters
c) $0.10		⭕ 2 nickels
		⭕ 10 pennies
		100 pennies
		⭕ 1 dime
d) $1.00		1 dime
		⭕ 10 dimes
		⭕ 100 pennies
		⭕ 20 nickels
e) $0.04		4 dimes
		1 quarter and 3 nickels
		⭕ 4 pennies
		40 pennies
f) $0.40		⭕ 4 dimes
		⭕ 1 quarter and 3 nickels
		4 pennies
		⭕ 40 pennies

2. The number line represents a map of a 3-mile trail. Graph each location on the line according to the information below.

a) Echo Lake: 1.5 miles from the start of the trail, called the *trailhead*

b) Rock Cliffs: 2.25 miles from the trailhead

c) Ranger Station: 0.66 miles from the trailhead

d) Highest elevation on the trail: 2.05 miles from the trailhead

e) Stream Crossing: 0.25 miles from the trailhead

f) Wild raspberry bushes: 1.33 miles from the trailhead

g) Meadow: 2.90 miles from the trailhead

Book 7: *Decimals* 5

CONTINUE THE PROBLEM SOLVING

Have students work individually to solve the problems on page 6. As they work, you may want to circulate and monitor their recorded answers. When students finish each problem, have them compare and discuss their answers with a partner. Then have each pair share their answers in a class discussion of the problem. Refer to the following **Teacher Notes: Student Page 6** for more specific ideas about each problem on the page.

As students work and report their conclusions, focus on these issues:

Facilitate Students' Thinking – You may wish to remind students that they can use estimation to get a ballpark sum to help them solve problem 3.

Help Make Connections – As students work through these problems, you might suggest that they use the same kind of thinking you modeled for them in the second concept introduction activity.

Validate Alternate Strategies – Encourage students to share and explain the strategies they used to solve the problems on this page. Have the class discuss how efficient these strategies are.

TEACHER NOTES: STUDENT PAGE 6

Problem 3: This problem requires students to use estimation and informal addition strategies to determine which combinations of amounts have a total value close to one dollar. *Teaching Strategy:* This is an excellent problem for sparking student discussion. Students will have various ways of estimating and combining the given decimals. By having them describe their methods, you will be able to get a sense of the sophistication of their understanding of decimals and how they can be combined.

Problem 4: While many students may have used estimation strategies for problem 3, they are explicitly asked to do so for problem 4. *Watch for:* Be attentive to the strategies students use as well as the numbers they choose to anchor upon as they complete their estimates. This problem is excellent for eliciting student discussion.

Student Page 6: Problems and Potential Answers

Section B: Formalizing Decimals and Beginning Operations Set 1

3. <u>Close to One Dollar</u> How close can you come to making one dollar? Choose and circle the combination of amounts that comes closest to $1.00. Write an addition sentence using the amounts you have circled. An example has been done for you.

   Example: $0.17 ($0.25) ($0.45) ($0.32) $0.09 $0.25 + $0.45 + $0.32 = $1.02

   a) $0.12 $0.23 $0.34 ($0.45) ($0.56) $0.45 + $0.56 + $1.01

   b) ($0.05) $0.12 ($0.53) ($0.23) ($0.18) $0.05 + $0.53 + $0.23 + $0.18 = $0.99

   c) $0.32 ($0.16) ($0.55) $0.48 ($0.29) $0.16 + $0.55 + $0.29 = $1.00

   d) $0.09 ($0.08) $0.12 $0.05 ($0.59) ($0.34) $0.08 + $0.59 + $0.34 = $1.01

   e) $0.77 $0.66 $0.55 $0.44 $0.33 $0.22   Each matched pair is $0.99: $0.77 + $0.22 = $0.99, $0.66 + $0.33 = $0.99, $0.55 + $0.44 = $0.99

   f) $0.01 $0.22 $0.03 $0.05 $0.08 $0.09 $0.01 + $0.22 + $0.03 + $0.05 + $0.08 + $0.09 = $0.48

4. Estimate each sum. <u>Explain how you estimated</u>. Explanations will vary.

   a) 0.75 + 0.75 + 0.75 + 0.75 + 0.75 + 0.75   Estimate: about 4.50

   Explain. _____

   b) $2.94 + $4.01 + $0.99 + $0.05   Estimate: about $8.00

   Explain. _____

   c) 0.33 + 0.10 + 0.89 + 0.66   Estimate: about 2.00, or 2

   Explain. _____

   d) $3.31 + $2.58 + $4.12 + $5.91 + $0.41 + $1.69   Estimate: about $18.50

   Explain. _____

Book 7: *Decimals*

CONTINUE THE PROBLEM SOLVING

Have students work individually to solve the problems on page 7. As they work, you may want to circulate and monitor their recorded answers. When students finish each problem, have them compare and discuss their answers with a partner. Then have each pair share their answers in a class discussion of the problem. Refer to the **Teacher Notes: Student Page 7** for more specific ideas about each problem on the page.

As students work and report their conclusions, focus on these issues:

Help Make Connections – You may wish to remind students of the work they did earlier counting sets of coins. Ask them to think about how they succeeded at doing so, and have them apply this knowledge to the problems on this page.

Facilitate Students' Thinking – You might remind students that, just as with whole numbers, multiplying decimals is the same as repeated addition or skip counting by a single interval.

Validate Alternate Strategies – As students discuss each problem, have them explain their strategies. Ask the class to determine whether these strategies are helpful in solving the problems.

TEACHER NOTES: STUDENT PAGE 7

Problem 5: Problem 5 offers students multiple opportunities to practice multiplying decimals. Because they are based on familiar contexts, these problems draw on students' informal and intuitive knowledge of decimals as well as monetary values. (For example, 3 nickels and 2 quarters gives students a context they know.) Toward the end of the page, there are several problems that are not nested in a money context.
Watch for: While some students will most likely solve these problems intuitively, others may choose to use multiplication algorithms they have already learned. You may choose to examine and discuss these algorithms at this point, although they are beyond the scope of this book.

Student Page 7: Problems and Potential Answers

Section B: Formalizing Decimals and Beginning Operations — Set 1

5. **How much?** Find the value of each combination. Show your work or explain your thinking.
   Explanations will vary.

   a) 5 quarters Value: $1.25

   b) 3 piles of pennies; each pile has 12 pennies Value: $0.36

   c) 7 nickels Value: $0.35

   d) 15 dimes Value: $1.50

   e) 15 pennies Value: $0.15

   f) 15 × 0.10 Value: 1.50

   g) 15 × 0.01 Value: 0.15

   h) 5 × 0.25 Value: 1.25

   i) 3 nickels, 6 quarters, and 22 pennies Value: $1.87

   j) 12 piles of dimes; each pile has 2 dimes Value: $2.40

   k) 12 × 0.20 Value: 2.40

   l) 5 piles of coins; each pile has 1 dime and 5 pennies Value: $0.75

   m) 5 × 0.15 Value: 0.75

   n) 5 × 0.25 Value: 1.25

   o) 16 × 0.25 Value: 4.00, or 4

SECTIONS A AND B ASSESSMENT (PAGE 8)

LAUNCH THE ASSESSMENT

Have students turn to the Sections A and B Assessment on page 8. An additional copy is found on page 115 of the Assessment Book. Have students work individually to solve the problems and write their explanations. As they work, circulate to be sure students understand what they need to do for each problem and that they are completing each part of the problem. For example, for problem 1, students need to estimate whether they have enough money to buy a set of items and then explain how they made their estimates. You may find it helpful to read through the directions for all the problems before students begin, discussing the types of responses they need to make for each problem.

Encourage students to use whatever space they need to explain their thinking. If the space on the page is inadequate, they should use an additional sheet of paper or the back of the page.

Refer to the **Teacher Notes: Assessment Problems for Sections A and B** for more specific ideas about the problems on this page.

Evaluate Student Responses

Use the assessment rubric on page 114 of the Assessment Book (pictured on page 181 of the Teacher Edition) to evaluate student responses. The Assessment Book has some general suggestions for using the rubric that you may find helpful.

TEACHER NOTES: ASSESSMENT PROBLEMS FOR SECTIONS A AND B

These assessment problems will indicate the degree to which a student is grasping the concept of informal combination of decimals. One of the best contexts to do so is that of money. *Teaching Strategy:* When possible, emphasize estimation strategies both as a way to begin the problem and also as a way to verify whether the results obtained are reasonable given the problem context.

Problem 1: *Watch for:* First, students should estimate the cents by combining amounts that are close to one dollar. For example, the combination of $0.78 and $0.26 is very close to one dollar. Then students can estimate the whole-dollar amounts. For this problem it is enough to estimate. The exact sum is not necessary.

Problem 2: *Watch for:* Students might use a variety of strategies to solve these problems. Some students may wish to use ratio tables (or other forms of repeated addition) to solve these problems. Regardless of the method, the key point is to see students estimating and working with benchmark amounts.

Student Page 8: Problems and Potential Answers

Sections A and B: Problems for Assessment

1. Estimate. Explain how you estimated.

   a) You have $12.00 in your pocket. You go to the grocery store to buy four items that cost $1.49, $2.94, $6.78, and $0.26.
   Estimate. Do you have enough money to buy all the items? __Yes, I have enough.__

   Explain your estimate. _____
   Explanations will vary.

   b) You want to ship a box of books. The box you are using can hold up to 11 pounds. The books weigh 1.18, 1.28, 1.25, 1.31, 1.20, 1.29, 1.25, and 1.23 pounds.
   Estimate. Can you ship all the books in the box you are using? __Yes, the box will hold the books.__

   Explain your estimate. _____
   Explanations will vary.

2. **How Much?** Find the value of each. Show your work or explain your thinking. Explanations will vary.

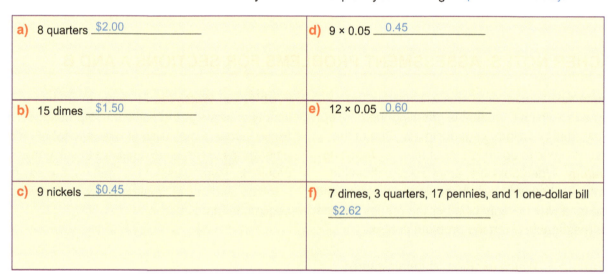

a) 8 quarters __$2.00__	d) 9 × 0.05 __0.45__
b) 15 dimes __$1.50__	e) 12 × 0.05 __0.60__
c) 9 nickels __$0.45__	f) 7 dimes, 3 quarters, 17 pennies, and 1 one-dollar bill __$2.62__

3. Label increments of 0.3 on the number line. Extend your labels through 3.0

0.0 0.3 0.6 0.9 1.2 1.5 1.8 2.1 2.4 2.7 3.0

How many 0.3's are there in 1.5? __5__   How many 0.3's are there in 3? __10__

8 Book 7: *Decimals*

SCORING GUIDE BOOK 7: DECIMALS

Sections A and B Assessment
For Use With: Student Book Page 8

PROBLEM DESCRIPTION	SCORING: WHAT TO LOOK FOR	SCORE AND COMMENTS
Problem 1a–b Estimate decimal sums. Level 3: Connection and Application	Do students: • Use benchmark or friendly decimals to help with estimating sums? • Articulate their thinking?	(3 points each) Points: _____ of 6
Problem 2a–f Find the value. Level 1: Comprehension and Knowledge Level 3: Connection and Application	Do students: • Understand money values? • Connect money context to decimal values? • Find correct sums?	(2 points each) Points: _____ of 12
Problem 3 Label a number line in increments of 0.3. Level 1: Comprehension and Knowledge Level 2: Tool use	Do students: • Have an intuitive understanding of decimals? • Correctly place numbers on the number line?	Points: _____ of 4

TOTAL POINTS: _____ OF 22

Section C: Measuring With Metrics

SECTION C PLANNER

THE MATHEMATICS CONTENT AND GOALS

GOALS
Students will:
- Solidify their understanding of decimal representations in a context other than money.
- Develop enhanced understanding of the way the metric system builds upon common decimal representations.

> **LANGUAGE DEVELOPMENT**
> **Mathematical language in this section includes:**
> *Metric System:* A measurement system in which the units and subunits are related by multiples of 10.
> *Meter:* The standard unit of length in the metric system, abbreviated m.
> *Centimeter:* One hundredth (0.01) of a meter, abbreviated cm.
> *Decimeter:* One tenth (0.1) of a meter; 10 centimeters, abbreviated dm.
> *Millimeter:* One thousandth (0.001) of a meter; one tenth (0.1) of a centimeter, abbreviated mm.

PROBLEM SETS: OVERVIEW

A common and helpful representation of decimals lies within the metric system of measurement. Like money, the metric system is an excellent context in which to explore decimals because of its real-world applicability and utility. Students are likely to have had some experience with the metric system. This section deals with metric units of length.

Set 1 (pp. 9–11; problems 1–9)
There is only one set of problems in Section C. The first few problems introduce students to the metric ruler and metric units or length: meter, decimeter, centimeter, and millimeter. Help students make connections between the money used earlier (pennies, dimes, quarters, dollars) and the metric system. With some prompting, students should notice that the denominations of our monetary system are not entirely structured around multiples of ten. Both nickels and quarters are common coins in our system, but neither is based on multiples of ten. In contrast, units in the metric system are all based on multiples of ten: 10 millimeters = 1 centimeter, 10 centimeters = 1 decimeter, 10 decimeters = 1 meter.

PACING

The projected pacing for this unit is 2 class periods (based on a 45-minute period).

CONCEPT DEVELOPMENT (PAGES 9–11)

INTRODUCE THE CONCEPT

ASSESS STUDENTS' PRIOR KNOWLEDGE
Begin this section with a discussion of nonstandard units of measurement.

Ask:
How wide is your desk? Measure it without using a ruler. Use any tool you choose. Report the measurement in terms of the tool you have used.

Listen for:
Students may use books, paper clips, chalk, pencils, etc. As they report the measurements, such as 10 pieces of chalk, 7 pencils, 3 1/2 math books, write them on the board. Discuss the variety of lengths listed. Explain that there is a need to have standard units of measurement as a common frame of reference.

MODEL MATHEMATICAL THINKING
Tell the class that there are two common systems of measurement used in the United States. The one we are most familiar with is the customary system, in which the units of length are the inch, foot, yard, and mile. The other system, used throughout most of the rest of the world, is the metric system.

Display a meterstick, and tell students what it is. Point out the centimeter and millimeter marks.

Ask:
How can we express the relationship between the millimeter and the centimeter?

Talk Through the Thinking:
I can count how many millimeters there are in one centimeter. There are 10 millimeters in one centimeter. So 1 centimeter is 10 times as long as 1 millimeter. I can write this relationship as 10 millimeters = 1 centimeter. Write this on the board. If 10 millimeters = 1 centimeter, then 1 millimeter is one tenth of a centimeter. Because we use decimals when we are talking about metric measures, I can write this relationship as 1 millimeter = 0.1 centimeter. Write this on the board.

Ask:
What are two ways to express the relationship between the centimeter and the meter? Allow students to examine the meterstick closely.

Listen for:
- 100 centimeters = 1 meter
- 1 centimeter = 0.01 meter

LAUNCH THE PROBLEM SOLVING

Have students work individually to read page 9 and solve the problems at the end of the page. As they work, you may want to circulate and monitor their recorded answers. When students finish each problem, have them compare and discuss their answers with a partner. Then have each pair share their answers in a class discussion of the problem. Refer to the **Teacher Notes: Student Page 9** for more specific ideas about the problems on this page.

As students work and report their conclusions, focus on these issues:

Allow Processing Time – Allow students extra time to become familiar with the metric units of length introduced on the page.

Help Make Connections – Stress the connection between the metric system of measurement and decimals. You may need to point out that decimals, especially tenths and hundredths, can be visualized on the meterstick.

Facilitate Students' Thinking – Use work with the metric system to reinforce that the decimal point helps keep track of the location of the ones (wholes) and the smaller units that make up one whole.

Allow Waiting Time – When students struggle to explain their thinking, be sure to allow them ample time to organize their thoughts.

Encourage Language Development – For those teachers working with students who speak Spanish as a first language, the metric measurement context provides a great opportunity to make a Spanish language connection. All of the prefixes of the metric measuring system (centi-, deci-, and milli-) share the same root with the Spanish names for these root numbers. For example, in Spanish, the word for 100 is *cien*, and groups of 100 are referred to as *centenas*.

Likewise, the Spanish word for 10 is *diez*, and groups of tens are referred to as *decenas*. Finally, in Spanish, 1,000 is written as *mil*, providing another natural connection to the English words used to define metric units. Capitalize on this natural language overlap.

TEACHER NOTES: STUDENT PAGE 9

The problems on this page introduce students to the metric ruler. It will be most helpful for students if they have access to rulers and metersticks as they explore the problems in this section. *Teaching Strategy:* Be sure to stress the connections between this model as an illustration of decimals and the money contexts used earlier.

Problems 1–3: *Teaching Strategy:* Encourage students to actually count the smaller units that make up the larger units in these problems.

Student Page 9: Problems and Potential Answers

Section C: Measuring with Metrics — Set 1

The metric system gives us an easy way to measure and compare amounts and distances. It is based on decimal units in groups of ten. Let's learn about metric units of length. We'll start with the meter.

A **meter** is about the width of a doorway.

One meter is made up of 10 **decimeters**. Here is a picture of a metric ruler. One **decimeter (dm)** is equal to 10 **centimeters (cm)**.

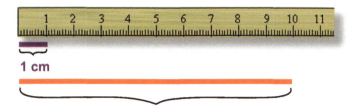

1 **decimeter** (1dm) = 10 **centimeters** (10 cm)

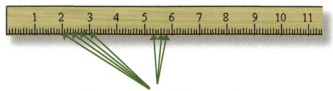

There are **10 millimeters** in each centimeter

If there are **10 millimeters** in each centimeter, and **10 centimeters** in each decimeter, and **10 decimeters** in each **meter**...

1. How many **millimeters** are in 1 **meter**? _____1,000_____

2. How many **centimeters** are in 1 **meter**? _____100_____

3. How many **millimeters** are in 1 **decimeter**? _____100_____

Book 7: *Decimals* 9

Decimals Teacher Edition 185

CONTINUE THE PROBLEM SOLVING

Have students work individually to solve the problems on page 10. As they work, you may want to circulate and monitor their recorded answers. When students finish each problem, have them compare and discuss their answers with a partner. Then have each pair share their answers in a class discussion of the problems. Refer to the **Teacher Notes: Student Page 10** for more specific ideas about the problems on this page.

As students work and report their conclusions, focus on these issues:

Validate Representations – Encourage students to compare and discuss their representations of millimeters, centimeters, etc., as fractions and as decimals. Have them determine whether all the representations are correct.

Help Make Connections – For problem 6a, you might suggest that students look for patterns in writing 0.1 and 0.01. They should apply this to expressing one thousandth as a decimal.

Facilitate Students' Thinking – Suggest that students use logical reasoning and their number sense to solve problem 7. You might ask them to think that if 1 cm = 0.1 m, then what would 2 cm equal?

Allow Waiting Time – When students struggle to explain their thinking, be sure to allow them ample time to organize their thoughts.

TEACHER NOTES: STUDENT PAGE 10

The problems on this page may be the most challenging in this book. *Teaching Strategy:* While it is possible to plug these fractions into a calculator to determine their decimal equivalents, be sure to engage students in discussion about the meaning of this operation (if you even allow calculators at all). These problems will allow you to assess your students' understanding of decimals. Be sure to have students share and discuss their understanding of each of these problems.

Problems 4–5: These problems review earlier material and set the stage for a similar process to be followed in the context of metric measurement.

Problem 6: Some of these problems will be more challenging then they first appear. The purpose of this problem is to give students practice representing a relationship between two related units as a fraction prior to finding its decimal equivalent. *Watch for:* For example, for problem 6a, students need to recognize that there are 1,000 millimeters in one meter. The representation will be a new fraction, 1/1,000, and consequently a new decimal 0.001 that has not yet been introduced in the book.

Problem 7: Encourage students to draw on their experience with problem 6 to solve this problem. *Watch for:* Students may wish first to represent these amounts as fractions prior to representing them as decimals. There are some challenging equivalents in these problems. *Teaching Strategy:* Be sure to encourage students to discuss their thinking and strategies, if not their uncertainties, in these problems.

Student Page 10: Problems and Potential Answers

Section C: Measuring with Metrics — Set 1

More on Metrics

We know that there are 100 centimeters in 1 meter. So, 1 centimeter is $\frac{1}{100}$ of a meter. This is like saying, "There are 100 pennies in 1 dollar. So, one penny is $\frac{1}{100}$ of a dollar."

4. How do we use a decimal to show that one penny is $\frac{1}{100}$ dollar?

   1 penny = __0.01__ a dollar

5. How do we use a decimal to show that one centimeter is $\frac{1}{100}$ of a meter?

   1 centimeter = __0.01__ meter

Here is what we know about the fractional relationships in the metric system:

> 1 millimeter = $\frac{1}{1000}$ meter
> 1 millimeter = $\frac{1}{100}$ decimeter
> 1 millimeter = $\frac{1}{10}$ centimeter
> 1 centimeter = $\frac{1}{100}$ meter
> 1 centimeter = $\frac{1}{10}$ decimeter
> 1 decimeter = $\frac{1}{10}$ meter

6. Write each fractional relationship in decimal form.

   a) 1 millimeter = __0.001__ meter
   b) 1 millimeter = __0.01__ decimeter
   c) 1 millimeter = __0.1__ centimeter
   d) 1 centimeter = __0.01__ meter
   e) 1 centimeter = __0.1__ decimeter
   f) 1 decimeter = __0.1__ meter

7. Rename each in decimal form.

   a) 2 cm = __0.02__ meter
   b) 2 cm = __0.2__ decimeter
   c) 2 mm = __0.2__ centimeter
   d) 4 dm = __0.4__ meter
   e) 50 cm = __0.5__ meters

CONTINUE THE PROBLEM SOLVING

Have students work individually to solve the problems on page 11. As they work, you may want to circulate and monitor their recorded answers. When students finish each problem, have them compare and discuss their answers with a partner. Then have each pair share their answers in a class discussion of the problem. Refer to the *Teacher Notes: Student Page 11* for more specific ideas about the problems on this page.

As students work and report their conclusions, focus on these issues:

Help Make Connections – Remind students that a ruler is a concrete representation of a number line, and that they can use a ruler to help them solve problems just as they use a written number line.

Look for Misconceptions – Be sure to emphasize that, for example, 0.5 of one unit is very different from 0.5 of another. You may also wish to point out that 0.95 of a smaller unit, such as a decimeter, is a shorter length than 0.5 of a larger unit, such as a meter.

Facilitate Students' Thinking – For problem 9, students may need to be reminded that each answer should be expressed as part of a meter.

TEACHER NOTES: STUDENT PAGE 11

The two problems on this page return to the familiar number-line construct used earlier in this book. Here, the number line is represented as a metric ruler. The connection between the number line and the ruler should be evident to students.

Problem 8: This problem is similar to others encountered earlier in this book. Students are once again given opportunities for practice in placing decimals on a number line. In this case, students use a scale drawing of a partial meterstick. *Teaching Strategy:* Be sure to confirm, or have students confirm, that this diagram is a scale drawing. These problems may be more difficult than they first appear. This is due primarily to the fact that they ask students to compare decimal representations of various units. For example, 0.5 decimeter is quite different than 0.5 meter. Students need to attend to both the decimal itself and to its meaning in context, as well as the units being compared. *Teaching Strategy:* This is a good opportunity to remind students that, like a fraction, a decimal only has meaning when they know the units that are being represented. If students finish this problem with that understanding firmly in place, they are well on their way to developing a rich understanding of decimals.

Problem 9: Using the meterstick again as the contextual backdrop, this problem provides opportunities for students to practice adding decimals. *Watch for:* Students should gradually move away from representing each decimal on the number line. Students should be aware that the answers to each of these problems should be expressed in terms of meters.

Student Page 11: Problems and Potential Answers

Section C: Measuring With Metrics Set 1

8. Imagine that this ruler is 1 meter long.

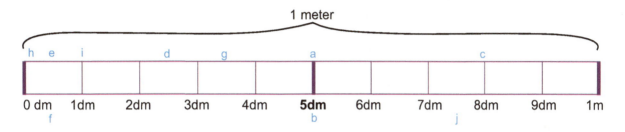

Label the ruler with the letter of each measurement below.

a) 50 cm   b) 0.5 meter   c) 0.8 meter   d) 0.25 meter   e) 0.5 decimeter   f) 0.05 meter

g) 3.5 decimeters   h) 0.01 meter   i) 0.1 meter   j) 75 centimeters

9. Suppose you could join two pieces of string together end to end. How long would the new length be? How long would a new length be if you cut off part of one piece of string? Use the ruler below to help you solve each problem. Then show each answer on the ruler. An example has been done for you.

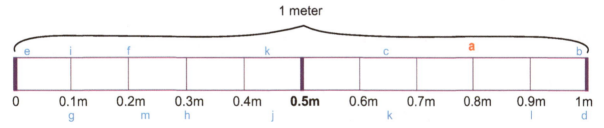

Example:

a) 0.3 meter + 0.5 meter = **0.8 meter**   h) 0.15 meter + 0.15 meter = 0.30 meter

b) 0.9 meter + 0.09 meter = 0.99 meter   i) 0.15 meter – 0.05 meter = 0.10 meter

c) 0.3 meter + 0.35 meter = 0.65 meter   j) 0.5 meter – 0.05 meter = 0.45 meter

d) 0.5 meter + 0.5 meter = 1 meter   k) 0.6 meter + 0.05 meter = 0.65 meter

e) 0.01 meter + 0.01 meter = 0.02 meter   l) 0.4 meter + 0.5 meter = 0.9 meter

f) 0.1 meter + 0.1 meter = 0.20 meter   m) 0.20 meter + 0.025 meter = 0.225 meter

g) 0.05 meter + 0.05 meter = 0.10 meter

Book 7: *Decimals* 11

SECTION C ASSESSMENT (PAGE 12)

LAUNCH THE ASSESSMENT

Have students turn to the Section C Assessment on page 12. An additional copy is found on page 117 of the Assessment Book. Have students work individually to solve the problems. As they work, circulate to be sure students understand what they need to do. You may find it helpful to read the directions before students begin, reminding students that a measurement in the right-hand column may be used more than once while other measurements may not be used at all. Refer to the **Teacher Notes: Assessment Problems for Section C** for more specific ideas about the problems on this page.

Evaluate Student Responses

Use the assessment rubric on page 116 of the Assessment Book (pictured on page 192 of the Teacher Edition) to evaluate student responses. The Assessment Book has some general suggestions for using the rubric that you may find helpful.

TEACHER NOTES: ASSESSMENT PROBLEMS FOR SECTION C

You may wish to encourage students to draw a representation of a meterstick and use it as they did for the problems on previous pages. The meterstick can function as a double number line, with one type of unit above and a different type of unit below.

Student Page 12: Problems and Potential Answers

Section C: Problems for Assessment

Match each measurement in Group 1 with its correct decimal form in Group 2. Answers in Group 2 may be used more than once.

Group 1   **Match**

a) 0.5 meter   2, 14

b) 25 centimeters   12, 8

c) 50 millimeters   10

d) 0.05 meter   10

e) 5 decimeters   2, 14

f) 0.01 meter   9

g) 1.5 meters   13

h) 0.002 meter   3

Group 2

1. 2.5 millimeters
2. 50 centimeters
3. 2 millimeters
4. 500 centimeters
5. 2 centimeters
6. 1 decimeter
7. 1.5 decimeters
8. 2.5 decimeters
9. 1 centimeter
10. 5 centimeters
11. 0.05 centimeter
12. 250 millimeters
13. 150 centimeters
14. 500 millimeters
15. 5 millimeters

Book 7: *Decimals*

SCORING GUIDE BOOK 7: DECIMALS

Section C Assessment
For Use With: Student Book Page 12

PROBLEM DESCRIPTION	SCORING: WHAT TO LOOK FOR	SCORE AND COMMENTS
Problem 1a–h Matching metric units. Level 3: Connection and Application	Do students: • Understand metric units of measurement? • Understand conversions between metric units (e.g., meters to centimeters)?	(1 point each) Points: _____ of 8

TOTAL POINTS: _____ OF 8

END-OF-BOOK ASSESSMENT (PAGE 13–14)

LAUNCH THE ASSESSMENT

Have students turn to the End-of-Book Assessment on page 13. An additional copy is found on page 119 of the Assessment Book. Have students work individually to solve the problems and write their explanations. As they work, circulate to be sure students understand what they need to do for each problem and that they are completing each part of the problem. For example, for problem 1, students must extend the number line in given increments and then determine how many groups of 0.5 there are in portions of the number line. You may find it helpful to read the directions for all the problems before students begin, discussing the types of responses they will need to make for each problem. Refer to the **Teacher Notes: End-of-Book Assessment, Student Page 13**, for more specific ideas about the problems on this page.

Evaluate Student Responses
Use the assessment rubric on page 118 of the Assessment Book (pictured on page 195 of the Teacher Edition) to evaluate student responses. The Assessment Book has some general suggestions for using the rubric that you may find helpful.

TEACHER NOTES: END-OF-BOOK ASSESSMENT, STUDENT PAGE 13

Problems 1–3: These problems review many of the concepts presented throughout this book. By providing students with opportunities to express their thinking and explain their strategies for these problems, you will get a much better sense of the richness of their conceptual understanding of decimals.

Decimals Teacher Edition

Student Page 13: Problems and Potential Answers

End-of-Book Assessment

1. Label increments of 0.5 on the number line. Extend your labels through 4.

   a) How many 0.5's are there in 2? __4__   How many 0.5's are there in 4? __8__

2. Label increments of 0.4 on the number line. Extend your labels through 4.0.

   a) How many 0.4's are there in 2? __5__   How many 0.4's are there in 4? __10__

3. Label increments of 0.2 on the number line. Extend your labels through 2.

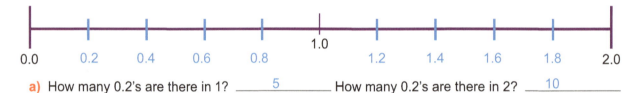

   a) How many 0.2's are there in 1? __5__   How many 0.2's are there in 2? __10__

4. After painting the outside of his house, Mr. Thomas tried to combine the contents of the paint cans. Each can holds 1 gallon of paint when full. Shade in the contents of each paint can and the total amount they would make when added together in the third paint can. Indicate each example in which the two amounts would overflow the third can.

   a)
   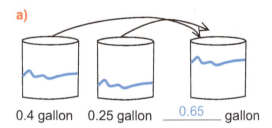
   0.4 gallon   0.25 gallon   __0.65__ gallon

   b)
   0.05 gallon   0.15 gallon   __0.20__ gallon

   c)
   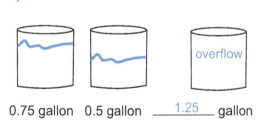
   0.75 gallon   0.5 gallon   __1.25__ gallon (overflow)

   d)
   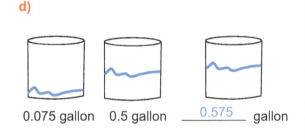
   0.075 gallon   0.5 gallon   __0.575__ gallon

Book 7: *Decimals*

SCORING GUIDE BOOK 7: UNDERSTANDING DECIMALS

End-of-Book Assessment
For Use With: Student Book Pages 13–14

PROBLEM DESCRIPTION	SCORING: WHAT TO LOOK FOR	SCORE AND COMMENTS
Problem 1 Label a number line in increments of 0.5. Level 1: Comprehension and Knowledge Level 2: Tool use	Do students: • Have an intuitive understanding of decimals? • Correctly place marks on the number line?	Points: _____ of 6
Problem 2 Label a number line in increments of 0.4. Level 1: Comprehension and Knowledge Level 2: Tool use	Do students: • Have an intuitive understanding of decimals? • Correctly place marks on the number line?	Points: _____ of 4
Problem 3 Label a number line in increments of 0.2. Level 1: Comprehension and Knowledge Level 2: Tool use	Do students: • Have an intuitive understanding of decimals? • Correctly place marks on the number line?	Points: _____ of 3
Problem 4a–d Combine amounts of paint as expressed in decimals. Determine whether amount exceeds 1 gallon. Level 2: Tool use Level 3: Connection and Application	Do students: • Have an intuitive understanding of decimals? • Use informal strategies for adding decimals? • Formally add decimals? • Compare quantities to 1.0 units?	(a) Points: _____ of 2 (b) Points: _____ of 2 (c) Points: _____ of 2 (d) Points: _____ of 2
Problem 5 Place four decimals on a number line. Use the number line to make a judgment in a real-world context. Level 3: Connection and Application Level 4: Synthesis and Evaluation	Do students: • Have an intuitive understanding of decimals? • Correctly place decimals on the number line? • Make sound judgment based on understanding of given data? • Articulate their thinking?	(Athlete #1) Points: _____ of 3 (Athlete #2) Points: _____ of 3 (Athlete #3) Points: _____ of 3 (Athlete #4) Points: _____ of 3

TOTAL POINTS: _____ of 33

CONTINUE THE ASSESSMENT

Have students turn to the End-of-Book Assessment on page 14. An additional copy is found on page 120 of the Assessment Book. Have students work individually to solve the problems and write their explanations. As they work, circulate to be sure students understand what they need to do for each problem and that they are completing each part of the problem. For example, for problem 5, students must label test results on the number line and then interpret the results of the tests. You may find it helpful to read through the directions for all the problems before students begin, discussing the types of responses they should make for each problem. Refer to the **Teacher Notes: End-of-Book Assessment, Student Page 14**, for more specific ideas about the problems on this page.

Evaluate Student Responses

Use the assessment rubric on page 118 of the Assessment Book (pictured on page 195 of the Teacher Edition) to evaluate student responses. The Assessment Book has some general suggestions for using the rubric that you may find helpful.

TEACHER NOTES: END-OF-BOOK ASSESSMENT, STUDENT PAGE 14

Problem 5: This culminating problem puts several of the concepts developed in this book in a real-world context. Students must label decimals on a number line and then interpret the meaning of these individual decimals. The evaluation component of these problems provides an additional opportunity for students to articulate their understanding of the relative magnitude of decimals. It is crucial that you spend some time introducing this problem to the students. Encourage students to discuss this problem to enrich their understanding of decimals. While the mathematics inherent in the problem is not different from what they have seen throughout the unit, the context may be new for some students. It is a good opportunity to highlight how decimals are often used in real-world contexts of significance.

Student Page 14: Problems and Potential Answers

End-of-Book Assessment

5. **Blood Test Readings.** Katie works in a laboratory that tests athletes' blood samples to make sure they are not using steroids. The test measures the number of foreign particles in the blood sample in parts per hundred (PPH) and then returns a score between 0 and 1. A sample is taken from each athlete on the first day of each month for three months in a row. Katie finds the sum of the three results and then looks at the scale below to determine whether or not there is anything suspicious that would require a second testing.

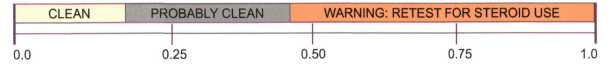

For each test result below, label the PPH scores on the scale. Then make an evaluation about whether or not the athlete should be retested. Write **Retest** or **No Retest**.

Athlete #1
PPH Scores: **0.10, 0.05, 0.22** ➡

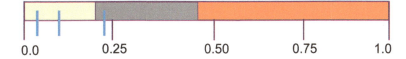

Evaluation: _No Retest_

Athlete #2
PPH Scores: **0.27, 0.39, 0.48** ➡

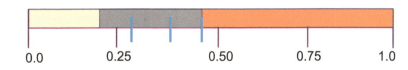

Evaluation: _Retest_

Athlete #3
PPH Scores: **0.82, 0.51, 0.15** ➡

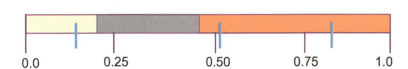

Evaluation: _Retest_

Athlete #4
PPH Scores: **0.48, 0.35, 0.44** ➡

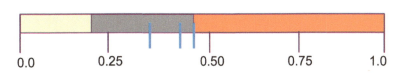

Evaluation: _Retest_

Book 8:
Fractions, Decimals, Percents

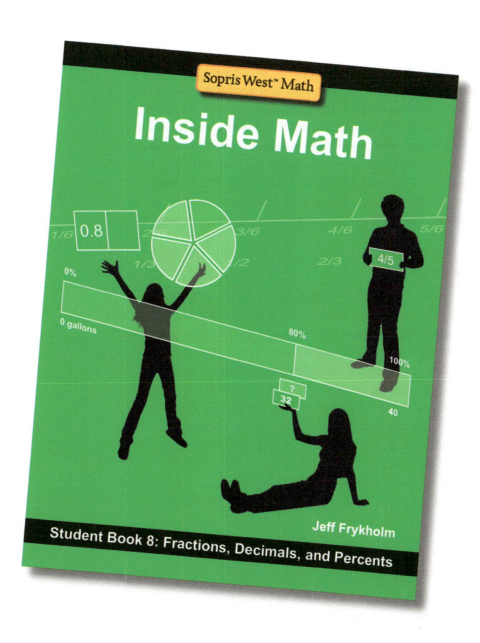

Book Eight Overview: Fractions, Decimals, Percents

Introduction

This is the final book in a series of eight that are geared toward helping middle-grades learners acquire both facility with, and understanding of, the basic mathematical procedures and concepts that lay the groundwork for more advanced mathematical study. In particular, this series cultivates understanding of a number of mathematical tools that children learn to use with facility in various mathematical and real-world contexts.

Book Focus

Book 8 engages students in contexts in which the implicit connections among decimals, fractions, and percents are made explicit. The development of students' understanding of percents is the priority for the book, which seeks to develop this understanding through the use of familiar tools and contexts seen in the earlier books on fractions and decimals. One of the driving forces for developing understanding of percent is the ratio table, used frequently throughout this series. Double number bars are also used quite frequently throughout the book as students become familiar with visual representations of percents and their meanings relative to familiar fractional and decimal amounts. Throughout the book, familiar contexts, such as tipping, sale prices and discounts, percent of versus percent off, are used to enhance students' understanding of percents.

How To Use This Book

There are two primary sections to each lesson in this book: an introductory discussion of the concept that is being introduced and a segment where students work problems with an accompanying teacher resource guide. Throughout the resource guide, you will be provided with insights into the mathematical content of each section of the book, pedagogical ideas to enhance teaching and learning, samples of anticipated student work, insights about student thinking related to the topics at hand, and ideas about assessment. This program is meant to be flexible and relies on the craft and knowledge of the teachers who will use it. To that end, the resource materials that accompany this text are not intended to be used as a script. Instead, the intent of this program is that teachers will apply their knowledge of students, their own experiences with some of these mathematical tools, and their intuition about teaching to make this program as effective as possible.

Models Of Implementation

This program has been designed to be as flexible as possible. While this series of books may be used as the primary curriculum for the classroom, it was not designed as the full curriculum for any given grade level. Rather, it was crafted to support you as you help students understand the number operations and concepts that precede more advanced work in algebra. You may therefore choose to use this program either as a guide for whole-class explorations or as the text for smaller, pull-out groups of students. In both cases, it is important to note that this program is designed on the principle that students learn mathematics in large measure through interactions with one another. Throughout the books, you will find numerous questions that ask students to explain their thinking. These occasions should not be taken lightly. It is in the sharing and comparing of solution strategies that students begin to build a firm foundation of understanding. The social dynamic of learning mathematics is important to recognize. Participation in mathematical discourse may be the most powerful impetus for learning mathematics available to young learners, and you should take advantage of every opportunity to encourage students to talk about their mathematical thinking and processes. Given a commitment to this principle, this program is likely to be most successful when students are progressing through the problems with their peers.

Addressing Issues of Language

There is no question that one of the greatest challenges facing teachers today is to make instruction relevant and accessible for second language learners. *Inside Math* has been written with this concern in mind. Careful consideration was given to the language that appears in directions, contextually based problems, and other sections of the book where text is necessary. When possible, for example, we have limited new vocabulary to only what is essential to the concepts being presented, and we revisit new vocabulary words and concepts repeatedly throughout the text. To assist you in making instruction accessible for English language learners, as well as other students for whom reading presents particular challenges, several supporting features were added to the teacher's edition. First, within the section planner that introduces each new major mathematical concept contained in the book, there is a heading that reads: *Language Development.* In this section of the overview, new vocabulary words are introduced and defined. Later in the text, when these words and concepts are introduced in a specific lesson, the teacher notes include additional information about pertinent language considerations and vocabulary. These notes appear as Encouraging Language Development under the Concept Development and Continue the Problem Solving headings.

Explaining Thinking

Throughout this series, and specifically in this book, students will be instructed to explain their thinking. The ability to articulate mathematical ideas and solution strategies is a feature of mathematics education that continues to grow in its importance. We see numerous examples in state, national, and international achievement tests in which answers alone are not enough. Students must also be able to express their thought processes, give rationale for answers, and articulate steps in any given strategy. As noted, in this book there are numerous opportunities for students to do likewise.

As this is often a new and challenging task for students, it is important for you to be able to model the process of making thinking explicit. At the beginning of each section in the book, there are suggestions for ways to introduce the content at hand, many of which are suitable for you to illustrate what it means to explain thinking in an intelligible way. Be aware of both the importance of this feature of the program, as well as the challenge it might provide students as they practice this skill for what might be the first time.

Assessment

At the conclusion of each section, you will find several problems that may be used for formative assessments. These problems review the key concepts discussed in the section. At the end of the book you will find additional assessment problems that cover the content of the entire book. These problems may be used as a cumulative assessment of student understanding of the key concepts in the book. The teachers' guide contains insights as to how the assessment problems might best be used and what they are intended to measure.

Assessment rubrics and scoring guides for every assessment may be found in Assessment Teacher Edition. Detailed instructions regarding assessment in general, and the use of the program rubrics in particular, are included in the introduction of Assessment Teacher Edition.

Professional Background

Overview

Both national and international mathematics tests, as well as dozens of other research studies, have revealed repeatedly that students in the United States have great difficulty with problems involving percents. On a recent national test (NAEP), for example, only about a third of our eighth-grade students could determine the final amount in a context that asked them to add a given percent of a number to an existing number. One of the big misconceptions so commonly seen in classrooms today was again revealed in this NAEP item. Many students incorrectly assume that a percent increase (for example, 10%) means they should add the number of the percent (10) to the quantity in question. As an example, if a teenager made $250 per month doing yard work and she decided to try to increase that amount by 10%, a majority of students will simply add $10 to the $250 for a total of $260. This is obviously not correct, because 10% of $250 is $25. Mistaking the percentage for raw data is one of several common misconceptions students bring to work with percents.

Given this misconception and other challenges having to do with the topic of percents, it is all the more important to reinforce conceptual understanding of percent by linking it to models and concepts that young learners already know. So in this book you will find percents linked to fractions and decimals through the use of appropriate models. Referring back to earlier work in this text series on ratios and proportions, you will also find examples that lead students to use proportional reasoning to develop percent sense and to compute with percents. Hence, the use of double number bars and ratio tables is essential, and will be highlighted in this book.

The Big Ideas

Big Idea #1: Connections Percents are intimately connected to fractions and decimals.

Big Idea #2: Representing the Hundredths Place Percents are simply decimals represented by the hundredths place value. The term percent can be thought of as another name for hundredths. Percent can be thought of as out of 100. Percents can be understood as another way to represent fractions with a denominator of 100 and decimals that are represented by tenths and hundredths.

Big Idea #3: Fractions, Decimals, and Percents Many models that were helpful in student understanding of fractions and decimals will be helpful for understanding percents. That should come as no great surprise, given the natural connections between all three number types. In particular, the double number line, or number bar, becomes very important in helping students visualize percents along a continuum from 0% to 100%. When you require students to use visual models, you help students develop a richer sense of percents.

Big Idea #4: Using Percent Models The use of models will allow students to quickly adopt mental strategies that are quite useful and efficient when working with percents. The most common example of this use of mental math is in the context of calculating a tip at a restaurant. Students learn that moving the decimal point is based on the 10-to-1 relationship discussed in Book 7. Once students learn how to determine 10% of any given amount, students can then double to find 20%. Then they can find the halfway point between 10% and 20% if they want to find the value of a 15% tip. The use of mental math associated with basic percent understandings is important to develop and comes quickly with the appropriate scaffolding.

Teaching Ideas

The book begins by addressing the common but understandable misconception that the use of percents implies that there were 100 data points in the original data sample. For example, earning a score of 70% on a test leads many students to believe that the person must have correctly answered 70 out of 100 questions. While that may very well be true, it is not necessarily the case. The test may have had 50 questions, and the student may have answered 35 of them correctly. As noted above, the use of ratio tables (proportional reasoning) can be very effective in these kinds of contexts, and it is toward this end that the first section of problems in the book is devoted.

For example, if a teacher decided that the cutoff for an A on an exam was 90%, how could we find how many problems would need to be done correctly to earn an A on a test with 80 problems? We can use proportional reasoning and a ratio table to do so. We might start by thinking that 90% means 90 out of 100. We can divide both 90 and 100 by 10, and by doing so find that 9 out of 10 is 90% correct. If 9 out of 10 is 90%, then, preserving the ratio, we can multiply the numbers in both the top and bottom rows by 8 (8 × 10 = 80 test items) to determine that 72 (9 × 8 = 72) correct answers would be the equivalent of an A, or 90%, on an 80-item test.

90	9	**72**	
100	10	80	

Another key concept in studying percents is the difference between percent of and percent off. Though semantically there appears to be very little difference here, there is a great conceptual difference as these two concepts relate to percents. A second model, one that should be familiar to students who have studied the concepts developed in the fraction and decimal books in this series, is used to illuminate this idea. That model is the double number line, or number bar, and builds on student understanding of fractional parts of a whole.

Consider the following problem:

A bathtub holds 20 gallons of water. Label the bar below to indicate how much water is in the tub if it is 25% full, 50% full, and 75% full.

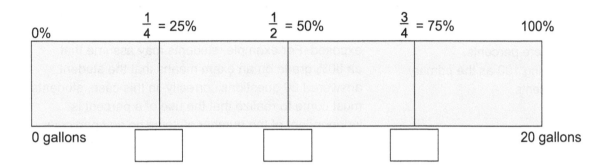

In this problem, students are presented with a double number line or number bar that includes benchmark percents and corresponding fractions on one scale and a range of 0 to 20 gallons on the other. Students can use their intuitive understandings of fractions or decimals to determine that ½ = 50%, and ½ of 20 gallons is 10 gallons. Therefore, 50% of 20 gallons must be the same as ½ of 20 gallons, or 10 gallons. As the problems become more challenging, students are pressed to develop even more complex number bars that can incorporate both fractions and decimals directly connected to the percents under investigation.

Throughout the remainder of the book, students are encouraged to use both of these models to solve problems with contexts that require the use and understanding of percents. As the book gradually moves to include more complex contexts and less familiar percents, you will have ample opportunity to observe how your students are progressing. As you do so, remember that realistic problem contexts offer the greatest opportunity for students to develop conceptual and procedural understanding of percents, and these contexts will give you the best window into the thinking and strategy use of your individual students.

Section A: What is a Percent?

SECTION A PLANNER

THE MATHEMATICS CONTENT AND GOALS

GOALS
Students will:
- Examine different representations of 80%.
- Use simple ratios to compare percents.
- Recognize the value of using 100 as the primary base for working with percents.

> **LANGUAGE DEVELOPMENT**
> **Mathematical language in this section includes:**
> *Percent (%):* A term that indicates hundredths; 32% means 0.32 or 32/100.
> *Percentage:* Percentage is often incorrectly used as a synonym for percent. In technical terms, a percentage is the result obtained by multiplying a quantity by a percent.
> *Proportion:* An equation stating that two ratios are equal.

PACING

The projected pacing for this unit is 1 class period (based on a 45-minute period).

PROBLEM SETS: OVERVIEW

In this brief introductory section, percent is presented to students through two contexts: an 80% grade on an exam, and 80% of the trees in a forest have burned in a forest fire. Through these two contexts, misconceptions students commonly hold about percents are exposed. For example, students may assume that an 80% grade on an exam means that the student answered 80 questions correctly. In this case, students must come to realize that the use of a percent is independent of the number of items on any particular exam. That is, in fact, why percent is so useful. It provides a meaningful measurement without having to consider each of the individual data points. In this first section, both double number bars and ratio tables are reintroduced, this time as tools for understanding percents.

Set 1 (pp. 1–2; problems 1–2)
There is only one set of problems in Section A. This section begins by examining two contexts in which the use of 80% is both familiar and relevant. For problems 1–2, students use proportional reasoning to discover that any percent can be represented by any number of equivalent ratios. For example, some ways to represent 80% are 4 out of 5, 8 out of 10, and 80 out of 100.

CONCEPT DEVELOPMENT (Pages 1–2)

INTRODUCE THE CONCEPT

ASSESS STUDENTS' PRIOR KNOWLEDGE

This section introduces students to percent (%) as a number that gives information about the relative size of one subset of items or data in relation to the entire set considered.

Write on the board: 1 cup of cereal provides 100% of your daily requirement of vitamin C. Explain that this information was on the back of a cereal box.

Ask:
What does this information mean? What percent of your daily vitamin requirement would you get if you ate 1/2 cup of the cereal? 3/4 cup? How did you find these percents?

Listen for:
Students should recognize that 100% represents the entire amount of the daily vitamin requirements. Their explanations for finding the percents in the 1/2 and 3/4 cup may vary but should reflect proportional thinking.
- You would get 50% of your daily vitamin requirement if you ate 1/2 cup.
- You would get 75% of your daily vitamin requirement if you ate 3/4 cup.
- I found 1/2 of 100% to get 50%. I found 3/4 of 100% to get 75%.

MODEL MATHEMATICAL THINKING

Ask:
Tamika needs to score 80% on the next test to get a B in math. How many correct answers does she need if the test has 100 problems? How many does she need if the test has 50 problems?
Draw this number bar on the board:

Talk Through the Thinking:
This bar represents percents, which are written above it, and the possible number of problems on Tamika's test. You can see that 100% of the bar represents 100 problems. How many problems would 80% represent? That's easy. 80% represents 80 problems. Tamika would need 80 correct answers on a test that has 100 problems in order to get a score of 80%. Erase the 100 at the bottom right of the number bar, and replace it with 50. *Now 100% represents 50 problems, and the 80% mark is in the same position as it was when there were 100 problems. How can I find 80% of 50? Well, I know that 50 is half of 100. So, I can find half of 80, the correct answers needed on a 100-problem test. Half of 80 is 40. Tamika would need 40 correct answers on a test that has 50 problems to get a score of 80%.*

Ask:
How many correct answers would Timothy need if he wanted to score 90% on a 100-problem test? On a 50-problem test? How did you find out?

Listen for:
Students should use proportional reasoning and generally follow your modeling of the thinking.
- Timothy would need 90 correct answers to score 90% on a 100-problem test.
- Timothy would need 45 correct answers to score 90% on a 50-problem test.

LAUNCH THE PROBLEM SOLVING

Have students read through page 1 on their own. When they finish, have them discuss the information on the page with a partner. Then have each pair share their insights and conclusions in a class discussion of the page. Refer to the discussion on **Percent and Proportional Reasoning** for more specific ideas about the problems on this page.

As students work and report their conclusions, focus on these issues:

Allow Processing Time – Allow students ample time to assimilate the information on the page. Encourage them to ask questions and to share their insights with their peers.

Look for Misconceptions – Be on the alert for students who mistakenly assume that all percents refer to a whole with a value of 100, or that the given percent refers to the whole. For example, a score of 75% on a test does not mean that there were 75 questions on the test.

Help Make Connections – Help students understand that percents are another way of representing quantities or numbers that can also be represented by decimals and fractions with a denominator of 100.

Allow Waiting Time – When students struggle to explain their thinking, be sure to allow them at least 20 seconds to organize their thoughts. (This may seem like a long time.)

Encourage Language Development – It is important early in this book to introduce and use appropriate mathematical language, in this case using words such as percent, percentage, and proportion.

Student Page 1: Problems and Potential Answers

Section A: What Is a Percent? Set 1

The key to understanding percent is in the word itself. <u>Percent</u> means *per hundred*, or *out of 100*. The percent symbol looks like this: %. Let's learn what that symbol means.

The statements below are different. But each statement uses a percent, in this case, 80%. What does 80% mean in each statement?

Statement #1: I got an 80% on the English exam.

Statement #2: The forest fire burned 80% of the trees in the national forest.

Statement #1: I got an 80% on the English exam.

- Does this mean that there were 80 questions on the exam? Not necessarily. There <u>may</u> have been 80 questions, but we don't know for sure.

- Did the student answer 80 questions correctly? Not necessarily. The student <u>may</u> have answered 80 questions correctly, but we don't know the exact number of questions on the exam, or how many were answered correctly.

Here is what the percent tells us in this statement: **IF** there had been 100 questions on the exam, the student would have answered 80 of them correctly.

Statement #2: The forest fire burned 80% of the trees in the national forest.

Does this mean that 80 trees in the national forest were burned? No. There were probably hundreds or thousands of trees that were burned.

Here is what the percent tells us in Statement #2. **IF** there had been only 100 trees in the forest, 80 would have been burned.

In the examples above, we do not know the actual number of questions answered correctly or the actual number of trees that were burned. But, we do know something about the proportion of questions answered correctly and the proportion of trees that were burned.

Now <u>there might have been</u> 100 questions, and <u>there might have been</u> 100 trees. But a percent does not tell us the actual numbers. A percent is a way to generalize the data to give us a rough idea of what the actual numbers mean. Sometimes a picture helps. Here is a representation of 80%. Think of the yellow part of the bar as 80 out of 100.

80 percent

100 percent

Book 8: *Fractions, Decimals, Percents*   1

Percent and Proportional Reasoning

Although there are no problems on page 1, the information on the page is a very important introduction to the concepts and models used in this book. The most important concept is that a percent is a measurement that can be useful in comparing sets of different sizes.

For example, what if a student wanted to know which was the better score on two quizzes, 21 correct answers out of 25, or 43 correct answers out of 50? One way to help students understand percents is to encourage them to ask themselves, "What if there had been 100… (questions, items, etc.)?" The key to having students understand percents is to help them recognize that they can use proportional reasoning (the work with ratio tables in previous books will greatly aid in this process) to weight the two sets of data equally. Students can ask, "What if there had been 100 questions, and the student taking the exam had continued to perform at exactly the same rate?" This is a good problem context to use to supplement the other introductory ideas for this first lesson.

21 correct out of 25… What if it had been out of 100?

We multiply 4 × 25 to get 100. So we multiply 4 × 21 as well.

4 × 21 = 84. So 21 correct out of 25 has the same value as 84 correct out of 100.

43 correct out of 50… What if it had been out of 100?

We multiply 2 × 50 to get 100. So we multiply 2 × 43 as well.

2 × 43 = 86. So 43 correct out of 50 has the same value as 86 correct out of 100.

Comparing the two, we see that 84 out of 100 (84%) is less than 86 out of 100 (86%), so the better score is 43 correct answers out of 50.

It is this kind of reasoning that students must engage in to understand percents and how they help us compare data sets that might otherwise look quite different from one another.

Be sure to call attention to the use of a double number bar as a way to represent percents.

On the Lookout for Misconceptions

Many students wrongly assume that if a particular statistic is represented as a percent (per hundred), it means that there were exactly 100 items, questions, objects, etc. Students will also make the mistake that the given percent, such as 80%, means that there were that number of items (80) under examination. So, when some students see that they got a 40% on an exam, they may think that they got only 40 problems correct. The discussion on page 1 is designed to help students understand that they could get 40% on a quiz that had only 10 problems.

Help students immediately recognize that percents are used to compare sets of different sizes. Percents allow us to examine various proportions of subsets within the whole group.

CONTINUE THE PROBLEM SOLVING

Have students work individually to solve the problems on page 2. As they work, you may want to circulate and monitor their recorded answers. When students finish each problem, have them compare and discuss their answers with a partner. Then have each pair share their answers in a class discussion of the problem. Refer to the **Teacher Notes: Student Page 2** for more specific ideas about each of the problems.

As students work and report their conclusions, focus on these issues:

Help Make Connections – Remind students of the work with ratio tables they have done earlier. Encourage them to remember the kinds of strategies they used to complete the tables (e.g., doubling, and halving).

Allow Processing Time – Allow students enough time to reacquaint themselves with ratio tables and the equal ratios contained within them.

Facilitate Students' Thinking – Encourage students to look for patterns in the ratio tables to help them develop strategies for completing them.

Allow Waiting Time – When students struggle to explain their thinking, be sure to allow them ample time to organize their thoughts.

TEACHER NOTES: STUDENT PAGE 2

Problem 1: The number bar was introduced on the previous page as a model for representing percents. For problem 1 on this page, the ratio table is reintroduced and will be a significant tool throughout the rest of the book. *Teaching Strategy:* Be sure to discuss the process involved in working through the ratio table.

As the context suggests, the ratio table is used to illustrate that there are many ratios of burned to live trees that can be expressed as 80%: 8 out of 10, 16 out of 20, and so on. *Teaching Strategy:* Help students understand that the ratio of 80% (80 per 100) is preserved in both the drawings and the ratios in the table. Be sure to allow students time to share the patterns they recognize in the table as a way to review the use of ratio tables.

Problem 2: The intent of this ratio table is to help students begin to understand that by using percents, they are anticipating the idea of per hundred. This problem also helps students recall the steps needed to complete a ratio table. *Teaching Strategy:* Be sure to illustrate or discuss each step of the ratio table. Also, be sure to emphasize the goal: to be able to express any ratio as an equivalent fraction that has 100 as the denominator. Time spent on this problem will pay dividends because the use of ratio tables will become a vital tool for students throughout the book.

Student Page 2: Problems and Potential Answers

Section A: What Is a Percent?   Set 1

More on Percents

Let's go back to the forest fire. We have no idea how many trees were in the forest. But regardless of the actual number of trees, 80% means the same thing. It illustrates a ratio between burned trees and total trees. Look at the three possibilities in the chart below.

	Burned Trees: 80%	Live Trees: 20%
Possibility 1	△△△△△△△△	△ △
Possibility 2	△△△△△△△△△△△△△△△△	△ △ △ △
Possibility 3	△△△△△△△△△△△△△△△△△△△△△△△△△△△△△△△△	△ △ △ △ △ △ △ △

1. Count the trees for each possibility above. Then fill in the table below. The first row has been started for you.

	Burned	Live	Total Trees
Possibility 1	8	2	10
Possibility 2	16	4	20
Possibility 3	32	8	40

What do you notice about the numbers in this table? Describe any patterns you see. _____
The ratios (e.g., burned to live, live to total, etc.) among the cases are the same. The numbers in each row are double the above row. Descriptions of patterns will vary.

2. Below is a ratio table that contains some of the same data in a slightly different form. Use the data you have already found to complete the ratio table. Some hints have been given to help you get started.

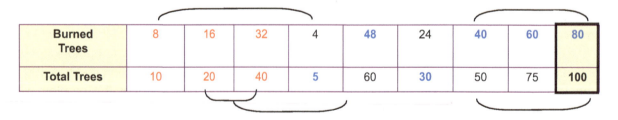

Burned Trees	8	16	32	4	48	24	40	60	80
Total Trees	10	20	40	5	60	30	50	75	100

Why has the last box been highlighted? What does this ratio table illustrate? _____
The last box has been highlighted to show how many trees would have burned if there were 100 trees in the forest. The ratio table illustrates 80% of different numbers of total trees.

2   Book 8: *Fractions, Decimals, Percents*

Section B: Ratio Tables and Percents

SECTION B PLANNER

THE MATHEMATICS CONTENT AND GOALS

GOALS
Students will:
- Use ratio tables effectively to compare equivalent fractions.
- Use ratio tables to express ratios in the form of percents.
- Use ratio tables to work backwards. Starting with a percentage, determine the original raw data.

> **LANGUAGE DEVELOPMENT**
> **Mathematical language in this section includes:**
> *Percent of (%):* In context, we often refer to the idea of a percent by asking the percent of a given amount or quantity. This refers specifically to the product of the percent and the original amount in the whole set.
> *Ratio Table:* A collection of equivalent ratios organized in a table.

PACING

The projected pacing for this unit is 3 class periods (based on a 45-minute period).

PROBLEM SETS: OVERVIEW

The goal of this section is to help students use ratio tables to understand the ways that percents allow us to compare sets of different sizes. What this means is that percents help students compare different sets of data by normalizing the data to 100. For example, as described earlier, the ratio 21 out of 25 can be expressed as a percent (84%) so that it can be more easily compared to a different ratio, 43 out of 50 (86%).

The ratio table becomes a very valuable tool in this process. Using ratio tables, the exercises in this section will help students determine the percent equivalent to a given ratio. Ratio tables will also help students find the whole when the percent is known. For example, if students know a score of 75% on a test and know that there were 80 problems on the test in all, students can use ratio tables to work backwards and find that 60 out of 80 is the same as 75%.

Set 1 (p. 3; problems 1–3)
These problems help students review the mechanics of using ratio tables.

Set 2 (pp. 4–7; problems 1–7)
The problems on pages 4–7 help students understand how ratio tables can be used to express a ratio in terms of 100, and, consequently, as a percent. On these pages are also problems that require students to work by starting with a percentage and then working backwards to the initial (equivalent) ratios.

CONCEPT DEVELOPMENT (PAGES 3–7)

INTRODUCE THE CONCEPT

ASSESS STUDENTS' PRIOR KNOWLEDGE

Draw this ratio table on the board (Answers are in blue print):

2	4	6	8	**10**
20	40	60	**80**	**100**

Ask:
What number belongs in the last cell in the top row? What numbers belong in the last two cells in the bottom row? How did you find these answers?

Listen for:
Students should recognize that the drawing is of a ratio table and that the ratios in each column are all equivalent. Some students may notice that as the numbers in the top row increase by 2, the numbers in the bottom row increase by 20.
- The number in the last cell in the top row is 10.
- 80 and 100 are the numbers in the last two cells in the bottom row.

MODEL MATHEMATICAL THINKING

Draw these ratio tables on the board:

1	2	3	5
20	40	60	100

6	30	60
10	50	100

3	15	30	60	75
4	20	40	80	100

Ask:
What do all three tables have in common? How can I get from one ratio to the next in the first ratio table?

Talk Through the Thinking:
One thing all three have in common is that the last number in the bottom row of each table is 100. Another thing the tables have in common is that in each table, all the ratios are equivalent. Let's look at the first ratio table. I know that all the ratios are equivalent because each ratio can be expressed in simplest form as 1/20. Now let's find out how to get from one ratio to the next. I can get from 1 to 2 by doubling 1, and I can get from 20 to 40 by doubling 20. If I add another 1 to 2, I get 3. If I add another 20 to 40, I get 60. Since 5 is the sum of 2 and 3, I can get the bottom number by adding the numbers in the bottom row below 2 and 3. 40 + 60 = 100. Ratio tables like these will help you in working with percents. That is because with percents, we always want to represent data as a ratio with a denominator of 100.

Ask:
How can you get from one ratio to another in the second table? How can you do this in the third table?

Listen for:
Students to work through the process in a way similar to the method you used in talking through the thinking.

LAUNCH THE PROBLEM SOLVING

Have students work individually to solve the problems on page 3. As they work, you may want to circulate and monitor their recorded answers. When students finish each problem, have them compare and discuss their answers with a partner. Then have each pair share their answers in a class discussion of the problem. Refer to the **Teacher Notes: Student Page 3** for more specific ideas about each problem on the page.

As students work and report their conclusions, focus on these issues:

Validate Alternate Strategies – When several students use different strategies to complete the ratio tables, have the class discuss whether all the strategies are valid.

Validate Representations – Have students share their completed ratio tables with the class. Ask them to analyze whether the tables are correct.

Help Make Connections – You may need to remind some students that ratio tables are not a new tool and that they can work with these ratio tables in the same way they used ratio tables earlier in the textbook series.

Allow Waiting Time – When students struggle to explain their thinking, be sure to allow them ample time to organize their thoughts.

Student Page 3: Problems and Potential Answers

Section B: Ratio Tables and Percents — Set 1

On the last page we used a ratio table to learn something about 80%. We can use ratio tables to help us understand connections among fractions, decimals, and percents.

As a quick review, complete each ratio table.

1. There are 12 oranges in each crate. Without using the shaded boxes, find how many oranges are in 4 crates, 6 crates, and 9 crates. Some of the ratio table has already been completed for you. (Remember, do not use the shaded boxes.)

Crates	0	1		4	5	6		9	10
Oranges	0	12		48	60	72		108	120

2. Use the ratio tables below. Find how many oranges there are in 14 crates, 24 crates, and 30 crates.

   a) 14 crates

Crates	0	1	10	5	15	14				
Oranges	0	12	120	60	180	168				

   b) 24 crates

Crates	0	1	10	20	5	25	24			
Oranges	0	12	120	240	60	300	288			

   c) 30 crates

Crates	0	1	10	20	30					
Oranges	0	12	120	240	360					

3. The owner of a store ordered 320 oranges. How many crates did it take to ship all those oranges? __27 crates__

Crates	1	30	3	27						
Oranges	12	360	36	324						

Book 8: *Fractions, Decimals, Percents*   3

TEACHER NOTES: STUDENT PAGE 3

The problems on this page provide practice for students as they recall the ways in which ratio tables are developed and used. These problems are very similar to others students have worked with in previous books. *Watch for:* It is imperative for students to recognize that there are often many ways to complete a ratio table successfully. *Teaching Strategy:* Be sure to encourage students to share their solution strategies. Call attention to those ratios that lend themselves to expressing a relationship in terms of a percent.

For example, if a student finds that a bottom number in the ratio table is 10, 25 or 50, remind them that it is relatively easy to compute the related percent:

10 → multiply the top and bottom numbers by 10
25 → multiply the top and bottom numbers by 4
50 → double the top and the bottom numbers

CONTINUE THE PROBLEM SOLVING

Have students work individually to solve the problems on page 4. As they work, circulate and monitor their answers. As students finish each problem, have them discuss their answers with a partner. Then have each pair share their answers in a class discussion. Refer to the **Teacher Notes: Student Page 4** for more specific ideas about each problem on the page.

As students work and report their conclusions, focus on these issues:

Validate Representations – Have students share their ratio tables for problem 1 with the class. Encourage them to discuss whether the ratio tables correctly represent the given information.

Validate Alternate Strategies – Ask students to describe the strategies they used to determine each percent. Have the class discuss whether these strategies lead to correct solutions.

Facilitate Students' Thinking – You may need to remind some students that they have had previous success in using ratio tables and suggest they use the same kind of thinking to solve these problems.

TEACHER NOTES: STUDENT PAGE 4

Problem 1: This problem gives students multiple opportunities to use ratio tables to find the percents for test scores. The test mentioned on the page consists of 40 problems. As the example below illustrates, the key to solving these problems is to use ratio-table strategies to find equivalent ratios that lead to a final ratio with a denominator of 100. Once students get to 100 in the bottom row, they will have found the percent that reflects the number of correct answers (in the numerator in the upper row).

Teaching Strategy: You may need to walk students through the example provided below to illustrate fruitful strategies.

1. Start with the given ratio: 32/40.

Score for Kevin	32			
	40			

2. We are trying to get the denominator to a number that is a factor of 100. One strategy we can use is to begin by dividing both the top and bottom rows by 2. One half of 32 is 16, and one half of 40 is 20.

Score for Kevin	32	16		
	40	20		

3. Following this same procedure, we can divide both 16 and 20 by two, leading to the third column in the ratio table.

Score for Kevin	32	16	8	
	40	20	10	

4. At this point, the denominator, 10, can easily be multiplied to result in a product of 100. 10 × 10 = 100. To preserve the equal ratios we must also multiply the number in the top row by 10. 8 × 10 = 80. So we end up with the final ratio, 80/100, which is equal to 80%.

× 10

Score for Kevin	32	16	8	80
	40	20	10	100

× 10

You may wish to work through one more strategy to ensure that students understand the goals of this exercise. For example, some students may prefer to divide 32 and 40 by 4 and then multiply by 10. There are many ways to arrive at a column with 100 in the bottom cell.

Fractions, Decimals, Percents *Teacher Edition*

Student Page 4: Problems and Potential Answers

Section B: Ratio Tables and Percents — Set 2

Ratio tables can be used to calculate percents. All the fractions in the ratio table below represent the 80% relationship: 8 out of 10 is 80%, 32 out of 40 is 80%, and 24 out of 30 is 80%, and so on.

Burned Trees	8	16	32	4	48	24	40	60	80
Total Trees	10	20	40	5	60	30	50	75	100

So, ratio tables can be used to calculate any percent as long as we know how many items we are considering and how many items there are in all.

1. <u>Test Scores</u> Mr. Salinas gives a science test every Friday. This week, if a student answered all the questions correctly, he or she would earn 40 points. What percent did each of the following students get on the test? Use ratio tables to help you find the percents. There are lots of ways to do them. An example has been done for you.

Name	Raw Score (out of 40)	Percent
Kevin	32	80
Michelle	18	45
Zach	22	55
Trina	40	100
Maria	39	97.5
Robby	24	60

× 10

Score for Kevin	32	16	8	80
Percent	40	20	10	100

× 10

Ratio tables will vary. Check students' work.

Score for Michelle							
Percent							

Score for Zach							
Percent							

Score for Trina							
Percent							

Score for Maria							
Percent							

Score for Robby							
Percent							

4   Book 8: *Fractions, Decimals, Percents*

CONTINUE THE PROBLEM SOLVING

Have students work individually to solve the problems on page 5. As they work, you may want to circulate and monitor their recorded answers. When students finish each problem, have them compare and discuss their answers with a partner. Then have each pair share their answers in a class discussion of the problem. Refer to the **Teacher Notes: Student Page 5** for more specific ideas about each problem on the page.

As students work and report their conclusions, focus on these issues:

Facilitate Students' Thinking – Some students may need to be reminded that when they use ratio tables, they can work both forward and backward. As an example, you may wish to point out their prior use of ratio tables to solve both multiplication and division problems.

Validate Representations – Ask students to share their ratio tables with the class. Have the class analyze the tables and decide whether all are valid.

Allow Waiting Time – When students struggle to explain their thinking, be sure to allow them ample time to organize their thoughts.

Validate Alternate Strategies – Be sure to have students share their strategies with their peers. Have them discuss the strategies and determine whether they all lead to the correct conclusions.

Student Page 5: Problems and Potential Answers

Section B: Ratio Tables and Percents Set 2

2. In Mr. Salinas's class, if you score less than 70% on any test, you have to take the test again. Mr. Salinas almost always has a different number of questions on his tests. So, he wanted to make a table to help let students know how many correct answers they needed on each test to score 70% or better. Use ratio tables to help him fill in the table below. (Hint: You will need to work backwards in the ratio table as shown in the example below.)

Number of Test Questions	Number Correct for 70%
100	70
80	56
60	42
50	35
40	28
20	14

70	35	7	42	
100	50	10	60	

In this example, we started with what we know. 70% is our target. We used a ratio table to work backwards until we reached a test that had 60 questions.

Strategies:

1) Half of 70 is 35; half of 100 is 50
2) 50 divided by 5 is 10;
   35 divided by 5 is 7
3) 50 + 10 = 60;
   35 + 7 = 42

So, 42 out of 60 is 70%.

Ratio tables will vary. Check students' work.

Book 8: *Fractions, Decimals, Percents* 5

TEACHER NOTES: STUDENT PAGE 5

Problem 2: For problem 1 on page 4, students were asked to start with the raw data. The example started with 32 out of 40. For this problem, students are given a percent–i.e., 70%–and asked to work back to the raw data to answer the question, "Given a test with n items, how many would you have to get correct to score a 70%?" This not only requires a different cognitive process, it also requires a more sophisticated understanding of ratios and percents. *Teaching Strategy:* Using the provided example as a starting point, engage students in a discussion about the fundamental differences between problems 1 and 2. Once students realize that the goal is to work backwards from 70/100 to the given denominator, they should come to the realization that the process for using the ratio tables is the same. The shift in thinking is that in this case, we start with a ratio that already has 100 in the denominator. The two examples of student work below illustrate this shift in thinking.

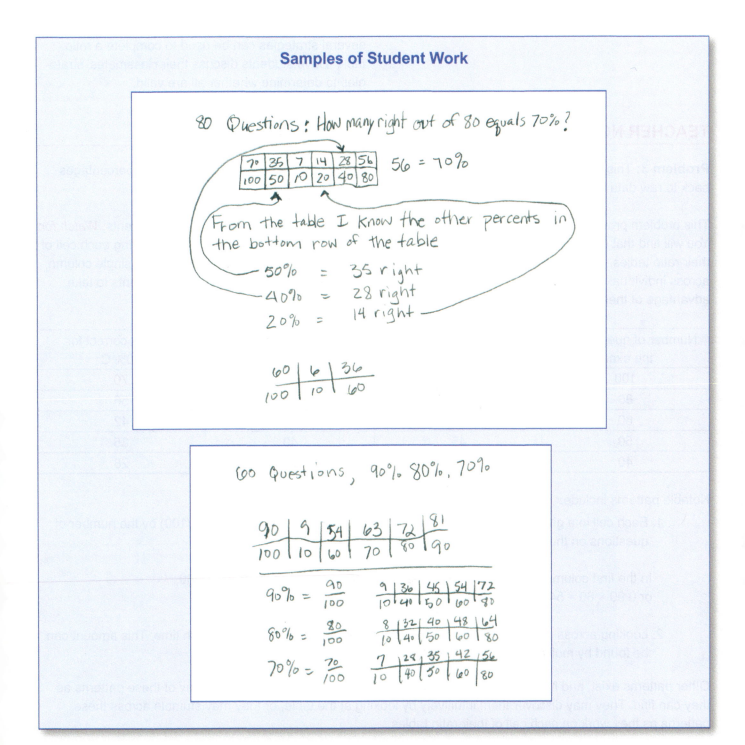

Fractions, Decimals, Percents *Teacher Edition*

CONTINUE THE PROBLEM SOLVING

Have students work individually to solve the problems on page 6. As they work, you may want to circulate and monitor their recorded answers. When students finish each problem, have them compare and discuss their answers with a partner. Then have each pair share their answers in a class discussion of the problem. Refer to the **Teacher Notes: Student Page 6** for more specific ideas about each problem on the page.

As students work and report their conclusions, focus on these issues:

Help Make Connections – Encourage students to look for patterns as they are completing both the table on the page and their ratio tables. Remind students of the key strategies for using ratio tables, such as doubling, halving, and multiplying by 10.

Validate Representations – Have students share their ratio tables with the class. Ask the class to decide whether each ratio table is correct.

Validate Alternate Strategies – Remind students that several strategies can be used to complete a ratio table. Have students discuss their classmates' strategies to determine whether all are valid.

TEACHER NOTES: STUDENT PAGE 6

Problem 3: This problem is similar to problem 2 on page 5. Students must work from the given percentages back to raw data for each of the given exams.

This problem provides opportunities for students to practice manipulating ratio tables to find percents. *Watch for:* You will find that discerning students will begin to notice patterns in the table as they are completing each cell of their ratio tables. For example, as you can see below, there are patterns that occur both within a single column, across individual rows, and across columns more generally. *Teaching Strategy:* Encourage students to take advantage of these patterns as long as they can explain where they come from.

Number of questions on the exam	Number correct for: 90% A	Number correct for: 80% B	Number correct for: 70% C
100	90	80	70
80	72	64	56
60	54	48	42
50	45	40	35
40	36	32	28

Notable patterns include:

1. Each cell in a given column can be found by multiplying the percent (e.g., 90/100) by the number of questions on the exam (e.g., 80).

    In the first column, with a total of 60 questions on an exam, one must get 54/60, or 0.90 × 60 = 54, correct in order to get a 90%.

2. Looking across a given row, the numbers decrease by the same amount each time. This amount can be found by multiplying 10% (1/10 or 0.1) by the number of exam questions.

Other patterns exist, and it is important that students be given time to recognize as many of these patterns as they can find. They may discover them intuitively by looking at the table, or they may stumble across these patterns as they work on each cell of their ratio tables.

Student Page 6: Problems and Potential Answers

Section B: Ratio Tables and Percents — Set 2

3. The students in Mr. Salinas's class want to know how many correct answers you need to get an A, B, or C on the exams. To get an A, you need at least 90% correct. To get a B, you need at least 80% correct up to 90% correct. To get a C, you need to at least 70% correct up to 80% correct. Use ratio tables to complete the table below.

Number of Questions on the Exam	Number Correct for: 90% A	Number Correct for: 80% B	Number Correct for: 70% C
100	90	80	70
80	72	64	56
60	54	48	42
50	45	40	35
40	36	32	28

Example: 90% on an 80-question exam:

×8

90	9	72
100	10	80

×8

In this case, we had to rename $\frac{90}{100}$ (90%) as an equivalent ratio for an exam that had a total of only 80 questions.

6 Book 8: *Fractions, Decimals, Percents*

CONTINUE THE PROBLEM SOLVING

Have students work individually to solve the problems on page 7. As they work, you may want to circulate and monitor their recorded answers. When students finish each problem, have them compare and discuss their answers with a partner. Then have each pair share their answers in a class discussion of the problem. Refer to the **Teacher Notes: Student Page 7** for more specific ideas about each problem on the page.

As students work and report their conclusions, focus on these issues:

Facilitate Students' Thinking – Students must be successful in solving problem 4 before they can go on to the other problems on the page. You may want to have them spend a little extra time on this problem before proceeding.

Help Make Connections – If students have difficulty with problem 6, remind them that they can follow the same procedure to solve it as they did for problem 4.

Validate Alternate Strategies – Be sure to have students explain their strategies to the class. Have the class discuss these strategies and determine whether they are pertinent to the solution of the problem.

Validate Representations – If students use different tables to solve the problem, have them analyze the tables to see whether all are valid.

TEACHER NOTES: STUDENT PAGE 7

These problems are contextually based application problems that require students to use ratio tables to work with percents. *Teaching Strategy:* Take time to make sure that students understand the contexts and what is required in terms of the use and treatment of the given percents.

Problem 4: This problem sets the stage for the others on this page. *Teaching Strategy:* Make sure that students are adequately invested in this problem before allowing them to continue. The procedure for solving this problem is the same as for problem 2 on Student Page 5. Students are given the amount that corresponds to 100%, in this case 400 minutes, and then are asked to find the corresponding number of minutes for each percent. *Teaching Strategy:* You may wish to introduce this problem before students complete the table by asking how many minutes the scooter could run if it were only 50% charged (which appears in the table). By this point, most students will recognize that 50% is 1/2 of the total time. Suggest that students work from this intuitive base to complete the more complex cells in the ratio table.

Problem 5: This problem is similar to problem 4. The first few columns of the ratio table should look familiar. What is different about problem 5 is that here students are asked to find percents given the number of minutes the scooter is ridden.

Problem 6: While the scooter context remains the same for this problem, there is a significant shift in what is being asked in problem 6. For this problem, students are asked to find the sale price of the scooter. The first two columns of the ratio table are completed, and the process followed is identical to that used for problem 4.

Problem 7: This problem mirrors problem 5, although the context is a continuation of the story line in problem 6. *Watch for:* The key is for students to recognize the importance of starting with 100% of the original cost.

Student Page 7: Problems and Potential Answers

Section B: Ratio Tables and Percents   Set 2

4. Hal's electronic scooter can run for 400 minutes when it is fully charged (100% charged). Complete the table below to find how many minutes it can run when it is only partially charged.

Percent Charged	100%	10%	1%	5%	50%	55%	60%	65%	66%
Running Minutes	400	40	4	20	200	220	240	260	264

5. One week Hal kept track of how many minutes he rode on his scooter. He started on Sunday, and by Thursday the scooter had run out of its charge. Hal had ridden the scooter for exactly 320 minutes before it ran out of charge. What percent charge did he have in the scooter before he started riding it on Sunday? _____80_____ %

Percent Charged	100%	50%	25%	75%	10%	5%	80%		
Running Minutes	400	200	100	300	40	20	320		

6. Hal bought his scooter at a sale. It normally costs $120. But at the sale, he bought the scooter for 80% <u>of its original price</u>. (Not 80% off, but 80% of the original $120.)
How much did Hal pay for the scooter? _____$96_____

Percent of Original Price	100%	10%	20%	40%	80%				
Dollars	$120	$12	$24	$48	$96				

7. A few weeks after Hal bought his scooter, Emma found the exact same scooter on sale at another store for $90. It also was originally priced at $120. For what percent of the original $120 did Emma buy the scooter? _____75_____ %

Percent of Original Price	100%	50%	25%	75%		
Dollars	$120	$60	$30	$90		

Book 8: *Fractions, Decimals, Percents* 7

SECTIONS A AND B ASSESSMENT (PAGE 8)

LAUNCH THE ASSESSMENT

Have students turn to the sections A and B assessment on page 8. An additional copy is found on page 127 of the Assessment Book. Have students work individually to solve the problems and create their ratio tables. As they work, circulate to be sure students understand what they need to do for each problem and that they are completing each part of the problem. For example, in problem 1 students need to complete the ratio table and then write the answer to the problem on a separate line. You may find it helpful to read the directions for all the problems before students begin, discussing the types of responses they need to make for each problem.

Encourage students to use whatever space they need to draw their ratio tables. If the space on the page is inadequate, they should use an additional sheet of paper or the back of the page.

Refer to the **Teacher Notes: Assessment**

Problems for Sections A and B for more specific ideas about the problems on this page.

Evaluate Student Responses

Use the assessment rubric on page 126 of the Assessment Book (pictured on page 228 of the Teacher Edition) to evaluate student responses. The Assessment Book has some general suggestions for using the rubric that you may find helpful.

TEACHER NOTES: ASSESSMENT PROBLEMS FOR SECTIONS A AND B

These problems are designed to help teachers determine whether students are grasping basic concepts related to computations with percents.

Problems 1–3: In each of these problems students begin the ratio tables by identifying an amount that corresponds to 100% in the first column. Students are then asked to find various percentages of this initial amount. In problem 1, students know that a 100% charge requires 8 hours. They are asked to determine what percentage of the battery will be charged after 6 hours. In problems 2 and 3, students are asked to determine the amount of gasoline that corresponds to a given percentage. In each problem, look for students to apply strategies common to solving ratio tables such as halving and doubling. In problems 2 and 3, students will be required to use decimals.

Problem 4: This contextually based problem requires students to apply their understanding of percents as they use a ratio table to determine various percentages related to miles driven versus gallons of gasoline used. Look for students to use common strategies such as halving, doubling, and multiplying by ten. Be sure that students understand the context adequately. They may wish to draw a diagram to help them effectively establish a ratio table and/or double number line.

Student Page 8: Problems and Potential Answers

Sections A and B: Problems for Assessment

Use ratio tables to help you answer each question.

1. Julie's new cell phone takes 8 hours to fully charge the battery (100%). In 6 hours, what percent charge will she have in the battery? __75%__

Percent Charged	100%	50%	25%	75%			
Hours of Charging	8	4	2	6			

2. John went to the gas station to completely fill (100%) his car's gas tank. The tank holds 14 gallons of gas. After two weeks of driving, the fuel gauge in John's car now indicates that the tank is 25% full. How many gallons of gas are left in the tank? __3.5__

Percent Filled	100%	50%	25%					
Gallons of Gasoline	14	7	3.5					

3. John decided to drive his car until the gas tank was only 5% full before he went to the gas station to fill it up.

   a) How many gallons of gas were in the tank when he arrived at the gas station to fill it up? __0.7__ gallon

   b) How many gallons did he need to pump to fill up his gas tank? __13.3__ gallons

Percent Filled	100%	10%	5%					
Gallons of Gasoline	14	1.4	0.7					

4. When the gas tank of John's car is full (100%), he can drive 450 miles before it is empty.

   a) John drove to visit a friend. He started with a full tank of gas. It was a 90-mile round trip. What percent of the gas was left in his tank after completing the trip? __80%__

   b) After another two weeks of driving, John noticed from his fuel gauge that only 5% of the tank was full. He then decided to go to the gas station. How many miles did he drive from the time his gas tank was full until the time he refilled it? __427.5 miles__

   Design and complete your own ratio table(s) to answer these questions.

Percent Filled	100%	10%	20%	80%				
Miles to Empty	450	45	90	360				

Percent Filled	100%	10%	5%					
Miles to Empty	450	45	22.5					

450 − 22.5 = 427.5

8 Book 8: *Fractions, Decimals, Percents*

SCORING GUIDE BOOK 8: FRACTIONS, DECIMALS, PERCENTS

Sections A and B Assessment
For Use With: Student Book Page 8

PROBLEM DESCRIPTION	SCORING: WHAT TO LOOK FOR	SCORE AND COMMENTS
Problem 1 Determine percent of total charge. Level 2: Tool use Level 3: Connection and Application	Do students: • Have an intuitive understanding of percents? • Calculate the correct percentage for 8 of the 12 hours? • Use strategies?	Points: _____ of 3
Problem 2 Determine percent remaining. Level 1: Comprehension and Knowledge Level 3: Connection and Application	Do students: • Have an intuitive understanding of percents? • Correctly calculate 25% of 14? • Use strategies?	Points: _____ of 3
Problem 3a–b Determine percent remaining and number of gallons needed to fill a gas tank. Level 1: Comprehension and Knowledge Level 2: Tool use	Do students: • Have an intuitive understanding of percents? • Correctly calculate 10% of 14? • Use strategies? • Correctly calculate the number of gallons needed to refill the tank?	(a) Points: _____ of 3 (b) Points: _____ of 2
Problem 4a–b Determine percent remaining and number of miles driven. Level 2: Tool use Level 3: Connection and Application Level 4: Synthesis and Evaluation	Do students: • Have an intuitive understanding of percents? • Have an understanding of context? • Understand percent calculations? • Understand the use of strategy?	(a) Points: _____ of 3 (b) Points: _____ of 2

TOTAL POINTS: _____ OF 16

Section C: Number Bars and Percents

SECTION C PLANNER

THE MATHEMATICS CONTENT AND GOALS

GOALS
Students will:
- Develop their understanding of the use of percent bars (number bars) as models for representing fractions, decimals, and percents.
- Deepen their understanding of the ways in which percentages normalize different data sets so that they can be compared.
- Understand the differences between the concepts of percent off and percent of.

> **LANGUAGE DEVELOPMENT**
> **Mathematical language in this section includes:**
> *Percent of (% of):* In context, we often refer to the idea of a percent by asking the percent of a given amount or quantity. This refers specifically to the product of the percent and the original amount of the whole set.
> *Percent off (% off):* Similar semantically to percent of, this concept of percent off is significantly different. The percent off an amount is found by determining the difference between the original amount and the product of the percent and the original amount. Percent off indicates subtraction of the percent of a given amount from the original amount. For example, 10% off $50 is equal to 50 − (10% × 50), or $50 − $5 = $45.
> *Estimate:* To approximate the amount, extent, magnitude, position, or value of some quantity.
> *Estimation:* The process involved in making an estimate.

PROBLEM SETS: OVERVIEW

This is an extremely important section of the book not only because the double number bar model is elaborated, but also because several very common real-world contexts are used to motivate the mathematics. The very important distinction between percent off and percent of is also treated in this section.

This section begins by introducing the number-bar model for percents and asks students to consider the relative amounts of water in large tubs. The number-bar model is used here because it is a visual model that corresponds to this kind of context ("Can you picture a tub that is 50% full? Can you picture a bar that is 50% shaded?"). Connections to the use of number bars in earlier books on fractions and decimals are important to emphasize.

The second set of problems involves visually estimating percents. The number-bar model is helpful here because it gives very explicit visual reinforcement to the idea that percents normalize sets of data of different sizes in order to make comparisons. Although two sets of data might look very different, the percents equivalent to these two ratios will look identical when represented with a number bar. For example, 10 out of 20 is the same as 300 out of 600.

The final set of problems addresses the important distinction between percent off and percent of. Several problems and contexts are utilized to help students make these distinctions. By the end of these problems, students should recognize the relationship that exists between these two ways to conceptualize and use percents. They should know that 75% of a price is the same as 25% off the price.

PACING

The projected pacing for this unit is 4 class periods (based on a 45-minute period).

Set 1 (pp. 9–10, problems 1–5)
These problems develop the use of number bars as students compare different amounts of water in tubs of varying sizes. The visual, number-bar model is used here because of its logical connection and representation of the context.

Set 2 (p. 11)
These problems ask students to interpret number bars by making estimates and drawing inferences from the visual representations.

Set 3 (p. 12; problems 1–7)
These problems explicitly address the distinction between percent of and percent off. The problems on this page particularly focus on percent of, which will then be contrasted in the following set of problems to percent off.

Set 4 (pp. 13–16, problems 1–10)
These problems use the context of sales to focus on the difference between percent of and percent off. Students have several opportunities to engage in the differences and similarities between the two.

CONCEPT DEVELOPMENT (PAGES 9–11)

INTRODUCE THE CONCEPT

ASSESS STUDENTS' PRIOR KNOWLEDGE
Draw the double number line below on the board. Fill in the numbers below the line as students respond correctly and as you model mathematical thinking.

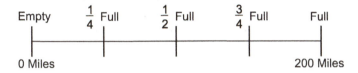

Ask:
The gas gauge on Mr. Martinez's car was broken. Mr. Martinez wanted to devise a way to tell when the tank was 3/4 full, 1/2 full, and 1/4 full. He knew that he could drive the car 200 miles on one full tank of gasoline. So he made a double number line like the one on the board. How many miles could he drive if he had 1/2 tank of gas? Explain your reasoning.

Listen for:
Students should use proportional thinking and recognize the value of the double number line.
- He could drive 100 miles on 1/2 tank of gas.

MODEL MATHEMATICAL THINKING
Model the thinking for another example by asking, *If Mr. Martinez drove 50 miles, how much of the gas in the tank would he have used? How far could he drive if he had 3/4 tank of gas?*

Talk Through the Thinking:
I already know that Mr. Martinez could drive 200 miles on one full tank of gas. And you found that he could drive 100 miles on 1/2 tank of gas. I know 50 miles is 1/2 of 100. So, I could find 1/2 of 1/2 tank of gas. That's 1/4 tank. Mr. Martinez would use 1/4 tank of gas if he drove 50 miles. Let's find how many miles he could drive on 3/4 tank of gas. 3/4 tank is halfway between one full tank and 1/2 tank. What number of miles is halfway between 200 miles and 50 miles? It's 150 miles. So Mr. Martinez could drive 150 miles on 3/4 tank of gas.

Ask:
Suppose Mr. Martinez could drive 300 miles on one full tank of gas. How would the number of miles for each fraction of a tank change on the double number line?

Listen for:
- Instead of 150 miles on 3/4 tank, he could now drive 225 miles.
- Instead of 100 miles on 1/2 tank, he could now drive 150 miles.
- Instead of 50 miles on 1/4 tank, he could now drive 75 miles.

LAUNCH THE PROBLEM SOLVING

Have students work individually to solve the problems on page 9. As they work, you may want to circulate and monitor their recorded answers. When students finish each problem, have them compare and discuss their answers with a partner. Then have each pair share their answers in a class discussion of the problem. Refer to the **Teacher Notes: Student Page 9** for more specific ideas about each of the problems on the page.

As students work and report their conclusions, focus on these issues:

Help Make Connections – Suggest that students think about how they can use ratio tables to help them solve the problems on page 9.

Validate Representations – Have students share their ratio tables and double number bars with the class. Encourage discussion about the representations, and have students determine whether they are all valid.

Allow Processing Time – Be sure to allow students enough time to actively engage in the problems on this page before you make suggestions and give further direction.

Student Page 9: Problems and Potential Answers

Section C: Number Bars and Percents Set 1

We can use ratio tables to help us understand the difference between "percent of" and "percent off". First let's review how to use double number lines, or number bars, as tools for figuring percents.

1. A bathtub holds 20 gallons of water. Label the bar below to indicate how much water is in the tub if it is 25% full, 50% full, and 75% full.

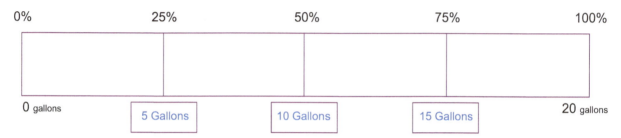

2. A larger hot tub holds 30 gallons of water. Label the bar below, filling in each gallon amount in the boxes provided.

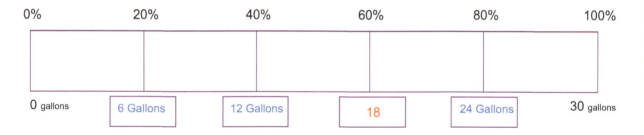

3. Use the bars in problems 1 and 2 to help you. Complete the bar below to show how much water would be in the hot tub when the tub is 10% full, 30% full, 50% full, 70% full, and 90% full.

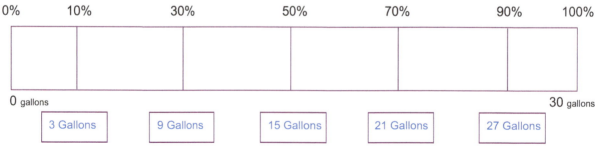

Book 8: *Fractions, Decimals, Percents* 9

TEACHER NOTES: STUDENT PAGE 9

Problems 1–3: These problems are similar in their design and intent, which is to encourage students to use visual models (number bars) and ratio tables to help conceptualize percentages. The problems begin with benchmark percents such as 50% and 25% that should be familiar to students.

Problem 2 is more difficult than problem 1 because it does not have a readily obvious way to find the number of gallons for the given percents. *Teaching Strategy:* You may want to encourage students to think about how ratio tables might also be used to solve these problems as a way to get them started.

Problem 3 is an excellent formative assessment item because it will allow you to see whether students can construct their own number bars.

CONTINUE THE PROBLEM SOLVING

Have students work individually to solve the problems on page 10. As they work, you may want to circulate and monitor their recorded answers. When students finish each problem, have them compare and discuss their answers with a partner. Then have each pair share their answers in a class discussion of the problem. Refer to the **Teacher Notes: Student Page 10** for more specific ideas about each of the problems on the page.

As students work and report their conclusions, focus on these issues:

Validate Representations – Have students compare and discuss their number bars with those of other students in the class. Ask them to determine whether each of the number bars accurately represents the given data and provide a solution to the problem.

Validate Alternate Strategies – You may want to have students who have drawn different number bars to explain how they completed them.

Help Make Connections – Have students discuss the similarities between ratio tables and number bars. This may help students who are having difficulty to gain some insights into the concepts and models on the page.

TEACHER NOTES: STUDENT PAGE 10

Problems 4–5: These problems are similar to those on page 9, with the difference that here they allow students greater freedom to construct their own number bars. *Teaching Strategy:* Encourage students to mark their number bars to help them find the amounts of water in each tub. *Watch for:* In so doing, they may begin to see how number bars are representations of the same calculations they would have made if they were using ratio tables. These problems provide a nice opportunity for you to explicitly make the connections between number bars and ratio tables. You may wish to illustrate this parallel by completing ratio tables for a subset of these problems.

Student Page 10: Problems and Potential Answers

Section C: Number Bars and Percents Set 1

4. An irrigation tank has 20 gallons of water in it. It is only 25% full. Use the bar below to find how much water the tank holds when it is completely full.

0%	25%	50%	75%	100%
0 gallons	20 gallons	40	60	80

5. Find how many gallons each tank holds based on the information provided.

How students use the bars will vary.

a) 0%, 10%, 100% — 0 gallons, 8 gallons — **80 Gallons**

b) 0%, 40%, 100% — 0 gallons, 8 gallons — **20 Gallons**

c) 0%, 5%, 100% — 0 gallons, 4.5 gallons — **90 Gallons**

d) 0%, 60%, 100% — 0 gallons, 30 — **50 Gallons**

e) 0%, 80%, 100% — 0 gallons, 32 — **40 Gallons**

CONTINUE THE PROBLEM SOLVING

Have students work individually to solve the problems on page 11. As they work, you may want to circulate and monitor their recorded answers. When students finish each problem, have them compare and discuss their answers with a partner. Then have each pair share their answers in a class discussion of the problem. Refer to the **Teacher Notes: Student Page 11** for more specific ideas about each of the problems on the page.

As students work and report their conclusions, focus on these issues:

Facilitate Students' Thinking – Be sure students understand that because the classes have different goals, a greater percent for one class may result in a lesser amount of money than a class that has attained a lesser percent of its goal. The goals are written at the top right of each number bar.

Help Make Connections – Help students understand that a vertical number bar works in the same way as a horizontal number bar.

Allow Waiting Time – When students struggle to explain their thinking, be sure to allow them ample time to organize their thoughts.

TEACHER NOTES: STUDENT PAGE 11

These problems represent a subtle change in the underlying objectives for students as they continue to develop their understanding of percents. For these problems, students are asked to read number bars and make inferences about the data behind the representations. The number bars on this page represent the relationship between the amount of money earned and the amount of money intended to be earned, the fund-raising goal. *Watch for:* This is an important section because we see this way of representing percents in publications, advertisements, propaganda, and so on. Students need to develop an ability both to interpret such bars and to make inferences about what the percents really mean given the underlying particulars of a situation.

Another important element of these problems is that they help students assimilate the idea that percentages are tools that can be used to normalize and then compare sets of data. In these problems, students are asked to think about how well each class is meeting fund-raising goals. While the goals and amounts of money raised differ across grade levels (as one would expect), we can still use percents to represent the progress of each group as it relates to other classes.

Teaching Strategy: This is an extremely important teaching point to emphasize. If students do not understand this fundamental concept on their own, they should be prompted to do so through discussion in small or large groups.

These problems are also important because they make explicit the connections between percents and fractions. The number bar, a visual model used to express both fractions and percents, is obviously an important connecting context for these two concepts.

Student Page 11: Problems and Potential Answers

Section C: Number Bars and Percents Set 2

Make an Estimate Jefferson Elementary School is having a fundraiser. The students in each grade have set a fundraising goal. They are using the number bars below to help them keep track of their progress. Help each class find the fraction and percent of their progress. You may need to make some estimates.

Kindergarden

100% $20

Fraction Earned: $\frac{1}{2}$

Percent Earned: 50%

Amount Earned: $10

0% $0

1st Grade

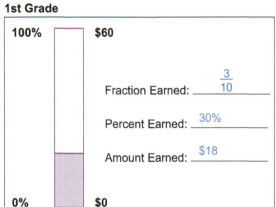

100% $60

Fraction Earned: $\frac{3}{10}$

Percent Earned: 30%

Amount Earned: $18

0% $0

2nd Grade

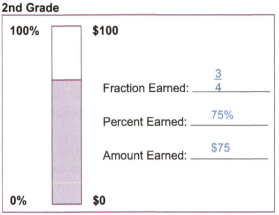

100% $100

Fraction Earned: $\frac{3}{4}$

Percent Earned: 75%

Amount Earned: $75

0% $0

3rd Grade

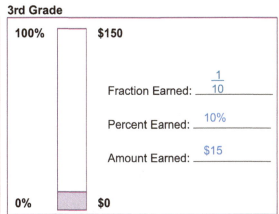

100% $150

Fraction Earned: $\frac{1}{10}$

Percent Earned: 10%

Amount Earned: $15

0% $0

4th Grade

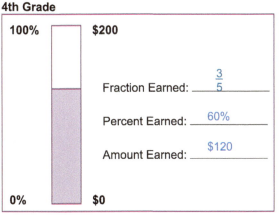

100% $200

Fraction Earned: $\frac{3}{5}$

Percent Earned: 60%

Amount Earned: $120

0% $0

5th Grade

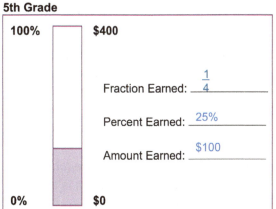

100% $400

Fraction Earned: $\frac{1}{4}$

Percent Earned: 25%

Amount Earned: $100

0% $0

Book 8: *Fractions, Decimals, Percents*

CONCEPT DEVELOPMENT (PAGES 12–16)

INTRODUCE THE CONCEPT

ASSESS STUDENTS' PRIOR KNOWLEDGE

Ask:
Suppose you want to buy a digital camera. Would you rather pay 20% of the full price of the camera or the cost if the camera were on sale for 20% off the full price? Explain your thinking.

Listen for:
Students may have only emerging understanding of the subtle difference between percent of and percent off and of the very different resulting amounts. Listen for students to use proportional reasoning. Watch for them to use a double number line to compare the percents.

MODEL MATHEMATICAL THINKING

Draw a number bar on the board. Above the bar, label the left end $0 and the right end $200. Below the bar, label the left end 0% and the right end 100%. Show the percents and amounts as you talk through the thinking.

Ask:
Suppose a digital camera costs $200. Is the better buy 25% of that price or 25% off that price?

Talk Through the Thinking:
I can use the number bar to find which is the better buy. 25% is equivalent to 1/4. That's 1/4 of the way to the end of the number bar starting at 0%. If the full cost of the camera is $200, 25% of that cost is $50. How can I tell where 25% off the price would be? This time I can start at 100% and come back 1/4 of the way. That puts me at 75% because 100% − 25% = 75%. So that means I pay $50 less than the full cost of $200, or $150. Even without knowing the original cost of the camera, the number bar clearly shows us that the better buy is 25% of $200.

Ask:
What if the choice were between 50% of the total cost or 50% off the total cost? Can you tell which is the better buy? Explain your thinking.

Listen for:
Students to refer to the number bar as they explain their thinking.
- Neither is a better buy because both 50% of the cost and 50% off the cost result in the same amount. If the original cost of the camera was $200, that amount would be $100.

LAUNCH THE PROBLEM SOLVING

Have students work individually to solve the problems on page 12. As they work, you may want to circulate and monitor their recorded answers. When students finish each problem, have them compare and discuss their answers with a partner. Then have each pair share their answers in a class discussion of the problem. Refer to the **Teacher Notes: Student Page 12** for more specific ideas about each problem.

As students work and report their conclusions, focus on these issues:

Facilitate Students' Thinking – Stress the importance of carefully reading the problems to distinguish between percent of and percent off.

Validate Representations – Have students share and discuss their number bars with the class to be sure that the bars reflect the given information and provide the correct answers.

Allow Waiting Time – When students struggle to explain their thinking, be sure to allow them ample time to organize their thoughts.

TEACHER NOTES: STUDENT PAGE 12

The problems on this page are designed to provide students with an intuitive basis for understanding the difference between percent of and percent off. *Watch for:* The approach taken in these problems is to motivate students to recognize the important principle that the sum of the percents of various outcomes for one event must total 100%. For example, if a student answered 75% of the problems correctly, she must also have answered 25% of the problems incorrectly.

Problems 1–7: These problems use number bars as a visual reinforcement to carefully walk students through the principle that the sum of the percents for a given event must total 100%. Problems 4–6 require students to create their own number bars to reflect this principle with differing number sets. Problem 7 asks that students state this principle. *Teaching Strategy:* Be sure to discuss this problem with students, allowing them to take the lead in the discussion.

Student Page 12: Problems and Potential Answers

Section C: Number Bars and Percents Set 3

"Percent Of" and "Percent Off"

50% of the students in Mr. Newton's 6th grade class play an instrument in the school band. There are 24 students in Mr. Newton's class.

0 Students   (12 in band)   12   (12 not in band)   24 Students

0%   50%   100%

In Ms. Wright's classroom there are 28 students. 21 of them are in the band.

0 Students   28 Students

0%   100%

1. What percent of Ms. Wright's class is in the band? __75%__

2. What percent of Ms. Wright's class is NOT in the band? __25%__

3. How did you find the answer for problem 2?
   Answers will vary.

Mr. William's class has 32 students. Only 25% of his students are in the band. <u>Complete the number bar below</u> to answer the questions:

4. What percent of Mr. William's class is NOT in the band? __75%__

5. How many students in Mr. William's class are in the band? __8__

6. How many students in Mr. Williams class are NOT in the band? __24__

0   8   16   24   32

0%   25%   50%   75%   100%

7. In each of these three examples, what do you notice about the percent of students IN the band compared to the number of students NOT in the band? Are there any patterns you see in the percents?
   They have a sum of 100%.

12   Book 8: *Fractions, Decimals, Percents*

CONTINUE THE PROBLEM SOLVING

Have students work individually to solve the problems on page 13. As they work, you may want to circulate and monitor their recorded answers. When students finish each problem, have them compare and discuss their answers with a partner. Then have each pair share their answers in a class discussion of the problem. Refer to the Teacher Notes: Student Page 13 for more specific ideas about each problem.

As students work and report their conclusions, focus on these issues:

Look for Misconceptions – Some students may still not understand that the size of the whole and the resulting number that represents the percent of the whole can differ, depending on the given information. For example, 50% of 100 is very different from 50% of 20.

Help Make Connections – When students struggle to find differences that may not exist when they find percent off and percent of, suggest that they use number bars. These visual aids will help students see that there may not be any differences.

Validate Representations – Have students share their number bars with the class. If some of the drawings are different, ask students to analyze whether they are all correct.

TEACHER NOTES: STUDENT PAGE 13

The problems on this page are designed to help students recognize that the sum of the probabilities for the outcomes of one event must equal 1. In this case, students are asked to compare the result of 80% of a given price with a 20% discount off that price. *Watch for:* The two number bars provided on the page will help students recognize that these two situations, though they may require different strategies for solving, are simply different representations of the same relationship.

Watch for: For problem 1a, be on the lookout for students who differ in their responses to the question of which is the better value, 80% of or 20% off. *Teaching Strategy:* Allow students to make their arguments in support of their assertions, and encourage students to look for, and articulate, the misconception that one calculation is better than another.

The number bars provided in 1b and 1c should help students see how the two problem statements result in identical answers. Students will probably use the number bars in quite similar ways. When they do, they are likely to see the similarities in the two ways of representing the same amount of money.

> ### On the Lookout for Misconceptions
>
> Revisiting an idea presented in an earlier book, remind students that we can determine how large (in number, size, amount, and so on) a given percent of a quantity is only if we know something about the raw data to which it applies. For example, in this problem we would not know how much to pay after the 20% discount has been taken (the final sale price) unless we know the original cost. This misconception is elaborated in subsequent pages.

Student Page 13: Problems and Potential Answers

Section C: Number Bars and Percents — Set 4

Stan's Sports Store: Clearance Sale
Stan decides it is time to have a sale on many items in his store. Use the number bars to help you answer the questions.

1. Stan has one bike model that normally sells for $100. He asks two of his employees to come up with a sign to help advertise the bike sale.

   Paul's Sign
   SALE!!
   Mountain Bike
   * 80% *
   Of the Original Price

   Sarah's Sign
   MOUNTAIN BIKE
   Clearance Sale
   20% OFF!!

   a) Stan is trying to decide which of these two signs advertises the better buy. What do you think? Which is the better buy? _Answers will vary._

   b) How much would you have to pay if Paul's advertisement is used? _$80_

   c) How much would you have to pay if Sarah's advertisement is used? _$80_

   d) What do you notice about "80% **of** the original price" and "20% **off** the original price?" _They result in the same sale price._

Book 8: *Fractions, Decimals, Percents*   13

242   **Fractions, Decimals, Percents** *Teacher Edition*

CONTINUE THE PROBLEM SOLVING

Have students work individually to solve the problems on page 14. As they work, you may want to circulate and monitor their recorded answers. When students finish each problem, have them compare and discuss their answers with a partner. Then have each pair share their answers in a class discussion of the problem. Refer to the **Teacher Notes: Student Page 14** for more specific ideas about each problem.

As students work and report their conclusions, focus on these issues:

Validate Representations – Most students will use number bars to help them solve the problems. Invite these students to share their representations with the class. Have students discuss whether they are all correct.

Facilitate Students' Thinking – As the more advanced students work through the problems, they may begin to recognize that there is a relationship between the models they draw and multiplication done by renaming the percent either as a decimal or as a fraction. Encourage these students to use this method.

Help Make Connections – Remind students that because 100% represents the whole amount, they can subtract the percent off from 100%. Doing so may make it easier for them to compare the final costs.

Allow Waiting Time – When students struggle to explain their thinking, be sure to allow them ample time to organize their thoughts.

TEACHER NOTES: STUDENT PAGE 14

Problems 2–4: These problems provide practice for students to determine the prices of products that are on sale at various rates of discount. *Watch for:* Students are likely to continue using number bars to solve these problems. They should be encouraged to do so for as long as they need to use the models. Other students may begin to see the relationship between the bar models and the algorithmic strategy in which they multiply the percent, renamed as a fraction or decimal, and the original cost of the item. *Teaching Strategy:* Look for opportunities to begin to guide students in this direction. A good way to start is to begin with several examples in which they need to find 50% of a given amount because they are more apt to recognize and be comfortable with the process when they are multiplying by 1/2 or 0.5.

Problem 5: *Watch for:* At this point, some students will notice immediately, without calculating, that the first advertisement represents the better buy. They should know this by comparing 30% off with 75% off. If they begin with 30%, students should recognize the relationship between 30% and 70% (they have a sum of 100%). If they begin with 75%, they should recognize the same relationship between 75% and 25%. Students can then compare 70% and 75%, or 25% and 30%.

Student Page 14: Problems and Potential Answers

Section C: Number Bars and Percents Set 4

Stan is considering using the advertisements below. Examine the ads. Then answer the questions.

ALL SKIS
75% of Original Price

2. What would a $220 pair of skis cost on sale?
   $165

ALL BIKE HELMETS
60% of Original Price

3. The most expensive helmet in Stan's store usually sells for $80. How much would this helmet cost at the sale price?
   $48

SWIM SUITS
30% off

4. What is the sale price of a swim suit that normally sells for $24?
   $16.80

IN-LINE SKATES NORMALLY $75
** NOW 30% OFF **

IN-LINE SKATES NORMALLY $75
75% OF REGULAR PRICE

5. Stan wants to know if these two signs would result in the skates being sold for the same price. Would they sell for the same price? If not, which advertisement is going to save the customer the most money? They would not sell for the same price. Sign 1 savings: $22.50 (greatest savings) Sign 2 savings: $18.75

14 Book 8: *Fractions, Decimals, Percents*

CONTINUE THE PROBLEM SOLVING

Have students work individually to solve the problems on page 15. As they work, you may want to circulate and monitor their recorded answers. When students finish each problem, have them compare and discuss their answers with a partner. Then have each pair share their answers in a class discussion of the problem. Refer to the **Teacher Notes: Student Page 15** for more specific ideas about each problem.

As students work and report their conclusions, focus on these issues:

Help Make Connections – Encourage students to use the same strategies, such as drawing number bars, for finding the final cost as they used when they compared final costs.

Validate Representations – If students use different number bars or other representations to illustrate the problems, have them analyze whether all are correct.

Facilitate Students' Thinking – You may want to suggest that students estimate the final cost before they begin their calculations. Remind them that an estimate can help tell whether their calculated answers are reasonable.

Allow Waiting Time – When students struggle to explain their thinking, be sure to allow them ample time to organize their thoughts.

TEACHER NOTES: STUDENT PAGE 15

These problems take a small conceptual leap forward and are probably a better example of what students may find in the real world. What makes these problems different and somewhat more challenging is that they ask students to compare transactions for items that have different original prices and different sale percents. This is in contrast to earlier problems in which they compared the relative cost of items that had the same original price but different sale percents, or problems in which the sale percents remained the same but the original prices differed. So in these problems, students must deal with both changing original prices and changing sale percents.

Problems 6–7: *Teaching Strategy:* Encourage students to use number-bar models (or other strategies) for each product. A helpful exercise is to ask students to predict ahead of time which product will be the least expensive. Doing so will help students develop the informed estimation skills that we often use in our daily transactions.

Student Page 15: Problems and Potential Answers

Section C: Number Bars and Percents Set 4

Which is the better deal? Use your knowledge of percents, fractions, and decimals to find which sale item in each group would result in the **lowest** price. Use number bars, ratio tables, or any other tool to help you.

No-Crack Ping Pong Balls
Regularly $9.99
Now, 10% off!

Ding Dong Ping Pong Table Tennis Balls
Regularly $12
Save 15% Today!

Sorry… Big Bounce Ping Pong Balls
ARE NOT ON SALE.
$9.25 per box

---

6. Which brand costs the least? No-Crack Ping Pong Balls: $8.99

    Explain. Ding Dong Ping Pong: $10.20. Big Bounce Ping Pong Balls: $9.25

RUNNING SHOES ON SALE
Trail Runner - Regularly $50
90% of Original Price

RUNNING SHOES ON SALE
Rock Hopper
Regularly $65
Take 15% off regular price

RUNNING SHOES ON SALE
Ultra Light Marathon
Normally $75
Now, 40% off!!

---

7. Which pair of shoes costs the least? Trail Runner: $45 and Ultra Light Marathon: $45

    Explain. Rock Hopper costs $52.25. This is more than both Trail Runner and Ultra Light Marathon, which cost the same.

Book 8: *Fractions, Decimals, Percents*

CONTINUE THE PROBLEM SOLVING

Have students work individually to solve the problems on page 16. As they work, you may want to circulate and monitor their recorded answers. When students finish each problem, have them compare and discuss their answers with a partner. Then have each pair share their answers in a class discussion of the problem. Refer to the **Teacher Notes: Student Page 16** for more specific ideas about each problem.

As students work and report their conclusions, focus on these issues:

Validate Representations – When students use number bars or other representations of the problems, ask them to share the representations with the class. Have the other students determine whether all representations are valid.

Facilitate Students' Thinking – You may wish to have students share their ideas on how to go about estimating the final cost of the items, particularly for problems 9 and 10.

Look for Misconceptions – Help students recall that a certain percent off a more expensive item results in a final cost that is greater than the same percent off a less expensive item. Additionally, even though a greater percent discount may be taken off a more expensive item, the final cost may still be greater than that of a less expensive item with a lesser discount.

TEACHER NOTES: STUDENT PAGE 16

Problem 8: This problem is similar to those on page 15. Encourage students to solve this problem with whatever tools they find are most familiar and successful. *Teaching Strategy:* As with the previous two problems, encourage students to estimate which product will be the least expensive.

Problems 9–10: These problems ask students to compare the final cost of the items without making any calculations ahead of time. This is an excellent formative assessment problem for you to use as you evaluate student comprehension. For problem 9, the percent off is the same for all the balls, but the original prices vary. *Watch for:* Students should recognize that if the percent is fixed, then the least expensive item will still be least expensive after the discounts are taken. Likewise, for problem 10, students should recognize that the prices of the jerseys are the same but the sale percents differ. In this instance, the jersey with the greatest percent discount will be the least expensive.

On the Lookout for Misconceptions

Some students run into a seemingly counterintuitive dilemma when applying fixed percent discounts to items with different prices. This type of misconception often occurs in situations similar to problem 9 (a 15% discount applied to three items, each with a different price tag). In these instances, the misconception actually emerges from solid mathematical reasoning. It goes something like this:

It can be shown that 10% of $20 ($2) is going to be a greater amount than 10% of $10 ($1). So when comparing the two situations, it is true that when the percent is the same, the greater amount results in a greater monetary discount. But, students need to remember that just because the actual monetary discount is larger in one case, the least expensive item to purchase is going to be the item that had the lowest original price.

Working several simple examples will help students confirm their understanding of this kind of proportional reasoning.

Student Page 16: Problems and Potential Answers

Section C: Number Bars and Percents **Set 4**

Shredder Mountain Bike Tires
Buy One at $30
Get the second at 50% off!

Everest Mountain Bike Tires
Regularly $40
Now, 40% off

Pro-Lite Mountain Bike Tires
Regular price: $60 (for two tires)
For a limited time, 60% of original price

---

8. Suppose you wanted to buy two tires. Which of the three brands costs the least? __Pro-Lite: $36__

Explain. __Shredder: $30 + $15 = $45. Everest: $24 + $24 = $48__

For the two sets of sale items below, determine which is the better buy without doing any calculations. Be prepared to justify your answer.

All Basketballs: 15% off
Play Ball Basketballs: $29.99
Ekin Basketballs: $35.00
Sadidda Basketballs: $32.99

Red Jerseys ($20) → Now 15% off
Black Jerseys ($20) → Now 20% off
Green Jerseys ($20) → Now 25% off

9. Which brand costs the least? __Play Ball__ How do you know without calculating?

Explain. __Lowest original price__

10. Which color jersey costs the least? __Green__ How do you know without calculating?

Explain. __Highest discount percent__

16 Book 8: *Fractions, Decimals, Percents*

SECTION C ASSESSMENT (PAGE 17)

LAUNCH THE ASSESSMENT

Have students turn to the Section C Assessment on page 17. An additional copy is found on page 129 of the Assessment Book. Have students work individually to solve the problems. As they work, circulate to be sure students understand what they need to do for each problem and that they are completing each part of the problem. For example, for problem 2, students need to find the sale price of each large pizza and then determine which is the best buy. You may find it helpful to read the directions for all the problems before students begin, discussing the types of responses they will need to make for each problem.

Encourage students to use whatever space they need to draw their models and representations. If the space on the page is inadequate, they should use an additional sheet of paper or the back of the page. Refer to the **Teacher Notes: Assessment Problems for Section C** for more specific ideas about the problems on this page.

Evaluate Student Responses

Use the assessment rubric on page 128 of the Assessment Book (pictured on page 251 of the Teacher Edition) to evaluate student responses. The Assessment Book has some general suggestions for using the rubric that you may find helpful.

TEACHER NOTES: ASSESSMENT PROBLEMS FOR SECTION C

These assessment problems are representative of the primary models and contexts that have been explored in Section C.

Student Page 17: Problems and Potential Answers

Section C: Problems for Assessment

1. The track coach is monitoring runners' workouts. Help her find how many more laps each runner needs to do to complete his or her workout, based on the information provided. Use the diagrams to help you.

   a) Gabrielle is a short-distance runner.

   b) Michael is a middle-distance runner.

   c) Jackson is a long-distance runner.

2. Which is the best deal? Use number bars, ratio tables, or any other tool to help you find which pizza place is offering the lowest price. Write the sale price of each pizza on the line.

   $11.99 $11.70 (Best Deal) $12.03

Book 8: *Fractions, Decimals, Percents*   **17**

SCORING GUIDE BOOK 8: FRACTIONS, DECIMALS, PERCENTS

SECTION C ASSESSMENT
For Use With: Student Book Page 17

PROBLEM DESCRIPTION	SCORING: WHAT TO LOOK FOR	SCORE AND COMMENTS
Problem 1a–c Find percent of total. Level 1: Comprehension and Knowledge Level 2: Tool use	Do students: • Use the tool appropriately to help determine the total? • Calculate correctly?	(3 points each) Points: _____ of 9
Problem 2 Determine the best deal. Level 2: Tool use Level 3: Connection and Application	Do students: • Understand context? • Calculate correctly for each deal? • Understand using strategies?	(2 points each calculation) Points: _____ of 6

TOTAL POINTS: _____ of 15

Section D: Tipping

SECTION D PLANNER

THE MATHEMATICS CONTENT AND GOALS

GOALS
Students will:
- Understand how to find 10% of any given amount both conceptually and procedurally.
- Apply the 10% procedure to problem contexts with differing percents.

> **LANGUAGE DEVELOPMENT**
> **Mathematical language in this section includes:**
> - *Tip:* A tip is extra money given in exchange for a service. It is usually determined by finding a percent of an agreed-upon price.

PACING

The projected pacing for this unit is 2 class periods (based on a 45-minute period).

PROBLEM SETS: OVERVIEW

This section includes problems that represent a familiar real-world context in which we use percents with great fluency: tipping. The process of moving the decimal point one place to the left to find 10% of a given number is developed in this section. Presenting this procedure has been held off until the last part of this text so that students will first have plenty of opportunities to develop their conceptual understandings of percent. Practice problems are provided to help students understand and use the 10% procedure and, perhaps more importantly, extend it to other situations in which its use may be of great benefit.

Set 1 (pp. 18–19; problems 1–6)
These problems develop the use of the 10% procedure (move the decimal point one place to the left) when finding 10% of a given number. The later problems in the set extend its uses to contexts that include percents other than 10%.

CONCEPT DEVELOPMENT (PAGES 18–19)

INTRODUCE THE CONCEPT

ASSESS STUDENTS' PRIOR KNOWLEDGE
Write the following on the board (Answers are in blue print.). Be sure students understand the idea of a tip as you explain the problem.

10% tip about $4   20% tip about $8
25% tip about $10   50% tip about $20

Ask:
A family is at a restaurant and needs some help figuring out the tip. The cost of the meal was $40.25. Estimate how much to tip the waiter using the percents written on the board. Explain how you estimated.

Listen for:
Students may use a variety of strategies to make their estimates. Listen for them to use proportional reasoning.

Students who have trouble estimating should be encouraged not to worry about the cents but to focus on the dollar amount and to use general strategies for making their estimates.

MODEL MATHEMATICAL THINKING

Ask:
What tools could you use to help you solve this problem?

Draw the number bar on the board. Add lines and labels to the bar as you talk through the thinking.

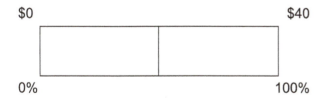

Talk Through the Thinking:
One tool I can use is a number bar. It can help me find about how much money to leave as a tip. The line down the middle of this number bar is halfway between 0% and 100%. So, I can label it 50%. What dollar amount is halfway between $0 and $40? It is $20. How can I find how much money a 25% tip would be? Well, 25% is halfway between 0% and 50%. So the dollar amount would be halfway between $0 and $20. That's $10.

Ask:
How can you use a number bar to help you find a 10% tip? A 20% tip?

Listen for:
Students should recognize that they can divide the bar into 10 equal parts for increments of 10% and label the parts accordingly. They should also understand that each part can be labeled in increments of $4 because $40 ÷ 10 = $4. They can then count one part ($4) for a 10% tip and two parts ($8) for a 20% tip. Students should also recognize that in this problem, the remaining 25 cents ($40.25) is insignificant in terms of calculating a rough percentage for a tip.

LAUNCH THE PROBLEM SOLVING

Have students work individually to solve the problems on page 18. As they work, you may want to circulate and monitor their recorded answers. When students finish each problem, have them compare and discuss their answers with a partner. Then have each pair share their answers in a class discussion of the problem. Refer to the **Teacher Notes: Student Page 18** for more specific ideas about the problems on this page.

As students work and report their conclusions, focus on these issues:

Validate Representations – When students use number bars, ratio tables, or other representations, have them analyze whether all are correct.

Allow Processing Time – Be sure to allow students enough time to assimilate the concepts developed on this page.

Validate Alternate Strategies – Different students may use different strategies to solve these problems. Have students compare and discuss their strategies to find those that are most efficient.

Allow Waiting Time – When students struggle to explain their thinking, be sure to allow them ample time to organize their thoughts.

Fractions, Decimals, Percents *Teacher Edition*

Student Page 18: Problems and Potential Answers

Section D: Tipping — Set 1

Finding 10% of any number is easy as long as you know something about how decimals work. Examine the following table and number bar:

10% of…	is →	
20	→	2
30	→	3
100	→	10
50	→	5

This number bar shows that 10% of 20 is 2.

Is the information in the table true? If you need help to find out, use a separate sheet of paper. Make a number bar similar to the one above for each line in the table.

What do you notice about how the numbers in the first column of the table are related to the numbers in the third column?   To find 10% of a number, drop the 0 in the ones place of that number.

1. Complete the table.

10% of…	is →	
20	→	2
10	→	1
15	→	1.5
30	→	3
25	→	2.5
10	→	1
9.9	→	.99
11	→	1.1

To find 10% of a number, divide the number by 10. Dividing by ten results in the movement of the decimal point one place to the left, as shown below.

What is 10% of 100? → 100 ÷ 10 = 10 (since 10 groups of 10 = 100)   1 0 0. 0 → 1 0. 0 0

What is 10% of $12.30? → $12.30 ÷ 10 = $1.23 (since 10 groups of $1.23 = $12.30)

2. What is 10% of 125? →   125 ÷ 10 = 12.5

3. What is 10% of 34.50? →   34.50 ÷ 10 = 3.45

18 Book 8: *Fractions, Decimals, Percents*

TEACHER NOTES: STUDENT PAGE 18

The introduction to this section invites students to think about the 10% relationship inductively. The table is provided so students can recognize through repeatedly looking at number bars that 10% of 20 is 2, 10% of 30 is 3, 10% of 40 is 4, and so on. *Watch for:* Students should definitely recognize this pattern. Be sure to evaluate their understanding before moving ahead too quickly. *Teaching Strategy:* If necessary, create number bars for each of the entries in the first table. This investment in time will be important later on in helping students understand the proportional thinking behind the use of the 10% procedure.

Problem 1: *Teaching Strategy:* Encourage students to use number bars as needed to be sure they complete the table correctly. *Watch for:* The entries toward the end of the table may be problematic for some students. At this point, if students have recognized that the decimal point may be moved one space to the left when calculating 10% of an amount, they will eagerly apply the rule in cases such as 9.9 or 11 when making a number bar is not easy.

Problems 2–3: Problems 2 and 3 are applications of the rule and provide additional practice using it. *Teaching Strategy:* You may wish to create one number bar for one of these problems as a whole-class activity in order to convince students that the 10% procedure works even with numbers that already contain decimal points.

CONTINUE THE PROBLEM SOLVING

Have students work individually to solve the problems on page 19. As they work, you may want to circulate and monitor their recorded answers. When students finish each problem, have them compare and discuss their answers with a partner. Then have each pair share their answers in a class discussion of the problem. Refer to the **Teacher Notes: Student Page 19** for more specific ideas about the problems on this page.

As students work and report their conclusions, focus on these issues:

Facilitate Students' Thinking – You may need to encourage students to articulate the relationship between 10% and 5% (5% is half of 10%) before they attempt to complete problem 5.

Validate Alternate Strategies – Have students discuss the strategies they used for problem 6. Invite them to compare strategies and to determine whether they are valid.

Allow Waiting Time – When students struggle to explain their thinking, be sure to allow them ample time to organize their thoughts.

Validate Representations – Some students may draw number bars or ratio tables to help them solve the problems on this page. Have them share their representations with the class and discuss whether each representation is correct.

TEACHER NOTES: STUDENT PAGE 19

Problem 4: This problem is similar to the table problem on page 18. *Watch for:* Students should be comfortable moving the decimal point one place to the left to complete this table.

Problem 5: Problem 5 asks students to make a conceptual leap as they apply the 10% procedure to 15%. *Teaching Strategy:* If students are having difficulty, illustrate this challenge with a ratio table or number bar, and follow a line of questioning such as the following:

Can you compute 10% of a number? Yes

What is half of 10%? 5%

What is 10% plus 5%? 15%

If you know what 10% of an amount is, how could you find 5% of that amount? *Divide the amount by 2.*

These questions should help students describe a process for finding 15% of any given amount. Find 10% of the amount, take half of that amount, then add the two amounts. The proportional reasoning students have done with ratio tables will help immensely in these problems, and with the task of determining tips in general.

Problem 6: This problem consists of practice problems with different amounts and different percents for tips. For example, for the second row students need to compute a 12% tip. *Watch for:* Students should follow the same kind of thinking and procedure they used to compute 15%—first use 10% and then make necessary adjustments. Students may need to develop a strategy for finding 1% of a given amount. While they could always create a number bar with 100 individual cells (tedious!), they might also use one of two other strategies. First, students might recognize that 1% can be found by taking 10% of the original amount, and then 10% of that amount again. Students may understand that the 10% procedure can be duplicated for 1%. For 1%, they must move the decimal point two places to the left. You may wish to discuss both strategies with your students.

As an example, the following line of thinking can be used to compute 12% of $30:

10% of $30 → $3.00

1% → 10% of 10%.

So 10% of $3.00 → $0.30

So 1% of $30.00 is $0.30.

Finally, 12% of $30 is equal to 10% + 1% + 1% of $30.

12% → $3 + $0.30 + $0.30 = $3.60

Student Page 19: Problems and Potential Answers

Section D: Tipping — Set 1

Tips given to waitstaff at restaurants can be quickly calculated using the 10% strategy.

4. Calculate the following tips at 10%. You may need to estimate some of these amounts

	Cost of Meal	10% tip
1.	10.00	1.00
2.	12.00	1.20
3.	24.50	2.45
4.	32.75	3.28
5.	50.00	5.00
6.	75.25	7.53

5. Most people today leave a 15% tip in a restaurant. What is a good strategy for calculating 15% of the total bill? _Answers will vary._

6. Complete the table below.

Restaurant	Tip%	Cost of Meal	Cost of Tip	Total Cost of Bill
TJ's Diner	10%	$20.00	$2.00	$22.00
Bob's Burgers	12%	$30.00	$3.60	$33.60
Pancake House	15%	24.80	$3.72	$28.52
Italiano	15%	$110.00	$16.50	$126.50
The Burrito Stand	10%	$15.00	$1.50	$16.50
Pizza Palace	18%	$24.00	$4.32	$28.32
Chicken Hut	15%	$40.00	$6.00	$46.00
The Salad Bowl	10%	$35.00	$3.50	$38.50

Book 8: *Fractions, Decimals, Percents*

SECTION D ASSESSMENT (PAGE 20)

LAUNCH THE ASSESSMENT

Have students turn to the Section D Assessment on page 20. An additional copy is found on page 131 of the Assessment Book. Have students work individually to solve the problems and write their explanations. As they work, circulate to be sure students understand what they need to do for each problem and that they are completing each part of the problem. For example, for problem 1, students need to find the percent that one amount is of another and then explain their strategies. You may find it helpful to read through the directions for all the problems before students begin, discussing the types of responses they will need to make for each problem.

Encourage students to use whatever space they need to explain their thinking. If the space on the page is inadequate, they should use an additional sheet of paper or the back of the page. Refer to the **Teacher Notes: Assessment Problems for Section D** for more specific ideas about the problems on this page.

Evaluate Student Responses

Use the assessment rubric on page 130 of the Assessment Book (pictured on page 261 of the Teacher Edition) to evaluate student responses. The Assessment Book has some general suggestions for using the rubric that you may find helpful.

TEACHER NOTES: ASSESSMENT PROBLEMS FOR SECTION D

These problems assess students' understanding of the 10% strategy. These problems are different from most of the other problems in section D because they require students to determine the percent used to calculate the tip, given the amount of the tip and the cost of the meal.

Problem 1: This scenario will reveal whether students know and understand the 10% strategy.

Problem 2: Problem 2 draws on students' understanding of ratio and proportions as they relate to decimals. Students must recognize that $3.20 is double $1.60 and then reason that the percent for the tip was also doubled from 10% to 20%.

Problem 3: This problem includes a tip that is halfway between the first two. While there are several strategies to use to get to this solution, students should understand that since the tip amount is halfway between $1.60 and $3.20, the percent of the tip should also be halfway between 10% and 20%, or 15%.

Fractions, Decimals, Percents *Teacher Edition*

Student Page 20: Problems and Potential Answers

Section D: Problems for Assessment

Meredith is a waitress at a restaurant. One night, three of her customers ordered exactly the same meal. The cost of the meal was $16.00. Meredith was interested in the different amounts that each of the three customers left for a tip. For each customer below, find out the percent of the cost of the meal that each customer left as a tip.

1. **Customer #1: $1.60 tip**

    What percent is $1.60 of $16.00? __10%__

    Explain your strategy. __Answers will vary.__

2. **Customer #2: $3.20 tip**

    What percent is $3.20 of $16.00? __20%__

    Explain your strategy. Answers will vary. Sample answer: Since I know that 3.20 is twice 1.60, then I have to double the percentage from 10% to 20% as well.

3. **Customer #3: $2.40 tip**

    What percent is $2.40 of $16.00? __15%__

    Explain your strategy. Answers will vary. Sample answer: I know that 2.40 is halfway between 1.60 and 3.20. So, halfway between 10 and 20 percent is 15%.

Book 8: *Fractions, Decimals, Percents*

SCORING GUIDE BOOK 8: FRACTIONS, DECIMALS, AND PERCENTS

Section D Assessment
For Use With: Student Book Page 20

PROBLEM DESCRIPTION	SCORING: WHAT TO LOOK FOR	SCORE AND COMMENTS
Problems 1–3 Use of 10% rule for computing with decimals. Level 2: Tool use Level 3: Connection and Application	Do students: • Understand the 10% algorithm? • Understand the doubling procedure to get 20%? • Understand that 15% is the midpoint between 10% and 20%? • Understand proportional reasoning?	Suggested 2 points per problem Points: _____ of 6

TOTAL POINTS: _____ of 6

Fractions, Decimals, Percents *Teacher Edition*   261

END-OF-BOOK ASSESSMENT (PAGES 21–22)

LAUNCH THE ASSESSMENT

Have students turn to the End-of-Book Assessment on page 21. An additional copy is found on page 133 of the Assessment Book. Have students work individually to solve the problems and write their explanations. As they work, circulate to be sure students understand what they need to do for each problem and that they are completing each part of the problem. For example, for problem 1, students need to find the amount of interest and then add it to the money already in the account. You may find it helpful to read through the directions for all the problems before students begin, discussing the types of responses they will need to make for each problem.

Encourage students to use whatever space they need to explain their thinking. If the space on the page is inadequate, they should use an additional sheet of paper or the back of the page. Refer to the **Teacher Notes: End-of-Book Assessment Student Page 21** for more specific ideas about the problems on this page.

Evaluate Student Responses
Use the assessment rubric on page 132 of the Assessment Book (pictured on page 266 of the Teacher Edition) to evaluate student responses. The Assessment Book has some general suggestions for using the rubric that you may find helpful.

Student Page 21: Problems and Potential Answers

End-of-Book Assessment

Bank Interest A bank is giving a deal on new customers' savings accounts. The bank manager tells you that on the last day of each month, the bank will determine how much money you have in your account. Then they will compute 5% of that amount and add it to your account.

1. If you had $400 on the last day of January, how much interest would the bank pay you for January? Interest: 5% × $400 = $20 What would be the new total amount in your savings account? New Amount: $400 + $20 = $420

2. Suppose you did not deposit or withdraw any money from your account during the next two months, February and March. How much money would you have in your savings account on the last day of March after the bank has paid the interest for the two months? New Amount at end of March: $441 + $22.05 = $463.05

   Explain. Interest in February: 5% × $420 = $21; New Amount at end of February: $420 + $21 = $441; Interest in March: 5% × $441 = $22.05; New Amount at end of March: $441 + $22.05 = $463.05

3. Do you think this is a smart plan for the bank? Answers will vary

   Explain why or why not. Answers will vary

Book 8: *Fractions, Decimals, Percents* 21

TEACHER NOTES: END-OF-BOOK ASSESSMENT

CONTINUE THE ASSESSMENT

Have students turn to page 22 of the End-of-Book Assessment. An additional copy is found on page 134 of the Assessment Book. Have students work individually to solve the problems and write their explanations. As they work, circulate to be sure students understand what they need to do for each problem and that they are completing each part of the problem. For example, for problem 5 students need to find the total amount of interest and then add it to the cost of the bike. You may find it helpful to read the directions for all the problems before students begin, discussing the types of responses they will need to make for each problem. Refer to the **Teacher Notes: End-of-Book Assessment, Student Page 22**, for more specific ideas about the problems on this page.

Evaluate Student Responses
Use the assessment rubric on page 132 of the Assessment Book (pictured on page 266 of the Teacher Edition) to evaluate student responses. The Assessment Book has some general suggestions for using the rubric that you may find helpful.

The problems in this final assessment are intended to provide you with an opportunity to measure student understanding of the uses and meanings of percents. The context used for the assessment problems is interest. This is an important context because it is one that is commonly encountered in daily life. This problem, like any good summative assessment, will stretch students beyond what they have done in the unit. Be sure to help students understand the starting principles of this problem and the specific goals they are to pursue in the problem.

Watch for: Look for students to use various methods for solving these problems, such as ratio tables, number bars, and the 10% procedure. Students will also need to demonstrate general conceptual understanding of the context in order to be successful with these problems. *Teaching Strategy:* You may want to encourage students to work in groups on these problems so they will be able to help each other as the context builds from one stage to the next.

Teaching Strategy: It may be helpful for you to work with students to begin completing the table in problem 4 so that they understand how the table is structured. Students should make their calculations working from the top of each column to the bottom. Then the new total at the bottom of one column is moved to the top of the next column, and a similar process is followed.

Student Page 22: Problems and Potential Answers

End-of-Book Assessment

4. You get a loan from the bank so you can buy an expensive bicycle. The bank lends you the money, but you have to pay back the bank in monthly payments. On the last day of each month, the bank will charge you 10% interest on the amount that you still owe.

   For example, if on the last day of the first month you still owe $100, the bank would add $10 (10% of $100) to that amount. So you would have to pay the bank $110. You agree to pay back the loan in six months.

   You borrow $1000 for the bike. The table below shows how much you paid each month and how much you still have to pay after the bank adds interest. Complete the table by filling in the purple shaded cells with the correct amounts. Use the information already in the table to get started.

	January	February	March	April	May	June
The Amount you Owe the Bank	$1000	$660	$484	$330	$220	$22
Your Monthly Payment Amount	$400	$220	$184	$130	$200	$22
Remaining Balance (what you still have left to pay)	$600	$440	$300	$200	$20	0
Bank Charges Interest at 10%	$60	$44	$30	$20	$2	0
New Balance on the account that you still owe	$660	$484	$330	$220	$22	0

5. The bike was supposed to cost you $1000. But you paid more than that because of the interest charged by the bank. How much <u>total interest</u> did you have to pay on the loan? $156   After all the payments, what was the total amount you paid for the bike? $1156

22   Book 8: *Fractions, Decimals, Percents*

Fractions, Decimals, Percents *Teacher Edition*

SCORING GUIDE BOOK 8: FRACTIONS, DECIMALS, PERCENTS

End-of-Book Assessment
For Use With: Student Book Pages 21–22

PROBLEM DESCRIPTION	SCORING: WHAT TO LOOK FOR	SCORE AND COMMENTS
Problem 1 Compute 5% interest on $400. Level 2: Tool use Level 3: Connection and Application	Do students: • Have an intuitive understanding of percents? • Correctly calculate 5% of 400? • Use strategies? • Correctly calculate total amount in bank account?	Points: _____ of 4
Problem 2 5% interest problem continued. Level 1: Comprehension and Knowledge Level 2: Tool use	Do students: • Have an intuitive understanding of percents? • Correctly calculate 5% of 400? $420? The other amounts? • Correctly calculate 5% on increasing monthly amounts in bank account? • Use strategies? • Correctly calculate the total amount in the bank account after several months?	Points: _____ of 4
Problem 3 Evaluation of problem context. Level 4: Synthesis and Evaluation	Do students: • Correctly interpret context? • Have an understanding of the use of percents in the problem context? • Articulate conceptual understanding of the context?	Points: _____ of 2
Problem 4 Compute compound interest over six months. Level 2: Tool use Level 3: Connection and Application	Do students: • Have an intuitive understanding of percents? • Understand context? • Correctly calculate 10% interest on remaining balance? • Find the correct sum for new balance? • Understand strategy use?	(11 individual answers at 1 point each) Points: _____ of 11
Problem 5 Summary of problem context. Level 3: Connection and Application Level 4: Synthesis and Evaluation	Do students: • Have a conceptual understanding of percents? • Understand percent calculations? • Have a conceptual understanding of problem context? • Articulate their thinking?	Points: _____ of 6

TOTAL POINTS: _____ of 27